Reassessing Egalitarianis

Also by Jeremy Moss

CLIMATE CHANGE AND SOCIAL JUSTICE (*editor*)
RISK AND RESPONSIBILITY (*edited with Greg Marston and John Quiggin*)

Reassessing Egalitarianism

Jeremy Moss
The Social Justice Initiative, University of Melbourne, Australia

First published 2014 by
PALGRAVE MACMILLAN

Palgrave Macmillan in the UK is an imprint of Macmillan Publishers Limited, registered in England, company number 785998, of Houndmills, Basingstoke, Hampshire RG21 6XS.

Palgrave Macmillan in the US is a division of St Martin's Press LLC, 175 Fifth Avenue, New York, NY 10010.

Palgrave Macmillan is the global academic imprint of the above companies and has companies and representatives throughout the world.

Palgrave® and Macmillan® are registered trademarks in the United States, the United Kingdom, Europe and other countries

ISBN 978-1-349-48144-6   ISBN 978-1-137-38598-7 (eBook)
DOI 10.1057/9781137385987

A catalogue record for this book is available from the British Library.

A catalog record for this book is available from the Library of Congress.

Transferred to Digital Printing in 2014

Contents

Acknowledgements

This book has benefited from numerous discussions and opportunities to present the material. For discussing parts of the book, I thank audiences at the universities of ANU, Beijing, Graz, Hong Kong, Lisbon, Oxford, Macquarie, McGill, Melbourne, Queensland, Sydney, UNESCO, and Wellington. The book was written in part while I visited the universities of Oxford and McGill, and they provided very congenial research environments. I particularly thank the participants of the Crash Course on Egalitarianism at Université catholique de Louvain in 2012 and Axel Gosseries for organizing it, as well as the participants of the Just Equality Workshop: Dan Halliday, Sanyar Sagal, Greg Bognar, Axel Gosseries, and Robert Young. I would also like to thank Graham Brown, Director of the Nossal Institute of Global Health, for his support during the research for this book. Some of the many people who have discussed parts of the book with me are Dave Archard, Dick Arneson, John Baker, Paula Casal, Tony Coady, Simon Caney, Garrett Cullity, Iwao Hirose, Simon Keller, Uwe Steinhoff, Adam Swift, Andrew Williams, and Jo Wolff. I thank them for their input. I also particularly thank Robert Young for many conversations on the topics collected in this book; they have been instrumental in making it a better work.

Earlier versions of some of the material have appeared in print as follows. I thank the publishers for permission to republish.

Moss, Jeremy. "Egalitarianism and the Value of Equality." *Journal of Ethics and Social Philosophy*, 2 (2009): 1–6.

Moss, Jeremy, "Against Fairness." *Journal of Value Inquiry*, 41 (2007): 309–324.

The book has also had the crucial support of a number of grants from the Australian Research Council – they enabled me to have time off for research and travel to other universities – in particular an ARC Future Fellowship and a Discovery grant, *Reassessing Egalitarianism*. I thank the Council for its generous support.

Introduction

This book aims to provide a critical overview and introduction to debates in contemporary egalitarianism. One of the main motivations for writing a book on recent egalitarianism is the richness of the material that has been produced over the last forty or so years in political philosophy. There have been genuinely new approaches to important questions and important extensions of old ones. Debates about equality's value or particular applications of egalitarianism to problems such as climate change have underscored the vitality of the field. Not only has the innovation occurred within egalitarian debates, but it continues to influence a wide range of disciplines and approaches to problems. This is perhaps clearest in the debate about the substance of a principle of equality. Amartya Sen's discussion of the "metric" or "currency" of equality initiated a very significant discussion that continues to have resonance outside philosophy in the fields of development, economics, and public policy.[1] Politically, the value of equality continues to have a primal appeal, as it has for several centuries. Equality of some sort – equality before the law, equal opportunities for jobs or education, and now equal access to a safe climate – has often been the linchpin of claims about justice. Claims to equal treatment in important spheres are also part of the contemporary political landscape. A powerful egalitarian demand has been that all those eligible to participate in political affairs be able to do so without the interests of one group dominating or excluding those of other groups. This kind of demand has historically been applied selectively to some groups (men, property owners) and not others (women, people of different races). Nonetheless, it is a claim with continued relevance when we consider that in many countries formal equality of participation exists but considerable informal barriers to the claims of many being heard in the political arena are still

1

present, let alone acted upon. This kind of appeal to equality is part of a specific conception of equality. For the most part, our interest is in what philosophers have to say about a broader concern with how people's lives go overall – equality of condition. What separates egalitarianism from just a commitment to equality is that egalitarianism focuses on a substantive conception of equality that concerns how people's lives actually go: whether they are equal to others in terms of key determinants such as health, education, and respect. This concern with equality of condition, as it is typically called, is very different from a commitment to formal equality, such as treating like cases alike, and is at the heart of egalitarianism.

The challenges that modern societies face raise important and interesting philosophical issues about equality's value, relevance, and scope and its relation to other values. Some of these issues are part of discrete debates that can usefully be discussed on their own. But there is also a considerable amount of overlap and dependence between areas that can be seen only when the debates are set against one another. One of the motivations for this book was to better understand these debates by drawing together all the major areas so that common themes in several of the debates, such as the role of individual choice and preferences, could emerge. The book aims to shed light on the role of some of these common themes that run across different parts of the philosophical discussion of egalitarianism both so that the connections can be understood, and to articulate when debates are at cross-purposes and thus to identify where there is disagreement as a result of misplaced assumptions.

A further motivation is that despite the range of interesting questions that egalitarian writers have raised, there is also a sense in which egalitarianism has not kept pace with the kinds of challenges that societies face. In setting out the shape of the philosophical debate, one of the aims of this book is to determine whether contemporary egalitarianism has adequately identified the kinds of inequalities that cause the most disadvantage. For instance, we consider whether contemporary theories have correctly identified the most significant kinds of inequalities for egalitarians. Are they instances of bad luck, or are they the kinds of inequalities of power and opportunity that social movements have identified? At any rate, one of the fault lines of recent debates concerns who has best captured the correct set of inequalities. Yet the main motivation for writing a book such as this is the belief that egalitarianism has something of value to offer as a theory of justice and that now is a crucial time in which to pursue the goals of substantive equality given the challenges of continuing poverty and climate change.

The value of equality

The modern philosophical discussion of egalitarianism can be divided into four separate but related topics: the value of equality, the currency of equality, the relationship between equality and responsibility, and global equality. The first of these, the value of equality, which is discussed in Chapter 1, is in many ways philosophically primary. Understanding the way in which equality is valuable would seem to be a necessary condition for exploring how it can be enacted, limited, or extended. In other contexts equality's value seems settled. It would make our task here a lot simpler if we could just assume that equality's value was beyond question. In terms of the recent debate about how we can value equality, equality's value has usually been seen to be either intrinsic or instrumental. When we say that equality just *is* valuable, this is close to what is meant by intrinsic value. A widely held view is that something is intrinsically valuable if it is valuable for its own sake and not by reference to some other value. Valuing it in this way of course does not settle the issue of its value in relation to other values, but it does place it on a very sound philosophical footing. Something that is intrinsically valuable cannot be easily trumped by another value. But this kind of valuation has run into problems. One prominent difficulty has led many to question whether equality is useful for accurately capturing disadvantage. Derek Parfit claims that if equality really is valuable for its own sake, egalitarians are committed to the view that there is something good about bringing the well-off down to the level of the poor – leveling them down – even if it benefits no one. Consider the situation in which there are very many people who lack the basic resources to live even a moderately good life when there are plenty of other people in the world who have more than enough. Egalitarians will argue that part of the injustice of this situation is that people are unequal. An alternative explanation is that what disturbs us about this situation is not the difference between the well-off and the poor but the actual condition of the poor. Thus the moral intuition is, in fact, not strictly an egalitarian one about how one group fares compared with another but a noncomparative claim about poverty. This kind of objection has led some to conclude that better principles are available for capturing how we should distribute goods. Parfit's own preference is for a prioritarian principle that gives priority to the worst off when distributing resources. Prioritarians think what should concern us is not a relative judgment about whether some have as much as others but an absolute judgment about whether a person's life is worse than it should be. A further response is to argue with Harry Frankfurt that what we should care about is whether a person has enough of what he or she needs. In his article "Equality as a Moral Ideal," Frankfurt claims that what we want for the poor is not that they have the same as the wealthy but that they have enough, or sufficient.[2]

In light of these and other objections, equality might have only instrumental value. Instead of seeing it as a stand-alone value that constrains other values, we should see it as having value because it contributes to other valuable outcomes. Take the example of inequalities of wealth and income. A common complaint about these inequalities is that they lead to some being excluded from having political influence or getting good jobs. Societies that have inequalities of this type might be less democratic or have deeper social divisions. If decreasing these inequalities would improve access to democracy or lead to greater social harmony, then it is something to be valued because it contributes instrumentally to one of these goals. This is a justification of equality that many support. Although it might be weaker in some philosophical senses than an intrinsic justification, it is nonetheless a powerful reason to support policies that encourage equality given the importance of achieving better participation in political life or social harmony. Nor is it, of course, impossible to think that some kinds of equalities are justified intrinsically and others instrumentally.

These two types of valuation have provoked a great deal of comment and response, which has led to a better understanding of what a commitment to equality entails. As we will see, ultimately we need to reassess this way of viewing the debate. One of the aims of Chapter 1 is to clarify how egalitarians can articulate the value of equality without being constrained by some of the traditional features of this debate. Nonetheless, the senses in which equality is valuable give a clear indication that there are several plausible and important ways in which to value equality.

Equality of what?

Understanding how we can value equality leads naturally to the question of the kind of equality in which we should be interested. This part of the debate, which has been called the "equality of what?" is discussed in Chapter 2. Importantly, whereas we might have equality in terms of all kinds of things – equality before the law, basic moral equality, and the like – typically egalitarians are concerned with a substantive understanding of equality that relates broadly to how well people's lives go, not just the formal equal freedoms people may have, important though these are. A focus on equality of condition, traditionally a defining feature of egalitarianism, is concerned with the "currency" or "metric" of equality: the kinds of things in terms of which we should actually be equal. The answers to this question fall into three broad groups – welfarism, resourcism, and capabilities – which we discuss in roughly chronological order.

The first metric is typically called welfarism. To promote equality of welfare is usually taken to mean that all people have their conscious states or preferences equally satisfied. In terms of the subjective preference approach to welfare, which is the main variant of the position, welfarists argue that we should equalize what really matters to individuals: their preferences as to how to live their lives. Ensuring that everyone's preferences are equally satisfied also has the virtue of respecting the different values and choices that people have, and it avoids paternalism by not telling people what is good for them and perfectionism by not asking individuals to conform to an ideal standard. Critics of welfarism point to its vulnerability to the adaptive preference objection. They note that people's preferences are formed by a range of influences formed by media, dominant social institutions, and their material circumstances. This is not in itself necessarily problematic, but it raises the issue of how to treat preferences that are harmful or that serve some other group's or person's self-interest. Critics have been particularly scornful of preferences that have been adjusted to fit the reduced expectations that accompany harsh circumstances, especially poverty. In a situation of severe poverty someone might form preferences that aim lower than those of a similar individual in a better situation. Sen has highlighted how a reliance on preferences that involve a "quiet acceptance" of deprivation can lead to a distorted set of preferences, which give reason to doubt their suitability as something to equalize as part of justice.[3] It also raises the issue of whether one of the chief attributes of the metric – that it preserves and respects agent autonomy – is in fact the case. A further major concern is that preference theories are vulnerable to a charge of unfairness. If one person's preferences are cheap and another's are expensive, then satisfying the more expensive person's preferences will use up a larger amount of available resources, which may be unfair. The difficulty of satisfying different people's sets of preferences might also vary greatly. Imagine that one person opted for a life of research into complex problems in mathematics and physics and another opted for a life spent collecting matchboxes. Satisfying the latter might be easier than the former, which raises the question of whether subjective welfarism is able to judge whether preferences have been satisfied in a way that is required by a theory of justice. One of welfarism's advantages was that it focused on ends and not the means to ends, thereby addressing directly what is important to people in a fundamental sense.

In contrast, resourcism as an answer to "equality of what?" attempts to identify all-purpose means that everybody conceivably might want irrespective of their conception of the good. The resourcist response comes in two main forms: an account of equality in terms of certain "primary goods" developed by John Rawls, and Ronald Dworkin's modification of Rawls's approach. Rawls's primary goods metric shifted discussion away from subjective metrics toward objective ones. Whereas some welfarists thought in terms of subjective preferences, the primary goods metric aims to make people equal in terms of items such as income and wealth, rights and liberties, and access to powers of office that are both easy to compare and all-purpose means that anyone might want to fulfill their broader goals. But it is important to note that the name "resourcism" captures a very broad class of things, most of which are not really resources in the standard sense of the term. What we commonly think of as resources are commodities – wealth, natural resources, and other types of portable, tradable things. But resources also include what Rawls calls "the social bases of self-respect" (essential things, such as the material means and political rights, that citizens need to pursue their lives) and assume a background of institutions and practices that are fair. Rawls's resourcism is less prone to the expensive tastes objection because everyone gets the same standard of primary goods, which they can then use for expensive or cheap goals depending on what best suits them. It is also not so tied to individual conceptions of the good to work out what to equalize because that standard is set independently. Its supporters argue that these features better enable it to fit the requirements of a public conception of justice. Similarly, Ronald Dworkin put forward a version of resourcism that differs from Rawls's yet maintains a focus on all-purpose means as an answer to the "equality of what?" question.

One of the positive developments of the debate about metrics has been the attention paid to issues associated with disability. Both Sen and Nussbaum argue that Rawls's metric considers only people with relatively normal ranges of human functioning, not people who are disabled or disease-prone. If we are really interested in inequality, then a situation in which some have to spend a disproportionate amount of their stock of primary goods just to achieve the same outcomes as the able-bodied is neither fair nor choice-promoting, according to Sen. Nussbaum's concern takes a different form. Her argument is that Rawls should not assume that everyone has the same level of intellectual, moral, and physical powers. Such a view misses our "animal" nature and ignores the natural growth and decline of our powers and fundamental interdependence.[4]

The result of these and other criticisms of welfarism and resourcism has been the capability approach to equality, the third of our metrics. This approach focuses on the ability to be and do various important things: being housed, safe, mobile, and so on. Having capability as the focus is meant to ensure that inequalities are sensitive to disabilities and to general human difference; it is not people's preferences that is the focus of resources but whether a person is equally able to do or be something. The focus on capability as the metric is meant to set the approach apart from the other two metrics. Like the others, it includes a range of interpretations of what a capability approach should entail. For instance, establishing the precise elements of a list of capabilities that can function as a metric for a theory of justice has left some skeptical about the approach's suitability. If the list preserves a strong role for people to have a say in its content, then it risks falling prey to all the objections that Sen and others made to welfarism. If the list is objective, like Nussbaum's version, then the worry is that it is perfectionist, in that it posits an ideal standard of what a human life ought to be like and does not respect the range of possible capabilities that a diverse society might value. Advocates of the capability metric also stress how sensitive their metric is to cultural differences. They claim it can do this because it focuses on capabilities and not achievements.

All the metrics have their own particular set of difficulties. One charge leveled against each of them is that in focusing on the constituents of metrics, we in fact equalize the wrong thing. Elizabeth Anderson has made the point that egalitarians have spent too long attending to their metrics and paid too little attention to the real goal of egalitarianism, which is to place people in relations of equality. Only some of the things in a metric will be equalized to achieve this broader goal. Clarifying the relationship of metrics to this broader goal is one of the more interesting challenges for contemporary egalitarianism.

Equality and responsibility

Recent egalitarianism most closely intersects with political debates in regard to the role of responsibility in determining which inequalities should be the concern of the state. The main focus of the debate has been on two general positions. On one side are "luck egalitarians," who defend a version of egalitarian justice that is motivated by the idea that it is fair that people should be compensated for those disadvantages that are a result of chance but not those that are a result of an agent's choices, reflecting their responsibility. It captures an important dimension of equality by removing (or at least mitigating the effects of) those inequalities that are out of our hands, such as poor genetic endowments or accidents, while at the same time acknowledging that we are agents who make decisions about our lives for which we can be held accountable. What this entails is that inequalities that are a result of choices, even if they lead to disaster, should not be compensated as a matter of justice. There may be a case for addressing these disadvantages for reasons of humanity or charity but not justice.

The idea that we should be responsible for the outcomes of our choices and not for those of chance has widespread appeal in political life and philosophy and is held by conservatives as well as egalitarians to different degrees. This ideal not only captures an important intuition but also has appeal because it respects a person's agency and, for egalitarians who support it, gets to the heart of which inequalities matter. Its detractors claim that incorporating the distinction between chance and choice in such a prominent way can also lead to disastrous consequences for those whose luck turns sour. Critics also worry that obtaining enough information to make these kinds of judgments will be excessively difficult. Another concern is that trying to get the right information and then applying it can be deeply disrespectful. For example, to get an unemployment benefit, a person might have to prove that he or she tried to get work but was not intelligent or talented enough to get a job. Forcing people into such a position does not respect them or place them in relations of equality with others, according to luck egalitarian's critics.

On the other side are "relational egalitarians," who claim that luck egalitarians hold a conception of equality that is too narrow and has lost sight of the true significance of egalitarianism. What egalitarianism should have as its goal is to place people in relations of equality and focus on the real causes of inequalities; for example, sexism, racism, or, indeed, excessive accumulations of wealth. If this is a better understanding of equality, then luck egalitarians are mistaken in elevating the distinction between chance and choice to the heart of their theories of justice. By ensuring that everyone is able to function in relations of equality, relational egalitarianism claims to be motivated by a more plausible set of ideals and to be closer to the egalitarian tradition.

In response, luck egalitarians have claimed that instances where people might foreseeably be treated with disrespect do not fundamentally alter the importance of responsibility but are just bad applications of good theory. A well-designed implementation of luck egalitarianism would avoid treating people disrespectfully. Moreover, properly designed social insurance schemes might avoid some of the destitution that can accompany poor choices. Pure luck egalitarians might respond to the disastrous consequences objection in the same way that "intrinsic" egalitarians respond to the leveling-down objection – by admitting that it is a consequence of their view but one that can be set aside in light of other considerations of value. While it is possible that society might deny medical care to the victims of bad option luck, it is likely that other values will override considerations of responsibility. Relational egalitarians might also be inviting some of the very criticisms that they made of luck egalitarians. For instance, Anderson and Samuel Scheffler both stress the importance of social relations being governed by reciprocity. For those who receive the benefits of cooperation but do not reciprocate, especially through choice, standard relational egalitarianism may not grant such people equivalent benefits – or any.[5]

As both relational and nonrelational positions cut across different metrics of equality, they provide excellent insights into the current state of egalitarian thinking about justice. But the positions' claims and counterclaims have masked some overlap. What is distinctive about the luck egalitarian position is not that responsibility matters – almost all egalitarians think it does – but that it should play a decisive and prominent role in determining the distribution of goods and when inequalities are acceptable. In fact, both positions have a significant role for responsibility. At stake is not only a set of issues about which inequalities are permissible but the goals of egalitarianism itself. A more fundamental set of differences – which also involves some overlap – concerns the role that luck egalitarian ideals play in their theories of justice. This is the most important objection that Anderson and Scheffler make against the luck egalitarians – that they have either the wrong ideal or, worse, no ideal at all.

Global egalitarianism

Defending the importance of reciprocity also sharply delineates where egalitarians stand in relation to whether egalitarianism can be globalized. When we consider whether egalitarianism should be confined to domestic justice given that egalitarians favor substantive equality and are commonly committed to claims concerning the equal moral worth of all people, one of the responses has been to argue that this claim depends on the right kind of reciprocal relations being present; for instance, those that obtain between citizens of one country who agree to impositions of laws, make sacrifices for one another, and so on. Others argue that global inequalities are simply so profound and disastrous to the poor that they cannot but command our attention. The debate about whether or not to extend substantive principles of equality beyond national borders to a large extent hinges on whether the duties we might have to others are properly duties of justice. Opponents of global egalitarianism might regard it as bad but not a matter of justice if those in a neighboring country are very unequal and hence not grounds for extending substantive equality. Those who hold that egalitarianism should not be extended do so for three main reasons. The most common justification is a relational one. Relational or associational egalitarians argue that for principles of egalitarian justice to apply globally, the right kind of relation between people must exist. An obvious example is that shared social and political institutions involving reciprocity and coop- eration must exist. Egalitarians committed to the importance of reci- procity support this claim. Others claim that duties of global justice are triggered when institutions have a "pervasive impact" on the higher- order interests of others. A third type of justification is the claim that the legitimate exercise of coercion is required to trigger duties of global justice. As we will see, much depends on what is meant by the "right type" of shared institutions. Relational views also hold that the kinds of practices that exist between people might also determine the value and type of certain sorts of goods that form part of the distributed outcome. Goods such as working conditions or relations with family might gain part of their significance because of the importance and meaning that one culture places on them.

Yet global egalitarians argue that these kinds of justifications are capable of yielding global and nonglobal results. For instance, nonre- lationalists charge that accounts of justice that require institutions to exist before duties of justice arise are conservative because they privilege the status quo. Just because a desirable feature of social interaction does not exist does not imply that it should not exist.[6] Similarly, if duties of justice are generated once some practice or institution has a pervasive impact on people's interests, then given the fact of globalization and its impacts, duties of justice are likely to arise. The coercion account also has difficulty confirming claims of justice to domestic contexts. For instance, according to Michael Blake, coercion is important because, constituting a threat to autonomy, it requires a justification. States do this through a system of laws and democratic practices, but there is no global equivalent to this system of laws.[7] While statelike laws are absent in the global sphere, coercion is not, and it has an often deadly effect on noncompatriots. If this is the case and if coercion arrangements are in need of justification because of these kinds of effects on our autonomy or other important values, then the coercion that exists in a global sphere also needs justification in the same kind of way.

Nonrelational approaches to global egalitarianism offer a quite different approach to the issue of justification. Nonrelationalists argue that there are basic features of moral personhood that ground global distributive principles of equality. So if everyone in the world shares morally relevant properties and we ought thus to treat everyone as mattering to the same degree, we ought also to extend our distributive concerns globally.[8] Nonrelationalists sometimes appeal to the idea of the moral arbitrariness of being born in one country rather than another to ground claims of global distributive justice. In the same way that people in wealthy countries should not be denied equal access to goods because of their location or skin color, the fact that one person was unlucky enough to be born into a desperately poor country with no resources and high mortality is simply morally arbitrary and should not determine the kind of life he or she has. Yet one matter of concern for these accounts is what we might call the problem of perverse implications. Moral personality accounts of global justice extend moral concern too far and in implausible ways. So, for instance, Darryl Moellendorf worries that unless we endorse the relational account, we will in principle be committed to duties of justice to intelligent beings on other planets with whom we have no contact. While we may have broader moral duties not to harm such beings, we do not have duties of justice.[9]

Assuming that we can justify extending principles of domestic egalitarianism globally, what would they look like? Do they face unique challenges because of the extra numbers and diversity of peoples and cultures? Does the lack of a common political system fatally wound the attempt to make egalitarianism global? Some of these uncertainties have been reflected in the overall more general discussion about metrics in relation to global justice. But many of the recent approaches to extending equality are more specific. Some have argued that there are specific types of goods that are particularly appropriate for global distribution. Two especially relevant examples are equal access to key natural resources and the ability to emit greenhouse gases as part of a response to climate change. This is an interesting development for global egalitarianism because it does not necessarily rely on a complete theory of global justice that distributes all or most valuable goods, instead focusing on a more limited approach to what can and should be distributed. This stems in part from the character of some types of resources. Consider the comparison between resources and natural talents. Rawls and others have argued that the distribution of talents among people is arbitrary from a moral point of view. Being born with a talent is not something a person deserves even if he or she works hard to make something out of that talent. Even so, talents are part of a person's identity, a part hard to morally separate out for purposes of distribution. Yet natural resources are importantly different from personal talents. For a start, resources are not part of a person's character in the way the ability to dance is part of a dancer's personality. The distribution of natural resources around the globe is arbitrary, not the hard work of someone in particular. Natural resources are thus not created by labor in the way that the outputs of manufacturing or farming are. We did not create the atmosphere through our labor, and so the justification of claims to its use will be different from that for products that result from someone's labor, which might justify unequal distribution.[10] The combination of claims about the arbitrary distribution of resources with the crucial role that resources play in the fulfillment of well-being in all societies provides several possible justifications for the claim that everyone should have an equal prima facie claim to resources.

Some rights theorists argue for such an equal claim. For instance, Hillel Steiner proposes that everyone is entitled to an equal share of the Earth's resources.[11] Where some have acquired a greater than equal share of initially unowned resources, they have undertaken a redistribution, and those with less than an equal share are entitled to claim back their fair share via some form of compensation. To distribute the entitlements to natural resources, Steiner proposes that we tax the market value of the untransformed resources as a kind of pooling of brute luck in resources. He claims that equality is a default norm at a fundamental level.

Responses by other egalitarians and by nonegalitarians to this kind of equal distribution take up some familiar themes. For instance, supporters of other metrics of equality argue that it does not aim at the right goals because it is not connected with people's welfare (welfarist egalitarians). Others claim that it does not fully address the difficult and different circumstances in which the poor find themselves (capability theorists) because as a libertarian proposal that tries to allocate a fair share of resources, it is not concerned directly with the further question of alleviating poverty. In addition, giving everyone an equal share might be less beneficial than creating public goods, for instance.

One particular resource offers an even more specific context in which to consider the application of a principle of equality to the global sphere. The distribution of the benefits and burdens associated with adapting and mitigating climate change has involved significant discussion of how to fairly approach this very important and complex issue. Egalitarians have several reasons to be interested in problems associated with climate change, ranging from how current decisions affect future generations to whether climate solutions ought to refer to broader egalitarian conceptions of how society ought to be organized. A particularly relevant discussion here involves what we can call the "carbon budget" problem, which concerns how we allocate emissions, given that there is a finite amount of carbon dioxide we can put into the atmosphere before we trigger dangerous climate change. If we are to avoid dangerous climate change, then an immediate and drastic reduction of worldwide total carbon dioxide emissions is needed. This raises the problem of how this budget is to be distributed among countries and people.

One approach has been to understand the atmosphere as a common good, which is not or should not be anybody's to own. Peter Singer writes, "Why should anyone have a greater claim to part of the atmospheric sink than any other?"[12] He conceives of this as a plausible starting point for discussion about dividing up our rights to emit. A related proposal that has widespread support is the equal per capita (EPC) approach; it simply divides the amount of carbon dioxide we can emit by the number of people in the world (usually adjusted to reflect a population baseline year), which yields a figure of how many tons of carbon dioxide–equivalent gases we could each emit as a baseline for allocating emissions entitlements. As its name suggests, the approach employs a principle of equality. The EPC approach faces a number of problems, such as whether it fixates on a small dimension of environmental justice – the ability to emit – and applies the principle of equality to this dimension alone.[13]

The debate concerning global egalitarianism highlights the importance of the issue of what kinds of actions and disadvantages fall under the concept of justice. Those who think reciprocity and cooperation need to be present will naturally seek to determine whether these kinds of interactions do in fact apply globally, which is largely an empirical question. Global egalitarianism also exhibits many of the same reservations concerning the need to achieve important outcomes.

The discussion of global equal opportunity, while obviously motivated by concerns about cultural diversity, seems even more insistent on avoiding outcomes as a focus. This seems particularly questionable in the case of the climate.

Considering the challenges that global injustice raises for egalitarianism is a timely reminder of how pertinent questions of the type, value, and scope of equality really are. Egalitarianism has been and should continue to be centrally concerned with removing the most important inequalities that persist in the modern world. Understanding these challenges and, importantly, egalitarian responses to them requires that we see what separates as well as unites the different responses. But it also hopefully will be beneficial if we appreciate the kinds of themes that run through egalitarian responses to injustice and appreciate whether they are on the right track. The themes should also tell us a great deal about the adequacy of current responses, what directions future debate should take, and where present debate has gone wrong.

Scope and focus

Egalitarian objections to inequalities have traditionally been couched in the language of justice. The fact that recently this has not always been the case has led to some problems. What quickly becomes apparent when reading the discussions of equality is that there is no consensus on how to define justice. It is not just disagreement about whether conceptions of justice should be left wing, should focus on self-respect, or should involve outcomes – such disagreements are to be expected – but about the concept of justice itself. Justice has variously been defined as applying only to society's basic structure, as entailing predominantly negative duties, as having to involve the possibility of coercion, as applying whenever a person's significant interests are affected, as being based not on association but on features of our moral personality, as invoked only when harms have a social cause, as involving only perfect duties, and as giving people their due. Justice might also be said to be remedial and transitional, as well as distributional. I will not attempt to settle this issue here, although I discuss it at greater length in Chapter 4. There are, of course, non-justice-based duties that can variously be described as humanitarian, general ethical duties, duties of charity, and so on. This distinction is crucial in several of the areas we will consider. For instance, some luck egalitarians see inequality that results from a person's choices as regrettable, even something in respect of which people should be assisted, but fundamentally not a matter of justice.

Some who support egalitarianism within a state support different distributive principles between people in different states. Or they argue that there might be strong duties to aid such people but they are not duties of justice. Similarly, there is disagreement regarding whether natural disadvantages, such as the existence of certain disabilities for which no one is responsible, should also be considered unjust. Despite this uncertainty over how to conceive of justice, what follows will be about justice and not ethics per se.

There are several good reasons for maintaining concerns of justice as a useful and important subset of ethics. For one, I think there is value in maintaining a language that has a resonance with past and current claims that have been invoked in struggles against inequalities. Keeping the language of justice maintains continuity with these origins. Connected to this reason is the thought that the language of justice captures a sense of urgency. A further reason is that justice tells us something about the things people can make a claim on in order for their life to go well. This is a major difference with a principle of charity or humanity, which depends in part on what others are willing to give for a redistribution to occur. Moreover, claims of justice are strong claims that can plausibly be seen as involving rights to the claim's subject, whether this happens to be resources of the earth or social products. These considerations are not intended as a full-blown defense of a focus on justice, but I hope they suggest that there are good reasons for keeping the discussion of egalitarianism within the scope of justice and for reconnecting the discussion of equality with that of justice.

In addition to appreciating some of the links and themes that permeate discussion of recent egalitarianism, it is useful to have an overview of each discrete section of the broader debate about egalitarianism and the shape it has taken over the last forty years. Yet any book that discusses a subject as broad as egalitarianism must exclude certain topics. I do not here discuss whether a principle of equality extends beyond humans to animals, for instance. Nor do I discuss the very difficult issue of the bases of equality – the degree and nature of those qualities (intelligence, ability to experience pleasure or pain) that make us equal. This issue is more often discussed in relation to straightforwardly ethical questions – such as whether some humans are "more equal" because of, say, greater intelligence – and has been a less prominent feature of egalitarian debate, although it is surely pertinent. With the exception of climate change and the issue of global resources, I leave aside any major discussion of the many applied issues where egalitarian thinking has been deployed. I am thinking here, for instance, of discussions of unemployment, incentives, or discrimination law. Nor does the book explicitly answer challenges arising from theories skeptical of large-scale redistribution in general, egalitarian or otherwise. Nonetheless, the book intends not only to be a critical discussion of the philosophical debate but to provide a useful set of tools for using egalitarian ideas to shed light on a range of urgent real-world problems.

1
The Value of Equality

1.1 Introduction

Equality is the central value for egalitarians. It is the value that defines and distinguishes egalitarianism from other political theories. However we understand the metric of equality – whether as comprising people's preferences, resources, or capabilities or as a mixture of opportunities and outcomes – any answer will assume that equality matters in some way. Why equality matters is a conceptually distinct question from the issue of which metric of equality is best or whether disadvantage caused by personal irresponsibility is a permissible reason to allow inequalities. However, if equality is the central value for egalitarians, then *why* it is of value should be an obvious starting point for any discussion of egalitarianism – and that is the subject of this chapter.

Equality has been valued for a range of reasons: because it promotes good health, reduces suffering, is part of a fair society, is how we treat people with respect, or is an ultimate value, like freedom. These and other arguments for equality raise the separate question of how to categorize the different types of arguments for equality. Of the several reasons to value equality mentioned a moment ago, all locate equality's value in relation to other values and hence raise the issue of how important equality is if it is used to support other, more important values. There are three broad ways in which the value of equality could be categorized. Equality could be valued intrinsically, in virtue of its own independent value. This is the strongest valuation of equality but also the most difficult for egalitarians to defend. It is difficult to defend because very few political values are justifiable without reference to some other, more fundamental value.[1] The obvious alternative to valuing equality intrinsically is to value it instrumentally because it contributes to or is necessary for some other valuable outcome. Some of the typical examples of valuing equality seem to fit this mold, especially the concern with excessively unequal distribution of income and wealth or the concern that inequality leads to poor health outcomes. A third type of valuation is to understand equality as not merely an instrumental value but nonetheless as deriving its value from its relation to other important values – what I call constitutive value. Moreover, equality's defenders also support equality for a range of personal and impersonal reasons. There is a clear sense that equality has a direct personal benefit if it achieves gains in people's health or welfare. But it might also be valuable because of its impersonal effects, such as making justice more widely achievable.

Clarifying which type of valuation is being used is obviously important philosophically, but it is important for other reasons as well. One reason is that each of the arguments for valuing equality is open to different objections. Valuing equality instrumentally increases the likelihood that a principle of equality will be overridden by a more important value, such as freedom. Intrinsic egalitarians, in contrast, face the objection that they have misunderstood the real concern for the disadvantaged, which is not to make people equal but to help the worst-off or give people enough of what they need.[2] Such criticisms also imply that this misunderstanding leads to unpalatable and absurd consequences, such as the idea that intrinsic egalitarians will have to "level down" the better-off to achieve equality. The leveling down objection occupies an important place in this debate, and it is discussed in more detail below. The objection concerns what some nonegalitarians think is a logical consequence of valuing equality intrinsically. Some argue that if equality really is important, there is something good about leveling down the well-off even if it does not directly benefit the worst-off.

These ways of valuing equality seem to present us with stark alternatives: either equality is valuable in and of itself, which is hard to establish, or it is valuable only because it has other good consequences. But even if equality is to be valued "merely" because of its instrumental features, this does not mean that there is not a very strong reason to promote equality. Equality might be strongly instrumentally necessary for the peaceful operation of social institutions and just outcomes.[3] But even setting this important point aside, we should not be too easily won over to this neat valuation of equality as either instrumentally or intrinsically valuable. The conceptual language in which to describe equality's value is richer than understanding equality as either intrinsically or instrumentally valuable in a straightforward way and allows a more nuanced assessment of how we should capture the value of equality. One thing we should also note here is that it is not the concept of equality alone that faces this problem. For instance, how we value freedom also faces a similar set of difficulties. Is freedom valuable because it leads to other important goods being realized, or is it just valuable in and of itself? Traditionally, egalitarians have understood equality as part of a bigger set of claims about social justice.[4] This valuation is echoed in the modern debate, where many of the most important arguments about why equality is valuable have occurred either in relation to discussion of another philosophically important value or in the context of a specific issue such as health. But in order to see that, we need to appreciate the kinds of reasons often advanced in favor of equality. As we will see, ultimately equality is important because of the broader role it plays in securing the conditions for living in a just society. In what follows, we explore the recent debate about why equality matters. This involves discussing some of the contexts in which equality is important – because it increases self-respect, for instance – but the main task is to understand the types of arguments that have been given for equality's value.

The importance of equality

One way of getting a sense of equality's value is to understand the types of advantages that are said to derive from having a more equal society. For instance, equality is often defended on the grounds that it is essential for promoting respect. In this sense, respect as used in egalitarian contexts often means what Stephen Darwall calls "recognition respect," where an individual or society gives appropriate weight to some important fact about a person and then regulates individual or institutional conduct in light of that fact.[5] When we grant someone recognition respect, we might do so by recognizing that she is owed respect because she is a person and has a unique moral status. In an institutional context, this might lead to people having equal rights to certain goods or forms of treatment. As the next two chapters show, achieving an equal distribution of important goods involves determining which metric of goods best suits the framework of justice. Many critics of inequality have pointed to how political and social practices fail to show people respect where significant inequalities exist. For instance, Elizabeth Anderson argues that many egalitarian political movements have objected to the demeaning stereotypes surrounding the disabled and other politically oppressed groups.[6] Welfare recipients, for example, often complain that the institutions with which they interact, as well as society in general, treat and regard them as citizens of inferior status. Receiving unemployment or parenting benefits is often said to have a stigma attached that generates disdain from others in society and may lead to discrimination in relation to other goods, such as jobs and housing. One of Anderson's major complaints against luck egalitarianism – a view that puts personal responsibility at the forefront of theories of justice – is that it subjects such citizens to demeaning and intrusive judgments about whether they are willing and able to look for work. Anderson speculates about what it would be like for benefits to the unemployed to be determined by inquiring of persons whether their disadvantage – disability, unintelligence, ugliness, or lack of marketable talent – is their fault or just a matter of a lack of natural talents. She asks us to imagine a letter, such as the following, from the State Equality Board that comes with the benefits to the naturally disadvantaged:

> To the stupid and untalented: Unfortunately, other people don't value what little you have to offer in the system of production. Your talents are too meager to command much market value. Because of the misfortune that you were born so poorly endowed with talents, we productive ones will make it up to you: we will let you share in the bounty of what we have produced.[7]

As far-fetched as this scenario is, Anderson's point is that treating people with respect should not involve being overly intrusive or forcing them to admit failings that they cannot help. Stigmatizing differences in status might also be manifested through cultural means – for instance, where a legitimate cultural practice is ridiculed or its participants forced to defend it against harmful attacks. Anderson claims that equality of the conditions of people's freedom is essential for respecting people in society and, as such, ought not to be overridden by a concern with making sure an account of personal responsibility is at the forefront of a theory of justice.

A related but different concern is that inequalities of income and wealth make it more likely that some will be subservient to others.[8] This is a traditional theme of egalitarian thought going back at least to the early English political movement, the Levellers.[9] Individuals who have vastly superior wealth may be able to dictate conditions of employment to others, influence the political process, set social agendas, or take advantage of scarce opportunities or resources otherwise unavailable. In commenting on whether his view of justice is egalitarian, one of the reasons that Rawls gives for why equality is valuable is that it does not involve some people being considered inferior by others and, importantly, by themselves.[10] Domination may or may not lead to feelings of inferiority on the part of those dominated. But insofar as it does, it introduces an extra dimension of harm because of its effect on the resilience and sense of self of those whom it affects. Attitudes of deference and servility may be damaging psychologically to those who internalize them and may produce attitudes in the dominators that are "great vices," as Rawls puts it.[11] For Rawls, a person's self-respect will be diminished when the institutional structures of society do not recognize important facts about people or groups of people and do not treat them as equal citizens.[12] For instance, where people are discriminated against because of their race, denied political rights because of their particular culture, or subjected to demeaning stereotypes, they are treated as publicly inferior. Here, the value of addressing inequalities of wealth and power derives instrumentally from how doing so contributes to the goal of giving individuals control over their lives. Inequality is bad not just because it is not part of what a proper democratic society ought to look like but because of the pernicious effect it has on dimensions of individual lives. On these accounts, whatever else it may be, equality is instrumentally good if it contributes to eliminating practices that treat people in disrespectful ways. But for Rawls, as we will see, equality is also good in itself wherever society makes use of fair procedures.[13]

Egalitarians also claim that high levels of inequality, especially in regard to income and wealth, may greatly increase the likelihood that some groups in society will increase the suffering of the poor. Referring to equality, Rousseau famously asserted that with regard to wealth, "No citizen shall be wealthy enough to buy another, and none poor enough to be forced to sell himself."[14] Where wealth in particular is more evenly distributed, people might have access to better health care, afford decent accommodations, or be employed in better jobs. Richard Wilkinson reports that in the United States and Canada, states that have more inequality show a tenfold difference in homicide rates.[15] The case for more equal societies is bolstered further by evidence about the impact of inequality on likelihood of voting, increased levels of stress, lack of cooperation, and health.[16]

One prominent reason for preventing inequality relates to the claims now made concerning the importance of health inequalities. A number of authors have developed an impressive body of research on the relationship between equality and a range of poor health and well-being outcomes. Much of the literature on the social determinants of health, as it has come to be known, has identified inequality as a major contributor to poor health outcomes. This is not simply the claim that poverty and deprivation are bad for one's health.[17] A large body of empirical evidence now points to the link between inequality across a range of indicies (work status, control at work, income) and poor health outcomes. Especially in relation to income inequality, it is claimed that it is not just the overall level of income and wealth in societies that matters for health outcomes but how that wealth is distributed. For instance, Michael Marmot's now famous Whitehall studies of British civil servants show a correlation between the grade of the civil servant and mortality and morbidity rates.[18] Each grade in the service does worse in terms of health outcomes than the one above it, yet none are in poverty. Allowing for genetic factors, age, and so on, Marmot's study points to the inequality between the different levels of civil servants as contributing to the difference in health outcomes. Others, such as Wilkinson, have posited strong correlations between inequalities of various types cited earlier. One example concerns the lack of trust and fraternity in very unequal societies. According to Wilkinson and Pickett, levels of trust are higher in countries with greater income equality.[19] They cite a number of studies which suggest that income inequality affects the level of trust in society. Where there is less trust, people are less willing to cooperate, are more reluctant to volunteer, and generally treat others with less respect.[20] If this research is accurate, its meaning in the context of this discussion is that more egalitarian societies do better than less egalitarian ones in terms of certain types of health outcomes. It also provides an interesting further argument for equality. At first glance this looks like a straightforwardly instrumental argument: equality is important because it leads to better health outcomes. But as we will see, research on the connection between inequality and health might also be understood as showing that equality is part of what makes for a just society in a more substantial way.

One of the areas in which the demand for equality has been strongest is in relation to politics. Ensuring that each citizen's views can be represented through equal voting rights or the ability to run for office and participate in the political process is at the core of modern democracies. While I do not here consider these kinds of demands in any detail, note that this demand for equality is a type of equal consideration that has other forms closer to the modern debate concerning egalitarianism. The demand that all citizens of a state get equal consideration from their government is, as Dworkin claims, the "sovereign virtue" of political community.[21] One of the most important ways in which this has been understood is in terms of ensuring that everyone has equal access to conditions for life to go well. This demand for equality is more than simply being free of oppression or domination. Rather, it is a demand for certain goods (being housed or mobile), opportunities (the ability to get an education), or even certain outcomes (e.g., concerning health) that allow people to lead meaningful lives. Identifying what these goods are has been the subject of the "metric" or "currency" debate and is one of the most important of the senses of what the demand for equality entails. The demand for equal access to the conditions required for people's lives to go well is also not limited to claims on fellow citizens. This demand has also been powerfully expressed in terms that do not depend on a person being a citizen of one country, as we discuss in Chapter 4.

A number of other reasons why equality is valuable are connected to other fundamental values. For example, equality has been strongly linked to the value of fairness in two ways that are significant here. Egalitarians object to inequalities because they want to "preserve the equality of starting places which is required by procedural fairness" and because "procedural fairness sometimes supports a case for equality of outcomes."[22] In the first case equality is required to ensure that fair procedures are not undermined in, for instance, the acquisition of property or competition for employment. The claim is that the institution of a "level playing field" or "fair race" sometimes requires equality.[23] But note that "treating like cases alike" itself is not uniquely egalitarian and will likely be endorsed by most theories of justice. Equality might also be valued intrinsically, just as freedom and other ultimate values are. As with freedom so with equality: the value of achieving it might not reside in whether people are directly benefited by the ideal. Equality is just one of those ultimate values we ought to try to achieve. This does not, of course, mean that it is the only value we should use to guide us in evaluating whether an action is just. As we will see, leveling down the well-off might not be the best course of action because other ultimate values, such as utility, should also guide us. The second case is more strongly egalitarian because it claims equal outcomes might also be a proper consequence of fair procedures. Such a principle might be invoked when individuals who are part of a cooperative scheme are said to have a claim to the benefits of that scheme. Outcomes matter because fairness often demands that if people have an equal claim to something, they have the same amount of that thing. We can also see this kind of claim at work in the global arena. Although we might have a claim to the products of social cooperation if we are cooperating members of a social scheme, our claims to a share of emission rights, for instance, need not be based on claims of cooperation because we did not create the atmosphere.

All these examples tell us something important about how equality is valued. Lessening inequalities in wealth may be necessary for having a society that is not plagued by social tension and discord. This is a powerful kind of instrumental reason for avoiding one kind of inequality. Perhaps the closest that equality comes to a stand-alone value might be where it is an important moral value. The moral imperative to treat people in ways that do not violate their dignity and freedom – say, by enslaving or humiliating them – in part stems from the fundamental respect in which people ought to be considered moral equals. Yet according to the framework outlined earlier, several of these reasons might plausibly fall into different categories. For instance, thinking of equality as important because it is a necessary condition for democracy might value it because it is a vital step to achieving democracy (an instrumental reason) or because it is part of what democracy includes (a constitutive reason). Equality might simply be valued as intrinsically valuable. These three reasons – intrinsic, instrumental, and constitutive – will be our focus in this discussion as they are crucial for understanding the contemporary philosophical debate about equality. In what follows we are interested in the defenses of and objections to these different ways of valuing equality. One of the most useful ways of doing this is by considering some of the main rivals to equality, especially to its having intrinsic value. Analyzing rival distributive principles will also help us assess whether it is a principle of equality or some other principle that is useful in explaining many different types of injustice.

1.2   Equality as intrinsically valuable

Egalitarians will recommend that the distribution of goods and resources and the structure of social relationships be organized so as to achieve equality in some significant respect. As we have seen, the justification for these views is connected to a broad range of arguments. Many of these justifications are recognizable concerns of the left and liberal left, which have evolved out of a mixture of the claims of social movements for justice and more traditional philosophical interests. Yet even though many of these goals might be widely held by people sympathetic to egalitarianism, it has been suggested that the insight that motivates such concern is not equality at all but something entirely different. To give an example, suppose that two groups in society have profoundly different lives. The individuals in one group are beset by poverty, physical insecurity, lack of education, an absence of basic health care, and so on. Individuals in the other group experience few or none of these disadvantages, and their lives go well. This description of suffering and inequality is characteristic of many countries in the twentieth century and is arguably becoming more prevalent. But critics argue that, in fact, egalitarians are wrong to suppose that they have a monopoly of ways of capturing what is unjust about this situation and to suppose that it is inequality that drives our concern. They object that egalitarians have focused on how the poor or disadvantaged do relative to the well-off. But is this really what attracts our interest? They argue that it is not the *comparative* judgment that some are better off than others but the *absolute* claim that some people do not have enough of what they need (sufficiency). Similarly, what might really motivate us to alleviate the condition of the disadvantaged in the preceding scenario is not a concern for equalizing the situation of the two groups but that in any future redistribution of important goods we ensure that those in dire poverty are given priority over those who are well-off (priority). In a distributive setting, sufficientarians claim that we should ensure that people have enough, while prioritarians advocate distributions that favor the worst-off. Both of these positions contrast with those favoring equality as the guiding distributive principle.

These two alternatives to equality – sufficiency and prioritarianism or priority – provide alternative ways of determining how to organize social institutions and distribute resources. Fundamentally, their supporters argue, our concern with poverty of the type described here is noncomparative rather than comparative; egalitarians get things wrong when they argue that what matters is the comparative judgment that one life goes as well as another; the more important question is whether someone has enough or whether we are directing our attention to the worst-off, even if they never have as much as others. This is not to say that sufficientarians and prioritarians have no place for equality in designing social schemes that would make people better off. Someone who believed that poverty ought to be reduced might very well argue that the best and most effective way of achieving this would be to institute free and equal health care or equal access to justice through the legal system. These egalitarian measures might garner wide support for their contribution to relieving suffering. But where such support differs from standard egalitarian claims is in how equality is valued. In these examples equality has no ethical significance of its own. These two views thus not only offer an alternative to egalitarianism (with their own foundation and set of philosophical difficulties) but provide a window on why equality is valuable. Each of these alternative views could be discussed as a stand-alone theory. Here I elaborate each, principally to highlight the issue of the value of equality.

1.3 Equality and sufficiency

Consider the situation in which there are very many people who lack the basic resources to live even a moderately good life when at the same time there are plenty of people in the world who have more than enough. Egalitarians argue that part of the injustice of this situation is that people are unequal. An alternative explanation is that what disturbs us about this situation is not the difference between the well-off and the poor but the actual condition of the poor. Thus, the moral intuition is, in fact, not strictly an egalitarian one about how one group fares compared with another but a noncomparative claim about poverty. In "Equality as a Moral Ideal," Harry Frankfurt claims that what we want for the poor is not that they have the same as the wealthy but that they have enough, or sufficient.[24] Frankfurt writes: "With respect to the distribution of economic assets, what *is* important from the point of view of morality is not that everyone should have *the same* but that each should have *enough*."[25]

Frankfurt argues that the sufficiency view, or sufficientarianism, captures what we find disturbing about disadvantage. Moreover, not only does sufficiency do better at capturing our intuitions, but equality itself is a dangerous ideal. What is bad about equality for Frankfurt is that it is alienating. A pursuit of equality suggests that we ignore what is really good for us as unique individuals and instead enjoins us to be satisfied with goods whose nature and numbers are determined by what others have.[26] He asks us to imagine the following example, which shows the moral unacceptability of egalitarianism. Suppose that there is enough of a crucial resource to enable some but not all of a certain population in a country to survive. For argument's sake, assume that the population of the country is ten people; each needs five units of the resource to survive, and only forty units are available. Frankfurt claims that the best approach in this situation is to ensure that as many people as possible have enough. We should, then, aim at sufficiency. If we apply a principle of strict equality in isolation, everyone should get four units, in which case everyone dies. Frankfurt argues that prioritarianism also produces implausible results here because prioritarians cannot appeal to the justification that saving eight and letting two die is benefiting the worst-off. Nor can they claim that "*where some people have less than enough no-one should have more than enough.*"[27] In a slightly different scenario, one where there are forty-one units of a good, giving the one unit extra to someone who was going to get nothing will still not improve his or her condition, according to Frankfurt, and indeed may worsen it by prolonging that person's starvation. So prioritarians such as Nagel alleg-edly confuse what is important about our motivations in responding to poverty.[28] For Frankfurt, when Nagel endorses Rawls's difference principle, whereby the needs of the worst-off are given priority, he has conflated being worse off with having urgent needs. The trouble with a view that focuses on the worst-off is that there is no reason to suppose that being worse off should be what attracts our moral concern because the worst-off may have no urgent moral needs whatsoever. Some indi-viduals might have less than other people but more than enough to lead the life they want, and whether they have less than others might well be a matter of indifference to them. For Frankfurt, once people have enough, others having more does not matter. Inequalities of money above the threshold are morally irrelevant.[29] Thus a sufficientarian such as Frankfurt makes two distinct claims: a positive claim that people have enough and a negative claim that additional distributive principles, such as equality, are not important.[30] The value of equality – if any – will be entirely dependent on whether it contributes to achieving sufficiency. But there are a number of difficulties with sufficientarian approaches. Two I focus on here are what we might call the *scarcity argument* for sufficiency and the *threshold problem*.[31]

Scarcity

One of the most intuitive arguments for sufficiency is that it is better able to cope with instances where a scarce resource must be divided such that not everyone can reach a threshold level. For instance, in Frankfurt's example, if there was only enough medicine to save five of a group of ten people, a sufficiency principle would do better than equality or priority principles, at least when construed as exclusive prin-ciples. According to Frankfurt, strict egalitarians will wastefully insist either that no one gets anything or that the medicine gets spread too thin to be of any use. Strict priority would tell us to benefit the worst-off even if they may not survive and the medicine would be better used on the less-badly-off. Casal notes that sufficientarians can appeal to two separate reasons when defending their claim. The first is that princi-ples other than sufficiency fail to get the people in scarcity cases to the required threshold. But this claim only proves the positive sufficien-tarian claim: thresholds matter. It does not establish that once everyone has enough, equality has no role. For instance, extending the medical case, Casal claims we could imagine that in a situation where patients had enough and there was a large donation to the hospital that provided extraordinary resources that could be used to greatly enhance medical treatment, it would be unfair of the hospital administrators to distribute it to just one or two people. If this is correct, then the sufficientarian has not established the negative part of his or her claim: once a threshold is attained, we should not care about equality.[32]

Appeals to the wastefulness and inefficiency of egalitarianism are also part of the sufficientarian armory, which is the second possible defense. In the medical case described earlier, sufficientarians argue that egalitarians are committed to an absurd view because they claim it is good in one way if we level down all the patients so that everyone has an equal but insufficient amount of the medicine. For sufficientarians, this shows the moral absurdity and wastefulness of egalitarianism. As we will see, egalitarians have several responses to leveling down. To prefigure one, several egalitarians claim that equality's value is conditional on its being part of other values, and where those values do not hold, equality should also not be implemented. Andrew Mason argues for a position such as this when he claims that equality's value is conditional on its benefiting some, and that is not the case in the medical example.[33] (We return to this issue later in discussing leveling down.) A second response is to argue that equality matters, but it is not all that matters. Egalitarians can claim that other values, such as utility, matter in this scenario and hence they will not be in the position of letting everyone die simply to ensure that equality is fulfilled.

Thresholds

In claiming that we should only be concerned about disadvantage below the threshold and not above it, sufficientarians must determine what the relevant threshold is. Frankfurt's claim is that thresholds are determined by whether people are content with what they have. He writes:

> If a person is (or ought reasonably to be) content with the amount of money he has, then insofar as he is or has reason to be unhappy with the way his life is going, he does not (or cannot reasonably) suppose that more money would – either as a sufficient or as a necessary condition – enable him to become (or have reason to be) significantly less unhappy with it.[34]

A person is at the threshold where he or she is content with (in this case) how much money he or she has. Frankfurt is at pains to note that his threshold is not at the level of just getting by but at a reasonably high level. There is an issue here about whether this method of delivering a threshold is vulnerable to a concern about adaptive preferences.

A person might be content with what she has because of having low expectations after years of disappointment and may have adapted her preferences to suit her (unsatisfactory) situation. Frankfurt might be able to escape this charge by insisting, as he does, that contentment is a matter of what we *ought reasonably to be* content with, which implies some sort of standard separate from a person's subjective preferences, in which case the threshold is no longer whether a person is content. Nonetheless, setting a threshold that does not rely entirely on people's preferences in a nonarbitrary way might prove hard to do. A further worry is that if a threshold is low, it may be meetable but insufficient for justice. If it is too high, it may not be meetable for all or even very many people. When the threshold is set high and not everyone can attain it, priority and ranking considerations are reintroduced.[35]

A more pressing objection is why getting people across a threshold is so important compared with achieving other improvements in people's lives. If crossing a threshold is more important than, say, merely achieving great gains for the worst-off, sufficientarians will be left with some counterintuitive results. For instance, transferring large amounts of resources from those above the line for a trivial gain to those below the line seems counterintuitive and to lack any sense of proportion. One might, as Roger Crisp does, specify that we should give absolute priority to those below the threshold where only nontrivial benefits count, leaving sufficientarians open to the charges of inefficiency and neglect of the worst-off.[36] But even here, we would still be required to exact huge sacrifices from many people above the threshold to make a small nontrivial benefit. Imagine an extremely expensive medical technology that would allow a small group of very old individuals to regain their hearing. In order to get the technology, say that a million otherwise well-off individuals would be reduced to just above the threshold. Where sufficiency is a "trumping principle," this would be what is required.[37]

1.4 Prioritarianism

Sufficientarian critics of equality worry that it fails to capture what motivates us in our concern for disadvantage and rests on a mistake about what we really care about. Sufficientarians try to capture that concern through the idea of raising people to a threshold. Yet we have seen that this approach is vulnerable to objections about how to determine and value a threshold and whether a sufficiency view can claim that equality is never relevant above a threshold. Prioritarians, on the other hand, claim that a better way to capture what we should care about is via the principle of prioritizing the worst-off. Instead of equalizing people's condition or raising them to a level of sufficiency, we should direct our resources to those whose lives are, in an absolute sense, worse than they should be: the worst-off.[38] Prioritarians thus claim that prioritizing the interests of the worst-off is the proper basis for our distribution of resources and is what we should really care about in the situation where there are inequalities. One advantage of the priority view over equality views is that it escapes the apparent difficulty that confronts egalitarians, especially intrinsic egalitarians, that there is something morally valuable about achieving equality even when the outcome is not good in other ways. Derek Parfit has provided the most famous articulation of this concern. His claim – that intrinsic egalitarianism is subject to a damning objection, the *leveling-down objection* – should, if correct, lead us to support prioritarianism. Parfit uses a number of distinctions to set up his argument. He divides egalitarians into two broad groups. *Telic egalitarians* believe that "it is in itself bad if some people are worse off than others."[39] As such, they value equality intrinsically, wherever and between whom it occurs, and not for some other reason. *Deontic egalitarians* value equality for some other moral reason. They may value equality because it would be unfair or unjust if two people with otherwise identical claims to some resource got unequal shares of it. For Parfit, deontic views are also connected with claims about injustice, where injustice is a special kind of badness involving wrongdoing. Thus, what matters when inequalities are unjust is that they have been produced in the wrong way.

Leveling down

If equality really is valuable for its own sake, then, Parfit claims, egalitarians are committed to the view that there is something good about bringing the well-off down to the level of the poor even if leveling them down benefits no one. For instance, Parfit claims that egalitarians must argue that there is something good in a society that takes away some people's sight to make them equal with the blind. On an egalitarian position that holds equality intrinsically valuable, an increase in inequality is bad in one way. If this is the case, then, as Parfit puts it, "its disappearance must be in at least one way a change for the better, *however this change occurs*," which Parfit finds absurd.[40] For Parfit, egalitarians are committed to the claim that inequality is bad even if it is worse for no one.

So on what Parfit calls a "strong egalitarian" position, this is true. Parfit provides an example of a simple case of distributive justice.

(1) All at 100.
(2) Half at 100, half at 101.
(3) Half at 100, half at 110.
(4) Half at 100, half at 200.

For Parfit's strong egalitarians, the move from (1) to (2) is bad because of the increase in inequality, as are the moves from (1) to (3) and so on. According to Parfit, strong egalitarians must regard the move from (1) to (2) as a bad outcome even though it is worse for no one. What he calls moderate egalitarians could accept at least (2) and (3) because they combine their commitment to equality with other values such as utility. Underlying Parfit's example is what he calls the "person-affecting claim," which is that if an outcome is worse for no one, it cannot be in any way worse. Moreover, according to Parfit, if telic egalitarians believe that equality has intrinsic value, they will be concerned with eliminating inequality whenever and wherever it occurs. This means that telic egalitarianism has an implausibly large scope. The plight of Inca peasants and Stone Age peoples should concern the telic egalitarian as much as the plight of the poor today. If telic egalitarians deny this claim and assert only an interest in inequalities within one community, this suggests that they are deontic egalitarians because a claim about social injustice is involved.

On Parfit's priority view, what matters is that "benefiting people matters more the worse off these people are." This is the crucial difference between prioritarianism and egalitarianism. Like sufficientarians, prioritarians are interested in how people's lives go in an absolute and not a relative sense. Prioritarians care that people are worse off but not because they are worse off than other people; only that they are worse off than they might have been. As Parfit puts it:

> People at higher altitudes find it harder to breathe. Is this because they are higher up than other people? In one sense, yes. But they would find it just as hard to breathe even if there were no other people who were lower down. In the same way, on the Priority view, benefits to the worse off matter more, but that is only because these people are at a lower *absolute* level. It is irrelevant that these people are worse off *than others*. Benefits to them would matter just as much even if there *were* no others who were better off.[41]

What concerns prioritarians is absolute disadvantage as opposed to relative disadvantage. As we saw, this difference has several implications, chief of which is that telic egalitarianism, at least, has a much larger scope than prioritarianism and is committed to leveling down. Note that prioritarians can still support equality but only for instrumental reasons. They might think that equalizing some distributional aspect of well-being, such as certain health outcomes or pension entitlements, is necessary for a society free of strife. Likewise, egalitarians might also be instrumental prioritarians in that they think that benefiting the worse-off in a noncomparative way is likely to increase equality in the long run.

Prioritarianism has obvious appeal as a way of allocating resources. It not only makes a claim to capture our motivations in dealing with disadvantage but also appears to avoid some of the moral difficulties that egalitarianism must overcome. A version of the priority view specifically applied to distributive justice can be found in Rawls's *Theory of Justice*. Rawls's difference principle seeks to capture the appeal of benefiting the worst-off on top of a baseline of equality. In relation to social and economic advantages, the relevant part of Rawls's second principle states that "social and economic inequalities are to be arranged so that they are both (a) to the greatest benefit of the least advantaged. ... "[42] The difference principle permits inequalities of wealth insofar as they are to the advantage of the least-well-off.[43] Rawls argues that the arrangement of institutions should follow the general principle of, first, maximizing the welfare of the worst-off, followed by the next-worst-off and so on.[44] If our distributive arrangements must benefit the worst-off, the better-off will have an incentive to benefit the worst-off when they increase their wealth and engage in economic activity. Without such improvements to the well-being of the worst-off, the resulting inequalities are unjust. The resulting distribution, according to Rawls, will be efficient and will conform to the "principle of Pareto-optimality": "A configuration is efficient whenever it is impossible to change it so as to make some persons (at least one) better off without at the same time making other persons (at least one) worse off."[45]

Like Parfit's view discussed earlier, Rawls's conception entails a departure from equality. Leaving aside the issue of the extent to which Rawls's overall theory is egalitarian or not, giving priority to the worst-off, as the lexical difference principle does, raises a number of issues for prioritarian distribution.[46]

It is important to note that prioritarianism is a kind of position that gives rise to many possible types of distributive principles. Rawls's difference principle and its leximin variant both assign absolute priority to the worst-off. Where a gain can be made for one of the worst-off, that person should be given priority in the distribution of resources for Rawls. One concern with this sort of absolute weighting of the needs of the worst-off is that it might lead to poorer and less efficient outcomes overall. For instance, where a huge cost is required to provide a small benefit to the worst-off, it may be better to use the resources to assist those who are not the worst-off (they might be the second-worst-off) but who could nonetheless benefit from the resources. For example, imagine a small group of people who are worse off than everyone else because of a rare medical condition that requires extremely expensive medical technologies to sustain them at a level of well-being just above adequate. What the medical technology example is supposed to show is that with what it would cost to enhance the lives of these people, we might be able to raise large numbers of worse-off groups to a very high level of well-being. Richard Arneson defends a kind of weighted prioritarianism that attempts to bypass this problem by assigning nonabsolute priority to the worst-off.[47] He argues that the value of prioritarianism comes from two features: that it assigns priority to the worst-off but only "provided that the total of benefits is thereby increased."[48] So a prioritarian can assign priority to the worst-off and be prepared to transfer benefits to the better-off if the gain in well-being is of a sufficient size.

1.5   Egalitarian responses

Pluralism

Prioritarian claims about leveling down might elicit several kinds of responses from egalitarians. The first kind is to claim that any plausible egalitarian theory of justice will not level down in most cases. This is the position taken by Larry Temkin. Temkin, in fact, has two types of reply, which we can call a *pluralist response* and a *fairness response*. The pluralist response is simply the claim that equality, while valuable, is not all that matters. So when confronted with the example of the blinding of the sighted discussed earlier, Temkin responds that equality matters, but so do other values: "But, the anti-egalitarian will incredulously ask, do I *really* think there is some respect in which a world where only some are blind is worse than one where all are? Yes. Does this mean I think that it would be better if we blinded everyone? No. Equality is not all that matters. But it matters some."[49] Temkin goes on to say that the leveling-down objection stems from being mesmerized by "pure equality's" terrible implications when there are always likely to be reasons why, all things considered, we would not choose to level down. Temkin is surely right to suggest that any egalitarian theory will appeal to other values in such cases. Any theory that recommends blinding the sighted just to achieve equality will be morally and politically unpalatable. If, for instance, egalitarians accepted a principle of utility that implied there is something morally better about individuals being better off, they might think that if utility were diminished significantly by leveling down, we would have an all-things-considered reason to not level down. The pluralist defense relies on weighing equality against other values that have an independent value. We might consider this an external defense because it relies on the relation of equality to values that are external to equality to enable us to determine when a principle of equality should be applied.

Fairness

Egalitarians might also respond in a different way by linking the value of equality to its relation to another value internally. To elaborate: pluralist responses show that egalitarians are unlikely to find themselves lumped with these kinds of difficult choices, yet the real issue posed by the leveling-down objection is whether there is *any* value in leveling down at all. Perhaps the most prominent response to the challenge posed by the leveling-down objection is to argue that equality can avoid the problems with leveling down because of the essential internal role it plays in connection with other values. Recall the list of reasons to value equality outlined in Section 1.1; they provided a map of the kinds of values with which equality has been linked. Rather than argue that leveling down will not occur because all-things-considered judgments will never endorse leveling down, approaches that locate equality's value within other values sometimes argue that there is something good in leveling down. This head-on approach is a direct challenge to Parfit's objection and, unlike the pluralism response to leveling down, links equality internally rather than externally to other values. Temkin's second defense of equality is of this form. He argues that there is *some* value in leveling down; his attempt to demonstrate this is what is interesting about his defense of equality as an intrinsic value. Temkin's response to the leveling-down objection has been to argue that the harm of inequality derives from the injustice it creates because the value of equality is part of the value of fairness. He argues that what underpins this Parfittian view is "the slogan" – the claim that "one situation *cannot* be worse (or better) than another *in any respect* if there is no one for whom it *is* worse (or better) *in any respect*."[50] Temkin's response to Parfit is thus to argue that equality is still valuable despite its not being person-affecting. Temkin's saints and sinners example (see Figure 1.1) is meant

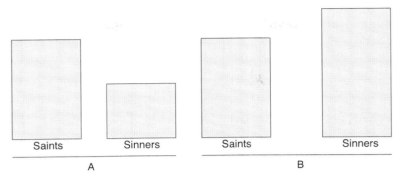

Figure 1.1 Temkin's "saints and sinners" example

to highlight that there are impersonal goods relevant to the assessment of the value of equality.[51]

The example compares situation A, in which the saints' lives are better than the sinners', with situation B, where the level of the saints' lives is the same but the sinners now have a better quality of life than the saints. That sinners' lives go better than saints' lives does not affect the self-interest of the saints, but it is a worse state of affairs, according to Temkin, because it ignores the connection between doing well and faring well – that is, it ignores proportional justice. Temkin's argument is that achieving proportional justice has intrinsic value, and so the slogan can be rejected on the grounds that there are impersonal principles that are relevant in assessing the goodness of outcomes, not just person-affecting ones. The ideal of proportional justice makes A preferable to B, because sinners do less well in A. But if the slogan is true, then B is preferable to A, because the saints are not less well off in B and the sinners are even better off. B is better for some people than A and worse for no one, so according to the slogan, B is better than A. Temkin claims, "Most people believe there would be *something* morally bad about the evilest mass murderers faring better than the most benign saints, even if there was *no one* for whom it was worse."[52] Temkin is claiming that there is a class of principles – for example, principles of retributive justice – where we accept their Pareto inefficient qualities.

Temkin's argument relies on attacking the slogan and on the claim that there are impersonal goods that matter. Leaving aside for now this issue in metaethics, one response to Temkin is to deny that the slogan is really what motivates us to reject leveling down. Temkin bites the bullet on this issue of whether telic egalitarianism does value equality intrinsically, though without offering an elaboration of how it is intrinsically valuable if it is part of another value. The implication of Temkin's view is a direct challenge to Parfit's objection that leveling down is absurd. Temkin sees some value in leveling down even though a pluralist will also have reasons not to level down.[53] Even granting the pluralism response, it might still leave the problem that equality should not be understood as being of intrinsic value, since it is part of another value, such as fairness, and relies on a notion of impersonal good.

Susan Hurley argues that it is not the person-affecting requirement that is the most plausible motivation for the leveling-down objection but "impersonal perfectionism and the value of excellence."[54] If leveling down occurs, then some good (health, wealth, or whatever it is) will be needlessly destroyed, and so it is the sheer wastefulness of leveling down to which we should object. She claims that the question that the slogan raises is whether or not equality could be better if it is better for no one, whereas she thinks that the most intuitively plausible reason why we should object to leveling down is that it wastes excellence. The implication is that the world is a worse place with the loss of excellence that leveling down involves.[55]

Another response that has been advanced to defend equality because it is part of some other value has been to defend it in relation to fairness, though for reasons that do not relate to impersonal goods. John Broome's response to the problem of whether or not inequality is valuable is to argue that inequality is a harm to someone because it is unfair. He argues that when we deliberate about whether a person should receive a good, we should be concerned only with those claims that we should provide to the person concerned. Claims are the object of fairness, and fairness in turn requires that claims be satisfied relative to the satisfaction of other people's claims.[56] With respect to equality, he argues, "Whenever people have equal claims to something, then fairness requires they should have equal shares of it."[57] Dennis McKerlie makes a similar point when he claims that when we see individuals as having a moral claim to a fair share of society's resources, an equal distribution of resources is implied. Determining what a fair share is requires that we compare them to other people's shares, and without a further principle to regulate distribution, this implies an equal division of resources. To divide resources unequally is to imply that some people have a greater moral claim, and this cannot be supported without appeal to other principles.[58] Some people make this kind of argument in relation to the distribution of rights to use the atmosphere as a carbon sink by emitting greenhouse gases (GHG). For instance, an argument discussed in Chapter 4 is that since no one owns the atmosphere and all need to use it to emit GHGs, fairness demands that we all have an equal claim to use the atmosphere as a carbon sink – that is, all have an equal right to emit GHGs into the atmosphere. To argue that some of us have a right to a greater share would require us to produce a special reason why we should be treated differently. A more intuitive approach to how we value equality if it is part of fairness or other values is to say that it has value but nonintrinsic value. This is the approach taken by Martin O'Neill. O'Neill defends a nonintrinsic version of egalitarianism, rightly pointing out that Parfit's division into telic and deontic equality does not capture all the varieties (and certainly not the most plausible versions) of what egalitarians should believe. He argues that Parfit's claim that it is in itself bad if some people are worse off than others is "obscure," "abstract," and merely an "arithmetical" goal for egalitarians.[59] Along with Temkin's, this nonintrinsic valuation of equality confronts the leveling-down objection by appeal to a broader impersonal value. For O'Neill, Parfit's telic egalitarianism makes a claim about the importance of states of affairs and of a certain conception of intrinsic value. He endorses the former while rejecting the latter. O'Neill claims that nonintrinsic egalitarianism offers a more plausible solution to Parfit's telic egalitarianism. His view is telic – in that he accepts that egalitarians should be concerned with states of affairs – but not intrinsic. O'Neill's view is that "distributive equality is valuable because of its effects, and specifically by virtue of the fact that it brings about states of affairs that are themselves intrinsically valuable for egalitarian reasons."[60] For O'Neill, Parfit's telic egalitarianism is too pure; it does not recognize the sense in which equality is part of some other important egalitarian value.

Drawing on Scanlon's work on inequality,[61] O'Neill also connects equality's value to a range of five more fundamental reasons, including that equality reduces excessive domination or disrespect. Deontic egalitarianism does not fare any better, according to O'Neill, in that egalitarians need not appeal to "some other moral reason" other than the value of equal states of affairs to claim that inequality is bad. By linking equality internally in this way to other egalitarian political values, we have at least one way of responding to problems concerning the excessive scope of a principle of equality.[62] If it does gain its value from its relationship to other values, then the scope of equality is fixed by the reasons that we have to value equality, such as its promotion of self-respect. If equality is valuable because of its role in promoting self-respect, then a principle of equality's scope will be restricted to instances where it is possible for social relations that promote self-respect to occur. O'Neill makes the point that it is one thing to claim that the plight of Inca peasants mattered as much morally as the suffering of those alive today, but this is different from arguing that their suffering matters because it made them unequal to people alive today.[63] One of the advantages is that egalitarians persuaded by the constitutive value of equality will not be troubled by claims to equality from previously unknown inhabitants of desert islands or faraway planets unless it can be shown that they are covered by appropriate relations of justice. More generally and positively, appreciating the noninstrumental value of equality adds weight to the reasons that egalitarians have to endorse equality.

1.6 Valuing equality

To return to our original question concerning how we can value equality: what these discussions of the leveling-down objection demonstrate is that Parfit's distinction, while productive, divides the ways in which we value equality in too neat a manner and does not capture the different possible ways of valuing equality. This is so because Parfit bases his valuation of equality on a particular understanding of the intrinsic/instrumental definition of value. Parfit's "straightjacket" is both too restrictive and too neat. We need to reassess the outline of the debate about how to value equality in light of the discussion that offers a more realistic response to equality's value. What several of the positions here attempt to do is locate the value of equality *relationally*. Broome and McKerlie, O'Neill as well as Temkin, link what is wrong with inequality to broader notions of unfairness or injustice, as does Scanlon, even though they differ on questions of impersonal value. The discussions here in fact present three ways of valuing equality: as intrinsically valuable in Parfit's sense, where equality is valued in itself irrespective of other values; as merely instrumental, where it is valuable purely as a means – for example, where it is valued by utilitarians because of diminishing marginal utility; and what we have seen as the valuation favored by many contemporary egalitarians – namely, a valuation of equality because of its role in achieving other central values, such as self-respect.

We can see that this sort of valuation of equality is what many of the authors discussed here may have implicitly had in mind. If equality has value because it contributes to the goal of citizens having self-respect, then it has extrinsic value. Similarly, where equality is necessary for fair procedures, it will have value in this way, too. Echoing Scanlon's argument concerning the importance of equality for procedural fairness, one of the examples that Brighouse and Swift discuss – the importance of certain positional goods to the value of fair competition – may also bolster the case for constitutive equality. Consider the case where someone is able to use his or her vast wealth to buy political influence; it will create an unfair advantage when competing for office. As Brighouse and Swift put it, "In competitive contexts, it seems plausible both that only a fair chance is enough of a chance and that only an equal chance is a fair chance."[64] This seems very like the type of fairness-based argument for inequality that we discussed previously. Where someone has a claim to a share of or participation in some aspect of society, unless there is another reason to supplant it, a fair share implies an equal share.[65] Without further reasons to make the competition unfair, arguing for the importance of fair competition is also a noninstrumental argument for the value of equality.[66] This example points to what some have labeled "constitutive value."[67] While we cannot discuss this position comprehensively, the crucial thing to note about constitutive goods is that they contribute to the value of the intrinsic good in the sense that they are one of the reasons why the good has the value that it does. The relationship here is one of part to whole. Something in such a relation is still noninstrumentally valuable because it is part of a whole and derives its value from some other value, but it is intrinsically valuable because of its relation to what is intrinsically valuable. On this account, literature or works of art may be worthwhile in themselves because of their role in a good life. For example, if a life that includes engaging with literature (or politics, sports, and so on) is part of what it is to lead a good life, then works of literature will be noninstrumentally valuable parts of a good life. They are, therefore, extrinsically good by virtue of their deriving value from something else but worthwhile in themselves because of the role they play in the good life.[68] The value of constitutive goods derives not just from their causally contributing to the existence of an intrinsic good but from their being part of what is valuable about an intrinsic good. By contrast, instrumental goods may well be causally necessary for an intrinsic good without being part of the goal or definition of the intrinsic good. For example, the good of food enables a person to lead a good life, but it does not thereby constitute the good life.[69] These examples indicate that there are other ways in which equality can be valued if we are not confined to Parfit's distinctions concerning deontic/telic and intrinsic/nonintrinsic value. While we might argue about which of the valuations is best, the terrain is conceptually richer than it first appeared.

1.7 Conclusion

However we value equality, contemporary egalitarianism offers a variety of responses to the challenge posed by the leveling-down and other objections to valuing equality. Notwithstanding the difficulties that the individual arguments for equality may have, collectively these approaches to the problem of how to value equality offer a way around the dilemma with which we began: that too often arguments about equality either take it to be only instrumentally valuable or are seen to rely on an unrealistically strong intrinsic valuation of equality.

Reassessing the debate in this way allows us to do a number of things. As will be seen throughout the discussion of egalitarianism, one of the ways in which the debate needs to be reassessed is in terms of reconnecting equality with the claims of justice that have often motivated egalitarians. Constitutive valuations of equality tend to connect the value of equality to these prominent justice-type claims, such as equality's importance for self-respect or nondiscrimination. Conceptually, understanding the value of equality to lie in its connection to other values makes the basis of equality's value clearer and more plausible. The conceptual language in which to describe equality's value is richer than understanding equality as either intrinsically or instrumentally valuable in a straightforward way and allows a more nuanced assessment of how we should capture the value of equality – avoiding Parfit's conceptual framework. In terms of individual conceptions of justice, it better allows us to connect specific types of equality with recognizable claims about what a just society ought to look like. This is important because a theme of recent discussion is that egalitarians have lost the connections with other important values that have given egalitarianism its moral and political force (see Chapters 2 and 3). If equality does derive its value from its contribution to the kinds of values discussed at the beginning of this chapter, it is likely to be a politically robust principle. Claims that the world is more unequal due to excessive accumulations of wealth, whether in one country or globally, should still be at the forefront of egalitarian concern. If excessive inequality of wealth remains important, new understandings of why equality is important are also conceptually and politically relevant.

Note that in one sense we should not be tempted to think that valuing equality instrumentally gives us only a weak reason to support equality whereas valuing it intrinsically gives us a strong reason, as the debate sometimes suggests. In fact, instrumental valuations implied by the need to promote equality to reduce domination are very strong reasons to support equality because of the importance of eliminating domination. When we combine these and other instrumental reasons in equality's favor with the reasons linked to its constitutive importance, we can see that there are several distinct and important arguments for the importance of equality. There is, of course, an unambiguously good outcome to these arguments, which is that equality remains a powerful and important political principle.

2
Equality of What?

2.1 Introduction

The "equality of what?" debate is concerned with articulating a "metric" or "currency" of equality that is part of a theory of justice. As we have seen, whereas we might have equality in terms of all kinds of things – equality before the law, basic moral equality, for instance – typically egalitarians are concerned with a substantive understanding of equality that relates broadly to how well people's lives go, not just the formal equal freedoms that people may have, important though these are. A focus on equality of condition has traditionally been a defining feature of egalitarianism. More recently debate about which is the best metric has also occupied an important place in defining what egalitarianism stands for. The assessment of the "equality of what?" debate must contain at least two dimensions: (1) which metric is best able to achieve a valuable type of equality as part of a theory of justice; and (2) whether it does so in a substantial enough way. The latter question is particularly important.

The discussion of which metric is best able to serve as a principle of equality typically yields one of three broad answers, with many variations and combinations. Briefly, the three answers are that equality should be understood in terms of welfare, resources, and capabilities. Having equal welfare, *welfarism*, is usually understood in terms of the ability to have appropriate conscious states or to have one's preferences equally satisfied. Welfarists claim that if we are redistributing resources, why not direct them to what really matters to people: their preferences about how they want to live their lives. What really matters, after all, is to be able to be and do the things we want. Such an approach also respects the different types of goods people value. But welfarism also has objective versions that claim we can define an objective list of what is good for people.

Welfarism's main rival, *resourcism*, is the view that equality should be seen in terms of a set of resources – anything from goods and income to institutional background conditions, such as fair opportunity to compete for jobs. Resourcists aim to provide a bundle of all-purpose means that any citizen will want regardless of more specific life plans. Resourcists also claim that providing all-purpose means respects the plurality of ends that citizens have and allows them to exercise their own choices over such ends. The final view, the *capability approach*, understands the currency of egalitarianism in terms of the ability to be and do various important things: being part of a community, being nourished, having bodily integrity and so on. Capability theorists see the advantage of their view as lying in its ability to deal with human difference and the "hard cases," such as disability. Understanding equality in terms of a capability to do something allows for extra resources to be directed to those with disabilities, for instance. These three views and their variations and combinations occupy most of the debate concerning the content of equality.

Before we discuss the metrics in any detail, we should be clear about the kind of issues around which the debate revolves and some of the background assumptions. There are two general issues to bear in mind. One is whether the debate concerning which metric is best is actually comparing metrics against similar criteria. For example, when a supporter of one metric claims that it better advances freedom than a rival metric, are the same kinds of freedom being compared? Each metric claims to have its own way to advance freedom, and one of the tasks of this chapter is to assess how it does so. A second issue concerns how to assess whether a metric is substantive enough to be egalitarian. The "equality of what?" debate raises a broader set of questions on this concern, which needs to feature in an overall assessment of this part of the debate and give it an important context. As we will see, this distinguishes the egalitarianism debate from more general debates and from nonegalitarian discussions about disadvantage or well-being. An egalitarian metric also must encompass the diversity of human needs in the right way. This is particularly important when the needs result from a disadvantage such as disability. Addressing severe disadvantage caused by certain types of disability is surely one of the key requirements of any metric. Sen's capability metric certainly makes this one of its aims, and he claims that one of the things in favor of his metric is that it can adequately address such disadvantage. Yet we ought to be aware that the best versions of other metrics might also be able to address concerns about disability. Resourcists such as Pogge claim that their approaches not only can but better capture concern for the disabled.[1]

As with the value of equality debate discussed in Chapter 1, the answer to the question "equality of what?" is also connected to broader debates in philosophy, albeit in a different way. Whereas the value of equality debate was closer to metaethical debates, the "equality of what?" debate is tied to debates between rival theories of justice. The connection to such theories is a descriptive feature of the debate but also something that is or should be part of the egalitarian discussion of equality. Thomas Pogge is surely right to emphasize that the question of which metric is best cannot be answered in isolation but only in conjunction with overall theories of justice.[2] This is, in fact, how the main advocates of the resourcist view, for instance, put forward their positions. Indeed, one of the main criticisms of the capabilities metric is that it cannot provide such an account. Being a part of a theory of justice also provides a specific context for what can be part of a conception of equality – what we can call the "constraints of justice." First, the type of equality we consider here is not a general moral theory of equality between people per se but part of what is due them as a matter of justice. The metrics typically do not concern what might be advantageous for people to have in equal measure for their well-being in general. Thinking of equality as part of a theory of justice introduces important constraints. Equality of the type relevant to a theory of justice is something citizens can demand (at least in the domestic case), even using coercion or sanctions, in a way that members of a group or association cannot demand of each other. As Anderson notes, making a claim of the form "the world would be better if state X were realized" does not imply that anyone necessarily has a duty to bring about state X or can coercively utilize the resources of others to achieve state X.[3] Liberal political philosophers also typically require that principles used to distribute goods be subject to publicity conditions; for instance, that society is effectively regulated by principles of justice and that citizens know this.[4] Again, this is a difference from non-justice-based conceptions of equality per se. Such restrictions will have an effect on what can form part of the metric. Given that citizens have diverse conceptions of the good, needs and handicaps, and so on, any metric will typically have to be of a form where what is equalized could be available to everyone in an appropriate form. As we will see, this is not equivalent to a claim that everyone ought to get exactly the same amount of "stuff"; some may get more of something in order to make them equal to others in terms of some broader goal, such as being able to be mobile, which may take more resources where someone is disabled. The metrics are also typically discussed in connection with distinctly nonlibertarian or conservative views of justice. This is really no surprise given that substantive equality – which is what the "equality of what?" debate concerns – is unlikely to be sought in libertarian theories of justice (with the exception of left libertarianism).[5]

As noted, how we compare metrics will depend in part on what the terms of our comparison are. One of the things to bear in mind in distinguishing egalitarianism from other families of views is whether they employ such a substantive definition of egalitarianism; this has not always recently been the case. For example, the term is often used in a much broader (and unhelpful) sense now. Will Kymlicka, for instance, takes up Ronald Dworkin's suggestion that the competing political theories do not, in fact, appeal to competing values. Dworkin's claim that every plausible political theory exists on an "egalitarian plateau" has gained wide acceptance. The claim is that every plausible political theory assumes that the interests of the members of the community matter – and matter equally. For instance, while claiming that all plausible approaches to the ethics of social arrangements require equality of something, Sen claims that all these theories are egalitarian. As he notes, such a definition would include Robert Nozick's libertarian *Anarchy, State, and Utopia* in the list of egalitarian theories because of Nozick's attempt to treat people as moral equals.[6] While we might agree that a concern for equality at some level is required of a plausible political theory, that does not then entail that all those theories that show such a concern should be called egalitarian. One author has even described "Right-Wing egalitarianism," by which he means egalitarianism of the political right.[7] But for a theory to be an egalitarian one, it needs a more substantial content than what we will call the weak egalitarian thesis of equal concern. The weak egalitarian thesis – a theory is egalitarian if it acknowledges some sort of basal equality – will not serve as a defining feature of egalitarianism.

The substantive dimension that a metric should satisfy is not always easy to articulate. Answering this "plateau challenge" is a difficult undertaking. It is not possible here to identify all the things egalitarians have been or should be concerned with because that would require articulation of a fuller theory of justice than is needed for our purposes. Moreover, there will be significant disagreement about what is on such a list and whether the elements are compatible. I leave such questions aside. But it is possible to give some indication of the kinds of issues that have been considered important from recent and historical debates. As we have seen, most theories share general requirements, such as not to discriminate in employment or in participation in political functions. But the types of equality discussed in the previous chapter are also relevant here to give substance to what would otherwise be an empty formal notion of equality. Other types of equality often cited as desirable include achieving equal status for different groups in society by eliminating stigmatizing practices. Equality of status, as it is sometimes called, is a clear substantive requirement.[8] Equality of power of different types has also been an important claim made by egalitarians. We have already noted one version of this claim in reference to having access to political office or the courts, but there are many other types. Having equal bargaining rights in a workplace is another traditional egalitarian concern. While a concern with basic needs not being met is not egalitarian per se – one could be a sufficientarian and object to material scarcity, for instance – it is certainly relevant for egalitarians. Insofar as inequalities contribute to material deprivation, they will be of interest and should be captured by the relevant metric. Two other substantive inequalities that often feature in egalitarian discussion are self-respect and, particularly, severe health inequalities.

What we will be principally interested in here is how to evaluate the different metrics as answers to the question of what should be equalized. But not all of the best metric defenses are themselves so committed to equality of the metric they advocate. We have to be clear that the metric – welfarism, resourcism, or capability – is distinct from the distributive rule with which it is combined. Nussbaum, for instance, advocates a mixed view: some capabilities are to be sought for people equally and others up to a sufficient level. Richard Arneson combines objective welfare with a prioritarian distributive principle. In taking these differences into account, I assume that these metrics can be combined with a principle of equality.

Finally, defenders of the metrics use several common criteria to assess them. One criterion is the scope of the theory of justice – a point that in practice is closely connected to the substantive content of egalitarian theories. By scope I mean the political constituency over which the egalitarian distributive principle is said to apply. For most of the authors discussed here, that scope is national, in the sense that their concern is with distributive principles that apply within a state. For some, such as Nussbaum, the metric applies globally. It often happens that advocates of equality at a national level do not change metrics when discussing global distributive justice but adopt different distributive rules – for instance, they advocate substantive domestic equality according to their favored metric but adopt, say, a sufficiency view globally.

2.2 Equality of welfare

What has come to be known as welfarism has a long history in philosophy and other disciplines.[9] In economics, some version of welfarism has long been the standard measure of well-being.[10] This has in part been so because of the influence of utilitarianism. In political philosophy its influence has been extensive but less so than in economics, reflecting the dissatisfaction with pure subjective preference accounts of equality and related debates about well-being and the impact of other metrics, especially Rawlsian-influenced ones. In relation to the "equality of what?" debate, the two key variants of the position are *success theories* and *conscious state theories* of welfare. Success theories of welfare propose that welfare is a matter of personal success in filling a person's preferences, goals, tastes, or ambitions. Conscious state theories hold that we should equalize some aspect of a person's conscious life, such as a feeling of happiness. The appeal of welfarism is not hard to understand. Payments or opportunities people receive as part of any redistribution are not ends in themselves but means to achieving other, more fundamental, goals that matter to them. Assisting individuals to fulfill their preferences or achieve various valuable conscious states matters more to the individual than the means that we provide for achieving those ends. What people really care about, welfarists argue, is whether we can achieve or have the opportunity to obtain what we want, and not the means that we use to get there.[11] Therefore, we should focus our metric on what really matters to us and not on mere means. The main focus of what follows will be success theories, which also form the most prominent and plausible conceptions of equality of welfare. Before we consider success theories, however, it is worth noting the arguments about conscious state theories of equality of welfare.

Conscious state theories of welfare hold that we should equalize the degree to which people have appropriate conscious states, such as experiencing pleasure or enjoyment. The influence of this view extends beyond classical utilitarianism to more modern theories of welfare economics. Yet, as a candidate for the currency of egalitarian justice, it is deeply problematic. For instance, imagine two people who both value success at the same type of job. They might differ in how much they are prepared to sacrifice to achieve success in their job – they might value the pleasure they derived from their work to different degrees, for example. So, while people might value positive conscious states, not everyone values them to the same degree, which is a limitation given that we are concerned with a metric that is supposed to be able to make interpersonal comparisons of people's condition. People might choose lives that overall contain less pleasure and more of something else that make it a better life to lead.[12] James Griffin cites the example of Sigmund Freud, who, near the end of his life, chose not to alleviate his painful illnesses with drugs so as to be able to think clearly even though he was in pain.[13] Further, imagine someone who thought that the best life for him or her was one that aimed at noble but impossibly high goals, such as trying to sculpt the perfect statue or write the greatest novel of all time. Let us suppose that many of the people who pursue such goals do so unsuccessfully and with a great deal of angst, stress, and sacrifice. Insofar as such pursuits involve frustration and a distinct lack of pleasure, then, the person will not derive many good conscious states. There may also not be one common type of pleasure that is experienced in every pleasurable experience. Derek Parfit makes this point when he claims that there is potentially no common element across common pleasurable experiences. Consider the pleasure derived from solving a mathematical problem, watching your sporting team win a final, or seeing your child graduate from high school. It is not obvious that all of these experiences have the same type of pleasure attached to them.[14] In terms of the broader debate about conscious state theories as an account of well-being, many have baulked at the emphasis on having to experience the relevant state. So if what matters is that a person has the relevant pleasurable state, this might be divorced from states of affairs in the world. Feeling happy that you are respected and liked might not reflect the fact that people really have a low opinion of you. The "experience requirement" of mental state theories can be problematic.[15]

Actual preferences

If the conscious state theory of welfare is an inadequate conception of equality, a preference-based theory might do better. The literature on preference based welfarism is large indeed. Here we will consider what are called "actual preference theories" and success theories of welfare as well as three objections (adaptive preferences, reasonable regret and expensive tastes). Preference or desire theories assume that people's lives go best when they are able to fulfill their preferences or desires. The simplest version of such a theory entails that what should be counted as a person's preferences are those the person actually holds. Actual preference accounts of equality have the advantage of placing the sovereignty of the individual at the forefront of our concern, since this account sees equality in terms of what people want. Moreover, when such an account is linked to market mechanisms, it offers a way of revealing people's preferences through their choices in the marketplace.[16]

In many ways, the actual preference theory is an ideal candidate for an egalitarian metric. One of its strengths is the plurality of goods it can account for. If all of us equally get what we most want, we can account for the enormous range of different things people want in their lives: my preference for a life spent helping others versus yours for the life of a hermit. It also potentially accords a high degree of autonomy to individuals if their preferences reflect their autonomy. Moreover, as Sumner points out, it does not rule out the possibility that there will be some things that help achieve everyone's preferences, perhaps certain basic resources, or even that some preferences will be common to many people, making the metric more suitable for a theory of justice.[17]

Yet if a preference-based welfarism is to be the currency of egalitarian justice, it will have to account for the ways in which people can get their preferences wrong. Perhaps the most pressing issue concerns the problem of individuals adapting their preferences to suit their circumstances in the wrong kind of way. Adapted preferences would be the wrong information base for social choice when they have been adapted for the wrong reasons. John Elster characterizes some of these preferences as having a "sour grapes structure," where individuals change preferences in light of perceived barriers and limitations of their circumstances, thereby not reflecting their first preferences.[18] We can also observe other adaptive mechanisms. Someone might form adaptive preferences because of harmful conditioning (religious, political, cultural) and not thereby be aware of alternative preferences he or she might otherwise choose. Where this is the case, preferences will not form a good guide to a person's well-being. Similarly, acceptance of deprivation might lead a person to lower expectations or claims to resources in a way that would not occur in less deprived circumstances. Both Sen and Nussbaum have discussed such cases at length. One example given by Sen concerns a survey of Indian widowers and widows conducted near Calcutta in 1944. Whereas 45.6 percent of widowers said their health was poor, only 2.5 percent of widows said so. Given that at that time in Indian society widows were far more likely to suffer disadvantage than widowers, it is a striking case of the former group adapting its view of itself to fit the circumstances. This kind of adaptation could, in turn, lead to less demanding claims for assistance because individuals did not believe they were unhealthy. For Sen, this type of reliance on preferences highlights how "quiet acceptance" of deprivation can lead to a distorted set of preferences and give us a reason to doubt their suitability as an information base of justice.

What the adaptive preference objection also highlights is that preferences are often a function of all kinds of inputs: social norms, government regulation, culture, and so on. This is not always a bad thing, but it does raise the issue of whether there is really such a strong link between respecting autonomy and respecting preferences. Preferences might not have been formed autonomously; people might have been misinformed or unduly influenced by exogenous factors. Or perhaps the preferences were a product of unjust background conditions.[19] Where this is the case, it seems odd to say that respecting preferences is also therefore respecting autonomy. Preferences may also be a function of the desire to avoid cognitive dissonance. Thinking that all the disadvantage suffered by the poor is a result of their own choices might help to make the distribution of the wealth in society seem more rational to the well-off, for instance. Having harmful preferences – say, those that pose health risks – might also be a factor (though not always a decisive one) in questioning their suitability.

Success theories

Even if one accepts these objections to political and impersonal accounts of preference-based views, one might still be attracted to another category of preference welfarism: equality of personal success (what many call *success theories*).[20] According to Dworkin, personal success theories hold that "a person's welfare is a matter of his success in fulfilling his preferences, goals, and ambitions, and so equality of success, and the conception of equality welfare, recommends distribution and transfer of resources until no further transfer can decrease the extent to which people differ in such success."[21] The proper focus of equality of welfare, then, should be equality of personal success. After all, the intuitive appeal of welfarism was partly based on its getting to the heart of what really matters to people, which is whether *their* preferences and plans are ultimately successful. But here, too, Dworkin objects that equality of welfare is untenable. He considers how we might measure a person's success in achieving his or her preferences. We might do so in two ways. The first is by judging individuals' success according to whether it measures up to their own assessment of achievement of their goals. On this conception of equality of welfare, resources will be distributed according to who has had more success in achieving their goals as they understand them – that is, by looking at a person's *relative success* in attaining what he or she thinks is valuable. According to equality of welfare, money will be taken from one person and given to another to achieve equality of a type that some may not value very much and others may not value at all. For instance, compare a person who has chosen to solve a complex scientific problem, has made some progress, but has got only 25 percent of the way to solving the problem. Such a person would require more compensation than one who had chosen to perfect his or her ability to whistle in tune and achieved 75 percent of his or her goal. What this highlights is that conceiving of equality of personal success in terms of people's own evaluation makes accurate and fair assessment of interpersonal comparisons of how well people's lives go difficult.

Even if we allow for judgments of success that remove some of the less reliable subjective interpretations people have of their own lives and contrive a situation in which they can accurately judge their lives according to their differing philosophical beliefs, equality of welfare still faces difficulties. One suggestion would be to change how we compare people's lives from what they think about them in light of their own philosophical beliefs to a standard of what "*should* have been, not merely of what conceivably might have been,"[22] which Dworkin calls judgments about the *overall* success of people's lives. This modification at least rules out the difficulty that people view their lack of achievements in an unreasonable way. For instance, it would be unreasonable to regret not being able to fly or to swim underwater without an oxygen tank; those things are impossible. But for Dworkin, the problem is that this account of welfare introduces a non-welfare-based measure of equality. This is so because what should have been for a person depends on the share of goods he or she should have received. But this assumes we know what an initial distribution of fair shares entails, which is a measure independent of equality seen as welfare. This puts the welfare theorist in a bind, according to Dworkin; we need the concept of reasonable regret in order to generate comparisons between how well people's lives have gone, but if we use the notion of reasonable regret, we are ultimately appealing to an independent (nonwelfare) idea of fair shares. Dworkin's claim is that when we start to specify the concrete conception of welfarism, we are left with alternatives that are too vague to establish welfarism's claims to be an egalitarian metric.

A further concern is that if we adopt welfarism as our metric, we are open to fulfilling a range of expensive tastes. For instance, Rawls posits a scenario involving two people, one who is easily satisfied with a diet of simple foods and another who has a taste for expensive wines and exotic dishes. The former has expensive tastes, and the latter inexpensive ones.[23] If we believe in equality of welfare, we will redistribute or compensate persons with expensive tastes so that they can increase their welfare. Rawls objects to this outcome because it ignores the sense in which citizens are responsible for developing and cultivating their own ends; as he puts it, it is unreasonable, if not unjust, to not hold such persons responsible for their preferences and to require them to make out as best they can.[24]

Responses

Dworkin's criticisms of welfarism focused on its unsatisfying abstractness and its inability to deal with the expensive tastes objection. In response, some have sought to argue that welfarism is not tied to a wholly subjective account of preferences and that incorporating a more robust theory of personal responsibility can account for the expensive tastes objection. There are several versions of objective welfarism that do not face the same objections as the subjective welfarism that Dworkin attacks. Indeed, many of these versions predate his discussion. For instance, Richard Arneson has tried to deflect the criticisms by claiming that although Dworkin is right to argue that when we specify some particular conceptions of welfarism, problems occur, not all conceptions fare as badly.[25] Arneson puts forward an objective version of the welfare metric that can provide an objective list of valuable opportunities for welfare (and some outcomes) from which a person can choose. He combines it with a prioritarian principle of distribution, which he claims is not subject to Dworkin's objections. Arneson claims his version of welfarism avoids the vagueness objection because it does not have to rely on personal preferences to come up with a basis of interpersonal comparison. It is objective because what counts as welfare is taken to be independent of a person's desires, preferences, or tastes. In a case where someone who is seriously mobility disabled has a sunny disposition that leads him or her to reject aid such as a wheelchair, the person's welfare should be determined objectively, not simply as a matter of subjective preferences. Dworkin's criticisms work best against conceptions of welfare that equate to subjective preferences. Arneson argues that if we replace subjective welfarism with an objective list theory of welfare, we will not be moved by Dworkin's attack. For once such a theory is adopted, a person's well-being is assessed by the extent to which he or she obtains what is "truly valuable" over the course of life.[26] Moving to an objective list theory allows us to avoid Sen's adaptive preferences objection and Dworkin's claim that welfarism is both vague and incoherent.

The expensive tastes objection can also be overcome, according to Arneson, by recognizing the extent to which we are owed opportunities to increase our welfare, not necessarily how those opportunities turn out if they are a function of our choices. He writes:

> The moral yardstick that measures my opportunities is calibrated in terms of the welfare level I could reach with those opportunities if I chose to use them to my advantage and if I used them as well as could

reasonably be expected. If I fail to behave as prudently as it would be reasonable to expect, no further compensation is owed me.[27]

He adds, where the opportunities I have are not merely ones judged valuable in terms of my subjective preferences but are "really opportunities for a genuinely good life."[28] With a move to the objective list theory, sorting the trivial and expensive preferences from the ones I genuinely should have is easier. Note that Arneson thinks his account is not unduly paternalistic, for while there is decision making at a societal level to make some opportunities and not others available to people, which ones an individual chooses to accept is up to him or her. In this sense Arneson's account is objective: society has an obligation and role in determining what kinds of opportunities count for living a good life. But for Arneson, responsibility is still in the picture because an individual can choose from among those options. So it is welfarist in the sense of maintaining a level of preference satisfaction, but it departs from the version of welfarism that Dworkin targets because of the societal filter that seeks to determine what the options for a good life actually are.[29]

Arneson's objective list account also addresses the reasonable regret objection that Dworkin makes against the welfarist. Recall that Dworkin claims that in order to know whether my life has gone well, I need a notion of reasonable regret. One cannot reasonably regret being unable to fly like a bird or run a one-minute mile; we need a measure of the fair shares to determine whether life has gone well. This harks back to a resourcist metric and away from a welfarist one. But the objective list account obviates the need for a theory of fair shares because we can compare the welfare of individuals independently of their subjective preferences via a full specification of the items on the objective list.[30]

The combination of an objective list and some role for individual choice has been developed by several authors, as we will see with Nussbaum's capability account. An objective list welfarism does seem to avoid some of the problems that Dworkin and others have raised for subjective welfarism. Not only does it introduce a criterion independent of people's subjective preferences; the right kind of list could also plausibly be taken to ensure that bizarre and idiosyncratic preferences are not part of any equalisandum. Objective list welfarists must nonetheless face two issues. The first is a very general concern about whether or not an objective list theory attaches in the right way to individuals. The strength of subjective welfarism is that it is a metric that links equality to what people really want. Objective list theories remove concerns about vagueness but at the cost of weakening the link with what people want by stipulating that what people should be equal in terms of is decided by criteria that may not pay enough attention to the distinctiveness of each individual's conception of the good. Potentially, an objective list may contain items an individual does not value, at least not very much (this objection is more forceful the more comprehensive the list). This is so even where individual choice has a role in selecting items for the list. A similar objection confronts this model of welfare as the one the revealed preference theory faces. Just as a situation in which choice of options may not reveal preferences where an individual really desires neither on offer, so choice of items on the objective list may not reveal what someone really wants if what is wanted is not on the list. Another concern, particularly for Arneson's response to these issues, is that moving toward an objective list theory raises the question of in what sense the theory is still preference based.[31] It is true that on Arneson's account there is a role for individuals' preferences because they are able to choose which of the objective goods they wish to pursue, but the goods forming part of the list are not valuable simply because they are the subject of a subjective preference and that should be the main criterion in determining whether or not a theory is welfarist.

As a metric, welfarism places people's preferences (objective or subjective) at the center of what they should receive from egalitarian justice. Dworkin's critique of subjective welfare highlighted several important problems, particularly its vagueness; while equality of welfare might have some appeal at an abstract level, when we start to specify what it actually means, serious difficulties appear. Categorizing subjective welfare as success in achieving preferences or conscious states just will not work when we get into the details. It is also problematic because it includes preferences that are beyond what a political society ought to fulfill as a matter of justice – what we called the *scope* objection. But his critique simply ignored accounts of objective welfarism that circumvented the expensive tastes objection and offered a substantially different account of what a welfarist metric could look like. In this sense, Dworkin's critique is too narrow, and to the extent that it represents welfarism as only subjective, it is misleading. Although it is not without its difficulties, objective welfarism offers a stronger account of what welfarism could be. It is important to note that the objections we considered concerning the difficulty objective welfarisms have attaching to people in the right way are not confined to welfarist metrics. Objective versions of the capability approach also face this problem. One of the things these assessments point to is that a plausible metric may need to be a mixed metric, incorporating features from several current metrics. This is a theme to which we will return.

2.3   Equality of resources

We have seen that the setting for the "equality of what?" debate is the issue of how we can make appropriate interpersonal comparisons of advantage of an equal and substantial kind. We noted that there were problems in measuring the types of subjective states we ought to compare, the intensity of these states, their costs, and their vulnerability to adaptation of the wrong kind. An obvious alternative is to select a currency of justice that is objective and focuses on things everybody conceivably might want irrespective of their conception of the good. So while welfare focused on ends, the resources approach selects a basket of things, a mixture of background conditions (rights, the social bases of self-respect) and goods (income and wealth) that are easier to compare and are all-purpose means anyone might want for the realization of different types of lives. In many ways resourcism is a bad name for the position it tries to describe. What we commonly think of as resources are commodities – wealth, natural resources, other types of portable, tradable commodities. Critics of resourcism are quick to point out that adopting a commodity-based approach to equality is fraught with difficulty. In debates about development, capability theorists standardly criticize those who seek to measure development via a focus on proxies for commodities and services, such as measures of GDP.[32] While there is no doubt much truth in criticisms of unduly narrow resourcist metrics focused on income, their philosophical counterparts are more sophisticated. What philosophical resourcists mean by resources includes income and wealth but also background conditions: legal institutions, trade regimes, and in some cases human talents. For this reason, I focus on the two most prominent examples of resourcist views, those of John Rawls and Ronald Dworkin. There are other types, such as Van Parijs's basic income approach and Ackerman's "stakeholder society" approach, along with variations of each, but it is fair to say that these two positions have been the most influential.[33] Each in its own way has determined the dimensions of the debate about the currency of justice and, indeed, of egalitarianism as well. It is hard to describe the views of Dworkin and Rawls without also describing their broader theories of justice. It is noteworthy that resourcists, more so than welfarists or capability theorists, tend to operate within the bigger picture of egalitarian justice. What resourcist positions share is a focus on all-purpose means as a way of achieving the right distribution.

Rawls and primary goods

We begin with Rawls: his political conception of justice, spelled out in *Political Liberalism*, is designed to answer the question of how to develop the most appropriate conception of justice for specifying the fair terms of social cooperation in the face of reasonable pluralism and where citizens are regarded as free and equal.[34] Rawls's response to the challenge is to develop a political conception of justice that can be the focus of an overlapping consensus involving people with different reasonable comprehensive views. People can achieve consensus because the principles proposed can be agreed upon even where participants' views about the good life differ. For Rawls, any account of what people should be equal in terms of has to respect the limits of a political conception of justice. His view is designed to avoid the problem of having to choose either different subjective preferences or advancing human excellence in a perfectionist sense – the view that there is a specific kind of good life we ought to promote. Even though citizens do not have the same final ends, we can assume a similarity in the structure of the conceptions of the good held by them, and Rawls's list of resources can be used to make interpersonal comparisons in a way he thinks subjective welfarism cannot. Rawls's primary goods are proposed as necessary means to whatever ends citizens may have. His list includes the following:

- basic rights and liberties;
- freedom of movement and free choice of occupation against a background of diverse opportunities;
- powers and prerogatives of offices and positions of responsibility in the political and economic institutions of the basic structure;
- income and wealth;
- the social bases of self-respect.[35]

The primary good of income and wealth most closely resembles what we think of when we use the term *resources*, but it has a broader meaning as a background condition. Rawls notes that income and wealth refer not just to personal holdings but also to the goods and services that government might provide (such as health care) or are various public goods (such as clean air).[36] The social basis of self-respect concerns those aspects of institutions that citizens need to have a sense of self-worth. The advantage of focusing on means and not ends is that a resourcist position is potentially better suited to standard conceptions of justice, those that aim to respect the different life goals citizens have. Moreover, resourcists claim that focusing on the kinds of means described below also shows greater respect for people's ability to exercise choice about how they use these resources. By focusing on means and not ends, Rawls thinks that we respect people's right to use the means as they see fit in pursuing particular goods. We do not thereby prioritize any particular conception of a good. Focusing on means rather than ends also lets citizens be responsible for choosing their own ends. This is important to the account because it both respects the autonomy of citizens to choose the kind of life they wish to lead and allows us to decide when inequalities that emerge as a result of particular choices are of concern to the state or merely private matters. Importantly, the list is objective in the sense that it is based on the objective features of the social circumstances of citizens. The list also has the advantage of being publicly debatable – a condition of Rawls's political liberalism. In addition, it observes neutrality regarding different comprehensive conceptions of the good that citizens may hold. A further advantage of the resourcist approach is that it offers something easier to evaluate because it is simpler to quantify. Providing everyone equal access to the same set of goods (rather than preferences, for instance) is easier to measure. Of course, as Rawls notes, just because something is easier to use as a basis of comparison does not make it the right metric. We have to have independent reasons for choosing equality of resources over equality of welfare.

Criticisms of Rawls's account of primary goods

One concern for Rawls's account is that the primary goods metric is too inflexible to serve as a measure of equality because it fails both to consider hard cases (disabilities and the like) and to fully appreciate human differences. For instance, how does distributing a standard set of primary goods to everyone in our population accommodate people who are outside relatively normal ranges of human functioning? The problem for someone with a disability, for instance, is that he or she will not be able to utilize his or her stock of primary goods as more able-bodied citizens can. If a person continually admitted to hospital for treatment of a debilitating disease has the same stock of primary goods as a healthy person, that individual will have less choice than the healthy person about how to use those primary goods and also will not be able to use them in the same way. For instance, if a person lacks mobility because of a disease or another cause, access to some goods or activities may cost that person more because, for instance, of the need to pay for special transport. These problems will be especially apparent when health care is the financial responsibility of the individual and not the state. Amartya Sen raises this question for Rawls's metric. Sen's point is that focusing on goods at the expense of what goods actually allow a person to do ignores the relationship between goods and people. [37]

The second type of criticism focuses on the extent to which Rawls shows an impoverished idea of human difference in the conception of the person he builds into his theory of justice. The primary goods metric is too inflexible; it cannot appreciate that normal citizens exhibit a vast range of relevant differences. Humans would have to be more alike for an index of primary goods such as Rawls's to be adequate. This deficiency in his account amounts to a fetishism with goods as such at the expense of what they do. What is at issue here is that Rawls ignores the *relationship* between goods and persons. According to Sen:

> Rawls himself motivates judging advantage in terms of primary goods by referring to capabilities, even though his criteria end up focusing on goods as such: on income rather than on what income does, on the "social bases of self-respect" rather than on self-respect itself, and so on. If human beings were very like each other, this would not have mattered a great deal, but there is evidence that the conversion of goods to capabilities varies from person to person substantially, and the equality of the former may still be far from the equality of the latter. [38]

At issue here is not just whether Rawls's resourcist metric captures the relationship between primary goods and what they enable people to do but also whether Rawls should include an issue such as disability within his conception of the person. Nussbaum makes this point in finding that Rawls's conception is too focused on the intellectual and rational features of our nature. [39] She wants to introduce instead a conception that acknowledges our "animal" features and recognizes disability as a part of our nature that ought not be ignored when designing principles of justice. The background to her discussion of primary goods is Rawls's postponement of the question of disability in the original position – the reasoning device that Rawls employs in order to think about theories of justice. She claims that Rawls's insistence that citizens have the minimum level of intellectual, moral, and physical powers to enable them to cooperate does not capture important features of humanness that should be part of a conception of a person. In turn, introducing primary goods as an account of the needs of citizens leads to a simplified account of the proper metric. Whereas if people are seen as having impairments and variability in their well-being across the different stages of their lives, it becomes harder to measure who is well off and who is not well off. This is especially true, according to Nussbaum, because of Rawls's reliance on income and wealth in indexing disadvantage.

At this point it is worth noting Rawls's response to some of these criticisms. In response to the charge that the primary goods metric occupies the wrong space because it does not understand what resources do for a person (i.e., it ignores the relationship between resources and people), Rawls claims that the account of primary goods does take into account basic capabilities. He has in mind that his account assumes citizens to have the two moral powers he understands as basic capabilities.[40] The index of primary goods is attentive to the relationship between resources and persons because the index is drawn up "by asking what things, given the basic capabilities included in the (normative) conception of citizens as free and equal, are required by citizens to maintain their status as free and equal and to be normal, fully cooperating members of society."[41] In response to the charge that the primary goods index does not account for human difference and the hard cases, Rawls's response, particularly to the latter in respect of health, is that these issues can be decided at a legislative phase after the principles are determined.[42] He also argues that the capability account violates the political nature of his liberalism by assuming a comprehensive theory of the good.[43] One might, as Norman Daniels does in his recent work, see the metrics as converging. Rather than find a "friendly amendment,"[44] as Daniels initially did, we might acknowledge that the two approaches are closer than they seem because there are more similarities than differences. We will be in a better position to assess the merits of each approach after a discussion of the capability metric itself. One thing we can note is that consideration of an issue such as disability had lead Rawls at least to acknowledge the importance of capabilities as a way of capturing important features of individuals. But it did not lead him to think that he ought to change his resourcist metric to a capability-based one.

2.4   Dworkin: auctioning resources

Like Rawls's, Dworkin's version of equality of resources is based on a mixture of background conditions and actual resources. The kinds of things that constitute Dworkin's metric include impersonal resources – which refers to those resources that are privately owned by individuals, such as their income and wealth, jobs, and property, *and* personal resources, such as a person's physical and mental health, general fitness, and capacities, including those capacities that can generate goods and services that others are prepared to pay for.[45] These are the kinds of things that make up Dworkin's metric of equality. Note that he does not include political power in his list but does include people's powers and capacities as something that should be compensated for in the case of those who have fewer internal resources. Many of the differences between Dworkin's resourcism and Rawls's relate to how Dworkin has sought to focus more explicitly on the importance of personal responsibility.[46] However, Dworkin's work also raises some interesting issues concerning the role of preferences in resourcist metrics.

Just as with Rawls's resourcism, Dworkin's account of his metric is guided by his broader commitments, which we need to mention in order to make sense of his ideas. Dworkin's theory is guided by two principles that shape his answer to the "equality of what?" question. The first is the principle of equal importance, where it matters equally that each human life goes well. The second is the principle of special responsibility, which each individual has for how his or her own life. These principles have the consequence that governments must adopt theories of justice that treat citizens in particular ways. The first requires that governments be insensitive to "who they [their citizens] otherwise are" (whether, e.g., they are of a particular race or have a handicap),[47] and the second requires that what happens to people reflect their choices. Dworkin's theory of equality in distribution aims to embody these principles by being ambition-sensitive (first principle) but endowment-insensitive (second principle). His theory of equality of resources tackles each part in turn.

To illustrate his idea for the initial division of resources, Dworkin asks us to imagine we are dividing society's resources for the first time. In this initial division we acknowledge that no one has prior rights to any of the resources; it also, crucially, meets what he calls the "envy test": "No division of resources is an equal division if, once the division is complete, any immigrant would prefer someone else's bundle of resources to his own bundle."[48] To escape unfairness in the division of resources, Dworkin proposes that the best way to distribute them is via an auction. Each person is given a certain amount of currency (clamshells in the original desert island example), which can be used to bid for the various lots of resources. Bidding in this way satisfies the envy test because if someone had envied another's bundle of resources, he could have purchased it instead of his own bundle. So someone who wanted to lead a lifestyle high in leisure but low in income might use the resources to purchase a leisure property, whereas someone who wanted to concentrate on earning money to fund expensive tastes is likely to purchase income-producing assets, which might require long hours of hard work to develop. This does not mean that everyone gets the same amount of welfare out of purchasing a bundle, but it does reflect people's preferences and, importantly, the costs associated with those preferences. Dworkin's auction model respects his two guiding principles in that everyone is treated equally in the auction and has responsibility for the consequences of the choices made. For those concerned about perfectionism, this aspect of Dworkin's theory is an advantage because it does not refer to ideal amounts of resources as part of the metric. It does not say that everyone has to have a certain amount of resources or resources for particular pursuits or goals. A further advantage is that background facts determine what equality of resources is – that is, the amount of resources available decides, in part, what bundles of resources people actually get. The bundles' value is also determined by how much others value them. If everyone wants country properties, their cost will go up as people are prepared to bid more for them.

Insurance and endowment insensitivity: Luck and handicaps

Dworkin thinks that his model of equality of resources can also accommodate two important issues for egalitarians: inequality of abilities, especially those resulting from handicaps, and the inequalities that are a result of people's choices. To take choices first: the auction is a device for the initial allocation of resources; it will not guarantee equality of resources once trade, people's willingness to work, and their preferences for leisure begin to alter the initial bundle of resources.[49] Dworkin distinguishes two types of luck that determine how people's lives go and to what extent other people should view differential individual outcomes as a matter of justice: "option luck," which is a matter of "how deliberate and calculated gambles turn out," and "brute luck," which is a matter of "how risks fall out that are not in that sense deliberate gambles."[50] The distinction between these types of luck corresponds, roughly, to situations and events that result from a person's choice and situations that result from a person's circumstances.[51] A person with expensive tastes will not attract egalitarian concern because these tastes are seen by Dworkin as falling on the option luck side of the divide; they are the responsibility of the person, not the political community. Similarly, disadvantage caused by choice will also not attract attention. The distinction captures the widely held egalitarian impulse to compensate people for the brute bad luck they suffer but not for the bad luck they suffer as a result of their own choices. How best to address the question of responsibility is left to Chapter 3.

The distinction between brute luck and option luck allows one way of determining when to compensate individuals for their misfortune. This distinction figures in equality of resources in a crucial way. Recall that Dworkin wants to ensure that people are not disadvantaged by a thing such as disability. He suggests that if there was a possibility of insuring against bad luck before the initial auction, people could choose whether they wanted insurance against a disability, for instance. The possibility of insurance links the two types of luck and is a way of compensating for endowment disadvantages. Importantly, equality of resources would not require a redistribution from the person who had insured to the one who had not if something went wrong for the latter.[52] The reason is that although an accident, a matter of bad luck, may have befallen both people, the decision to insure is a matter of option luck. The idea of a market in insurance provides a counterfactual guide to the problem of handicaps we face in the real world. As we know, people do not start off with the same level of disabilities. Nonetheless, Dworkin thinks we can proceed by imagining the total number of handicaps that develop in a given community by asking how much insurance a person would take out to insure against developing various handicaps.[53] We would reason, say, that the average person would have purchased insurance at the appropriate level, and those who did develop handicaps would be compensated out of some common fund generated by the proper level of taxation, which we could use to duplicate the results. As he puts it, it would establish "a hypothetical insurance market that they effectuate through compulsory insurance at a fixed premium for everyone on the basis of speculations about what the average immigrant would have purchased by way of insurance had antecedent risk of various handicaps been equal."[54] The hypothetical insurance market, then, seeks to remedy the shortfall in someone's life because of birth with a handicap; it cannot completely remove the disadvantage. As Dworkin notes, "it seeks to remedy one aspect of the resulting unfairness."[55] Note that he thinks that obsessions and cravings can be seen as handicaps in that a person may be better off without a strong craving for sex or money or power; that is, life would be better without such cravings. If these cravings are not part of what a successful life would be, Dworkin assigns them to a person's circumstances, where we treat them as we would treat handicap generally.[56]

The advantages of Dworkin's account of equality as equality of resources, as he sees it, are, first, that it avoids many of the pitfalls of equality of welfare generated by its vagueness, inappropriate scope, and expensive tastes. Further, it recognizes the role of individual choice in determining how someone's life goes and therefore the respect in which a community consents to compensate people when life has gone badly (choice sensitive). But it is also able to compensate for undeserved misfortune through its insurance scheme modeled on a system of taxation (endowment insensitive), thus allaying some of the concerns discussed in relation to Rawls's approach. As such, his scheme represents a "second-best" approach to justice because we cannot fully eliminate disadvantages such as handicaps. It also respects people's choices in another way: in acknowledging that choices are important and providing resources for people to pursue their different goals and preferences. It thus treats people as autonomous agents in both a negative and a positive sense. Dworkin's account of equality recognizes the importance of choice and preference, but choices and preferences are not themselves the currency of justice.

Dworkin's equality of resources: preferences and the market

Dworkin's resourcism is characterized by its eschewal of welfarism. But it seems that both preferences and mental states can and do have a role in his account of equality and, as noted at the beginning of the chapter, all of the metrics we are considering have *some* role for preferences at least. In relation to Dworkin, we need to ask two questions: first, despite Dworkin's objections to welfarism and the merits of his own theory of equality, it remains to be seen whether welfarism should play a greater role in a theory of equality; and, second, where preferences especially do play a role, whether the conception of preference employed is plausible. On the first issue, we might ask whether Dworkin's view is too narrow to capture the range of disadvantage with which egalitarians should be concerned. For instance, Cohen asks us to imagine someone who lacks mobility and needs an expensive wheelchair because of a disability.[57] It does not matter, according to Cohen, if Tiny Tim is actually happy in his pre-wheelchair state. Happiness and welfare are not the only considerations that should concern egalitarians. They will want to compensate him for his disability, not just because of his welfare deficit or, importantly, his opportunity for welfare, which might also be high.

Cohen thinks that a modified version of this example also shows that some welfare considerations are relevant in addition to resource concerns. So imagine further that the person in the wheelchair can move his arms normally (in fact, he has above-normal ability), but it causes him pain to do so. Now Cohen's point is that we cannot just describe Tiny Tim's disadvantage in terms of the resource deficiency. After all, Tiny Tim has the ability to move his arms; he can do so without difficulty, yet it is costly for him because he cannot do so without pain. Cohen claims that most egalitarians would agree that if there was a medicine to relieve the pain, Tiny Tim should be given it. If this is true, we cannot maintain a purely resource-based view of egalitarian justice because relieving pain is not a resources deficit. The resulting deficiency is a welfare deficiency (not one based on preferences); that is, it cannot just be reduced to a resource deficiency. Cohen writes, "There is an irreducible welfare aspect in the case for egalitarian compensation in real-life disability examples."[58] Moreover, these would be people whom Dworkin describes as having expensive tastes.[59] Cohen's point is that two dimensions of the disabled person's condition need attention: one, his lack of ability to move, which is a resource component, and two, the pain he feels with movement, which is a (mental state) welfare component.

Dworkin on the market and the role of preferences

Dworkin's heavy reliance on the mechanisms of the market to achieve equality of resources, a controversial feature of his account, tells us something further about the role of preferences in his metric. For Dworkin, the role of the market is crucial for egalitarian justice because it can measure the value of goods to people and deliver them in an envy-free way through the device of the initial auction. Importantly, the market can accurately measure the importance of goods to people because they bid for what is most important to them. Choice in the market also illustrates the role that Dworkin's account gives to individual preferences. The role is not as the substance of the metric but in choosing the alternative bundles of goods each person wants. But as Colin Macleod points out, there is no guarantee that the resources people want and, hence, bid for will contribute to the possibility of their leading a good life.[60] This is so because, as Dworkin has noted in his criticism of welfarism, subjective preferences do not neatly track individual interests. Because the results of the auction are a function of subjective preferences in a market situation, the resulting distribution may fail to deliver the results Dworkin thinks will be achieved. For instance, if during the auction I purchase worthless goods, thinking they are what I really want, while you purchase things you do really want, at the end of the auction you will have a more valuable bundle of goods than I will. I might have mistakenly adopted the wrong conception of the good life, or there might be nothing wrong with the conception, but I have misunderstood the resources that are needed to facilitate the conception. Either way, the envy test will have been satisfied, but people's bundles of goods will not be equally valuable. Here the problem is fundamentally the lack of fit between subjective preferences and human interests. We might modify Dworkin's account, as Macleod suggests, to adopt an objective account of human interests in place of the subjective preferences used in Dworkin's auction model. Nonetheless, this would significantly change the approach. It also might violate his stipulation that treating people as equals requires that we allow them to formulate their own life plans because this is what it is to treat them with respect. Moreover, the subjective preferences might be required because of the endorsement constraint; the importance of a resource to an individual would depend on the sense in which it contributes to a good because of the good life that the individual has endorsed.

A further and more damning objection to Dworkin and his reliance on the market is that his initial distribution assumes that people already have determined preferences,[61] whereas, as Dworkin initially describes it, the auction does not take into account the conditions required for the adequate formation of preferences. The basic problem is that if we require the preferences to be formed in the right way by having, in Dworkin's terms, the appropriate conditions of authenticity, we need a distribution of goods that is prior to the initial auction and does not depend on individual preferences. For example, we might require that a certain amount of money be given over to education, culture, the arts, and so forth; only what is left over might be the subject of an auction. This tells us that the role of the market, as Dworkin concedes, will be more limited. This is not to say that markets and individual preferences play no role; rather, their role is most useful once the conditions of preference formation have been adequately secured.[62] As we saw in Chapter 1, the role of preferences can also indicate the importance placed implicitly or explicitly on metrics' legitimacy. Dworkin's metric tries to achieve this via the auction, where individuals can endorse their purchase of bundles of goods. Yet the drive to ensure legitimacy comes at the cost of there potentially being a mismatch with what might be in somebody's interest.

The limited focus on ex ante equalizations of resources both in the initial auction and in an ongoing postauction policy sense means that Dworkin's theory relies more on ex post measures to correct inequalities. This has struck some as being the wrong way around for egalitarian justice. Having some means to ensure that inequalities of endowments do not occur or are lessened in the first place strikes many egalitarians as a greater (if more difficult) contribution to egalitarian justice.[63] Getting the causes of inequality right is surely one of the things we should demand of an egalitarian metric. Moreover, we might question how substantive his theory is likely to be given that what he ends up recommending turns out to be rather limited. Dworkin's theory may not do much to alleviate some of the more pressing concerns when he focuses on ex post distributions rather than on the much more challenging and important equalizing of ex ante endowments and resources. By setting up his metric in such a way as to ensure that the chance/choice distinction is central, it may place too much weight on opportunities at the expense of key outcomes. As we will see in Chapter 3, such an approach may lead to unacceptably bad outcomes.

We should be aware that using preferences as our metric can take different forms. At one end of the spectrum is the pure preference view, which puts forward any type of preference as the basis of a metric. We might call this the "saturation" view, where preferences are all that matter. But we have seen that actual preferences will not work as a metric because they fall prey to various objections about their scope and are also not a good guide to what is best for people when adaptive preferences are taken into account. What we might call a "selective" view is the view that only success-type preference theories should be adopted. Nonetheless if Dworkin is right, these too are problematic. In the final type of preference view, a "mixed" view, individuals get to exercise preferences but only on options selected objectively. This at least preserves a role for preferences, albeit in a limited way. So in assessing preference views we need to distinguish between versions that see preferences as constitutive of the metric and versions that see preferences' role as crucial but limited. Saturation views give preferences a foundational role, whereas mixed views accord them an ancillary role. These two levels of preference use in the welfarist metric are importantly different. Despite his rejection of welfarism, Dworkin's view is arguably closer to a mixed view because of the role of preferences in the auction.

2.5 Capabilities

Sen and capabilities

Our final candidate as a metric of equality is the capability approach to justice, the most recent of the three approaches. Primarily developed by Amartya Sen and more recently by Martha Nussbaum, the capability approach has been very influential outside as well as within philosophy. Indeed, Sen's discussion of equality in his "Equality of

What?" article reignited debate about the metric question.[64] According to Sen, adopting welfare as the sole measure of equality faced a number of problems because it failed to account for human diversity and how people's welfare could be distorted. Resourcists also faced the problems of accounting for human diversity and the hard cases, such as disability. Both Dworkin's and Rawls's schemes also faced the objection that they provided only means to equality, not important ends. Nussbaum, too, makes these and other objections to resourcism and provides her own version of the capability approach.

Sen's answer to these problems – the capability approach – steers a middle course between the other metrics we have examined. Sen's response to "equality of what?" concentrates on what goods or states of affairs *do* for a person rather than on the person's welfare or bundles of primary goods.[65] The aspect of a person that matters here is what Sen calls his or her "functioning." Functionings are the various things that people can be or do. They vary from a simple state like being nourished to a complex condition such as being part of a community. They include things one is actively able to do, such as reading and writing, and things that are passive states, such as being free of disease. Functionings fall between the other metrics of equality; they are neither measures of welfare nor some sort of distributive resource. They are certainly produced by goods (nutrition by food, knowledge by education, and so on), but they are prior to the utility generated by being able to use these states. To take an example, suppose a person is well nourished due, in part, to the food that he or she is able to consume. In turn, the state of being well nourished allows him or her to enjoy other activities essential to the person's overall well-being. What the state of being nourished provides here is a (very) basic functioning, which might then be used in a number of ways, including being combined with other valuable functionings.

The ability to achieve these functionings is what Sen thinks should be of interest, not just the functionings themselves. When assessing the information base of justice, the capability approach focuses not just on actual achievements of well-being but on the *freedom* to achieve functionings. As Sen puts it, "The capability approach to a person's advantage is concerned with evaluating it in terms of his or her actual ability to achieve various valuable functionings as a part of living."[66] Equality of capability entails that individuals have equal freedom to achieve relevant "beings" and "doings."

Sen is at pains to stress that the capability approach allows us to focus on individual freedom. He sees the advantages of expanding the information base to include freedom and not just achievement as twofold. First, including freedom allows us to appreciate the opportunities a person had to achieve various functionings. If a person has only one option, because perhaps of being ill or homeless, he or she is option poor and in a clear sense disadvantaged compared with a person with many options. The different options will be reflected in the different sets of functionings an agent chooses. The second reason freedom is important is that choosing itself may be directly relevant to a person's well-being. Having the freedom to choose between various sets of functionings acknowledges the important place of choice in a person's life and what might also be relevant for redistribution claims. Sen proposes a simple example to illustrate his claim. Imagine two people who are equally malnourished. The first is malnourished because he is poor and cannot buy enough food. The second is malnourished because he has chosen to fast in accordance with his religious beliefs; in fact, he is wealthy. All things being equal, both have equivalent nourishment, but the freedom they exercised in being malnourished is potentially relevant to whose nourishment deserves the most attention according to egalitarian justice or at least those versions of it that incorporate a form of the chance/choice distinction.[67] One person is not capable of being nourished; the other one is. Capability thus captures the sense we have of the functionings we enjoy or lack and the extent to which they are ours through the exercise of freedom. Moreover, as Sen points out, it could matter equally in a given situation whether the freedom concerned is the freedom to or freedom from in ensuring that a person has the capability to achieve a certain desired level of functioning.[68] For example, a person's freedom might be brought about through their having certain abilities that they can exercise as well as because threats to their health and safety have been removed. Capabilities can also be both active and passive. For instance, being free of disease might be a capability achieved by the efforts of the individual or through the foresight exercised in the implementation of preventive health programs. When Sen writes of capabilities, he often does so in the context of articulating a broad approach to evaluating well-being. As part of this broad approach he discusses what he calls "well-being goals" and "agency goals." The latter concern what Dworkin would refer to as impersonal or political goals, which are broader than just what would increase an individual's well-being. It is often not clear whether Sen would include agency goals in his description of capability equality that would be the subject of egalitarian justice (he indicates in a number of places that they would not be included).[69] Note, too, that for Sen at least, it is more accurate to talk of achieving combinations of capabilities, not merely individual ones. This is so because there will be numerous capabilities that a person will deem valuable, and there will be trade-offs between them.[70] One further point: for Sen, these capabilities are very general and must be applied so as to take into account the culturally relative variations that will inevitably occur. So what is required for the capability to be sheltered will vary according to, for instance, the climate or geography of a region in addition to the cultural preferences of the population.

For Sen, the capability approach makes its chief contribution to social justice by identifying an information base to determine individual advantages. It need not be combined, as here, with a distributive principle of equality. Moreover, articulating the "space" of evaluation does not tell us anything about how we select and weight the different capabilities within that space. As we will see, this has been a source of criticism of the approach. A further important feature of it is whether it could employ an objective or a subjective method of determining which capabilities are most valuable. For instance, Nussbaum's approach selects an objective list of capabilities that should form the basis of claims individuals have (though she does not think all of these should be distributed equally). Sen, on the other hand, is noncommittal about whether a list of capabilities should be objective or subjective, preferring to argue that either approach is possible within the space of capability analysis.[71] Sen insists that it is not the job of the theorist to select a list of capabilities. Such a task is more properly left up to the citizens of a democracy. He writes:

> What I am against is the fixing of a cemented list of capabilities, which is absolutely complete (nothing could be added to it) and totally fixed (it could not respond to public reasoning and to the formation of social values). I am a great believer in theory. The theory of evaluation and assessment does, I believe, have the exacting task of pointing to the relevance of what we are free to do and free to be (the capabilities in general), as opposed to the material goods we have and the commodities we can command. But pure theory cannot "freeze" a list of capabilities for all societies for all time to come, irrespective of what the citizens come to understand and value. That would be not only a denial of the reach of democracy, but also a misunderstanding of what pure theory can do, completely divorced from the particular social reality that any particular society faces.[72]

This is the single largest difference between the two versions of the capability approach.[73] Sen's insistence on vagueness in relation to the selection issue may seem to some to sidestep messy methodological issues that make it difficult to actually assemble a concrete list of capabilities.[74] In some ways, Nussbaum's approach provides a more detailed answer to the "equality of what?" question than Sen's because it directly addresses the question of what a metric would look like when applied to a theory of justice rather than when deployed for general evaluative purposes. It is worth taking a closer look at her account.[75]

Nussbaum and capabilities

Nussbaum argues that capabilities can form the basis of constitutional claims that citizens may have. While her approach directly addresses political concerns, it is much broader than the egalitarian metrics we have been considering in that it is a specifically global view. While she addresses problems in the welfare approach to equality, the main focus in her recent work is on an engagement with the work of Rawls and the primary goods metric. She understands capabilities as providing the basic underpinning of an account of the fundamental things to which people are entitled and which should be respected by all governments. She outlines a list of ten capabilities she thinks could fill such a role. Her position is motivated by the intuitive idea of the importance of living a life worthy of human dignity and argues that the ten capabilities are implicit in a life so lived. They are not just means to realizing this life, but constitutive of dignity.[76] Everyone in society is entitled to these capabilities, and each should be held to a minimum threshold (only sometimes entailing equality), with no trade-offs between capabilities. If people do not have these capabilities up to a certain threshold, truly human functioning has not been achieved, and justice has not been done. Nussbaum's approach to justice is only partly egalitarian in that only some capabilities must be held equally, while others can be held to a sufficient level. For instance, the social bases of self-respect, nonhumiliation, and nondiscrimination are things that people should hold equally, she argues.[77] She adds that political, religious, and civil liberties (perhaps education, too) can be secured adequately only if they are equally secured. However, some capabilities are required only to a level sufficient to maintain human dignity. The capabilities of being equally housed and, presumably, healthy are required up to a level that maintains human dignity.

Nussbaum's is an Aristotelian account of the good insofar as it stipulates proper human functionings that are not arrived at procedurally in Rawls's sense. The primary difference between her approach and Rawls's is that hers is an outcome-oriented rather than a procedural approach to justice.[78] Her Aristotelian notion of the good is thus not an outcome of a contractarian-type decision procedure but something that regulates and guides such procedures. Nonetheless, Nussbaum wants to combine her Aristotelianism with Rawls's political liberalism. She thinks her list of capabilities *can* be the focus of an overlapping consensus, but it is not a product of one. Her view can achieve this goal, she claims, because it is meant to be freestanding; that is, it does not rely on metaphysical and epistemological doctrines, such that citizens could endorse it no matter what their other comprehensive ethical views are.[79] Importantly, being the focus of an overlapping consensus is only really a secondary justification for the view. In *Women and Human Development*, she argues that the primary justification "remains with the intuitive conception of truly human functioning and what that entails."[80] Moreover, how Nussbaum values each capability is important to note. As we saw, each capability must be available to citizens in every country, with no capabilities traded off against others.

Sen's understanding of how we weight the different capabilities is different again to Nussbaum's. As we noted, he argues that because the idea of equality of well-being might be ambiguous, it may be a mistake to look for a total or complete ordering of the substantive elements within a theory of equality. Thus, it may be a mistake to think that out of a list of ten or twelve capabilities, we may be able to achieve a complete ranking for all people. Second, even if a complete ranking is possible, practical considerations may prevent us from arriving at it.[81] Sen's solution is to advance a "partial ordering" of different capabilities. A partial ordering can be achieved even where we do not have full agreement on the relative weights for different capabilities. So where people are engaged in weighing a good such as health against another good – say, mobility – and there are four divergent views on the weights (one-half, one-fourth, one-fifth, one-third), then there is agreement that the weight should be no more than half and no less than one-fifth. In this case we have a partial ordering of at least some capabilities.[82]

According to capability theorists, a focus on resources leads Rawls and other resourcists to miss the point of what really matters to egalitarians when the concern is the distribution of social benefits and burdens because it focuses on ends rather than means. Indeed, this is Sen's response to Dworkin's claim that the capability metric is simply resourcism using a different language. According to Sen, the approaches must be different if for no other reason than that capabilities represent not just a means to an end but (at least some) ends themselves.[83] This not only distinguishes the approaches but arguably represents an advantage for a theory of justice in that there is a presumptive reason to think in terms of ends rather than means.[84] This is Anderson's defense as well. She argues that there is a presumption in favor of articulating principles of justice in terms of ends rather than means. She writes, "Why choose an indirect measure when a direct measure is available?" For Nussbaum the notion of capabilities as ends is even stronger: they are directly constitutive of human dignity, and life without these capabilities is a life without human dignity.[85] These kinds of criticisms, if correct, imply that Rawls's theory fails to address important inequalities in a substantive enough way. In terms of addressing important inequalities caused by disability and certain kinds of difference, Rawls's metric leaves out a significant set of factors that make people unequal. Not only may there not be the same opportunities for those with disabilities, but unacceptable outcomes may also result.

2.6 Assessment of the capability approach

We have seen that what separates the capability approach, according to its supporters, is its flexibility with respect to human diversity, especially disability. But flexibility and apparent respect for disability are among the chief sources of complaint about the approach. While there are more objections than can be dealt with here, the main problems are whether the approach does more to maximize freedom than the other metrics, selection and weighting, a disrespectful attitude toward disability, costliness, and concerns about perfectionism.

Freedom

Sen claims that a strength of the capability approach is its focus on freedom, that by adopting capabilities as a metric, we increase people's freedom in important ways. Sen is surely right that this is a feature of the approach. But is it a unique feature of the capability approach? Consider a resourcist response to the charge that capabilities maximize freedom in a way superior to resources. The resourcist might respond that providing all-purpose means was exactly what was required to maximize freedom in a democratic society. Given a set of resources everyone wants, people would then be free to do what they like with them in line with their life plans. It might be true, as Sen and Nussbaum claim, that resourcists focus on too narrow a set of resources and ignore things such as how social factors influence self-respect and environmental concerns. While resourcists have not, in fact, taken some of these items into account, nothing prevents them from doing so. As we noted earlier, resourcism is a bad name for a metric that includes background conditions, institutional arrangements, and so on. For example, in terms of variations in a social climate, Sen highlights how the conversion of personal resources into quality of life is influenced by social conditions (public education, crime, violence, and pollution), all of which influence how people can use the resources at their disposal. Thomas Pogge responds that a resourcist like Rawls might see such social determinants as making insecure some basic liberties.[86] Whether or not all resourcists do this or only Rawls in particular is not the point; the point is that resourcists can incorporate these concerns, and taking any one resourcist approach that may lack this focus does not mean the metric itself is inferior to the capability approach. While the approach is freedom-promoting, the real differences with the other metrics lie elsewhere.

A further freedom-enhancing feature of the approach is the focus on capabilities and not functionings. Both Sen and Nussbaum are emphatic on the advantages of capabilities over functionings.[87] But the critical issue is not whether the capabilities approach provides more freedom or less than other metrics but whether the freedom it provides is really as important as Sen claims and whether capabilities as opposed to functionings are the appropriate focus for a metric of equality. Many liberal egalitarians hold that in arguing for equality, we should focus on ensuring that individuals have the freedom to choose between different opportunities for well-being (the opportunity view) rather than equal achievements or outcomes (the achievement view). The opportunity view cuts across preferences for the various metrics of equality. Egalitarians who support opportunity views over achievement views do so for several reasons. We might prefer opportunities because of uncertainty about what the most important types of valuable lives really are (epistemological). Alternatively, opportunities might be our focus because to allow the state or some dominant group within it to advance some types of lives or choices risks centralizing power in the hands of some over others (domination). We might also argue that a focus on allowing individuals to choose between different options allows them to exercise their responsibility, which might be important in deciding whose disadvantage deserves assistance (responsibility). Finally, we might prefer opportunities to achievements because we think doing so avoids being unjustifiably paternalist (paternalism).[88]

There is not the space here to give a full account of why functionings might also form part of the list. But we can note two types of arguments, one concerning the importance to individuals of functionings, the other their political significance. The first kind argues that there is a range of specific functions that might be too important for individual well-being to be left to choice. Health is one obvious candidate; in particular, the dimension of health that relates to health and safety. If we allow health to be compromised because of unsafe work practices or untested medicines, we are compromising individuals in an unacceptable way. Health is too instrumentally important for other goods to allow individuals or society to engage in practices that would imperil it and, therefore, many of the other things they value.[89] Indeed, Nussbaum mentions this kind of argument without fully modifying her approach to reflect the departure from capabilities. She writes, "In general, the more crucial a function is to attaining and maintaining other capabilities, the more entitled we may be to promote actual functionings in some cases ...."[90] We can call this type of claim the argument from *individual good*, because it relates specifically to individuals' own good or well-being, independent of what others may require of them.

The second broad type of argument relates to what we might demand of individuals as citizens. First of all, if we are really interested in whether citizens can function in an equal way within a society, they are likely to be required to have certain functionings, especially when some functionings are necessary for other capabilities to occur, as may be the case with basic education levels, for instance. Let me illustrate this by reference to one element of a list that is plausibly part of a metric of capabilities and functionings. Central to the idea of a democratic culture is being able to participate in public debate by weighing arguments for principles of justice, assessing competing claims, and so on. These tasks require a kind of autonomy, albeit an autonomy suited to political purposes. This is especially true if political participation is thought of in terms of what we owe each other if we adhere to a moderately strong sense of political obligation. If living in a democracy requires a certain level of participation – debating policies, voting, and the like, which are crucial to a shared political enterprise – then having an autonomous citizenry is an important political goal. Autonomy is important insofar as it is a necessary feature of being able to think and reason about justice in a political setting, which is part of the framework of social life – "the very groundwork of our existence," as Rawls puts it.[91] At the very least, the importance of political autonomy to the political process is strongly instrumental; it might also be constitutive insofar as participating in political life is an important part of individuals' account of the good, at least on certain conceptions of the good, although this is likely to be controversial. More generally, it will be constitutively good to a great many individual conceptions of the good.[92]

Selection and weighting

One of the major difficulties facing capability theorists attempting to use their approach as a public criterion of social justice is that it looks to be difficult to actually select a list of capabilities that will do the job in an adequate way. Some critics have objected that the capability approach is unable to deal with the enormously varied possible valuable capabilities.[93] The claim here is that the capability approach, when confronted with the vast range of capabilities, will have no way of distinguishing between significant and insignificant capabilities. As Arneson puts it:

> Whether or not my capabilities include the capability to trek to the South Pole, eat a meal at the most expensive restaurant in Omsk, scratch my neighbor's dog at the precise moment of his daily maximum itch, matters not one bit to me, because I neither have the slightest reason to anticipate I ever will have any desire to do any of these things and myriad other things. Presumably only a small subset of my functioning capabilities matter for moral assessment, but which ones?[94]

The answers given by both Sen and Nussbaum to this question highlight the way in which capability theorists are pulled in different and incompatible directions. On the one hand, Sen's insistence that selection of a list is not a function of the theorist but a democratic task and his partial ordering approach preserve pluralism by not providing a definite list of capabilities that can be used to assess comparative claims of disadvantage. But it comes at a cost, which is that selecting and ranking capabilities may be limited when we need clear public criteria to arrange redistribution or compensation. Allowing a democratic (and informed preference) way of determining which capabilities are to be selected preserves the space of capabilities – one is still selecting capabilities and not, say, income – but admits a higher degree of importance to preferences. A similar "reductionist"-type objection is made by Dworkin, who argues that when we take into account Sen's determination to move away from welfarism, the best way to understand capabilities is as resourcism but with a different vocabulary.[95] If what is really important for Sen is that governments equalize individuals' abilities to achieve such a complex personal goal as being happy and focus not on personal deficits that are a result of choice but on individuals' personal and impersonal resources, this is merely equality of resources by another name.[96] A potentially more damaging reductionist point is that Sen's arguments about selection and weighting show that his approach is in fact a subjectivist one.

At some points Sen seems to suggest that the political collective decides which capabilities are to serve as the currency of justice.[97] But at others he suggests that individuals will decide which capabilities to select.[98] If the second route is taken, surely his approach falls prey to the reductivist objection that what is really important is the subjective preferences that people express about the capabilities they will choose. If this is the case, his view is vulnerable to the objections he himself made about subjectivist views, in particular about the potential for preferences to be adaptive. Nonetheless, his view could be a combination of subjective and objective features. It could, for instance, allow a collective to decide which capabilities are important, which may be on an objective list, and then let individuals separately decide which capabilities are best for them.[99]

On the other hand, Nussbaum's approach provides a definite objective list but runs the risk of being overly perfectionist, even though she claims that her list can be the subject of an overlapping consensus. Broadly speaking, the difficulty of seeing capabilities in terms of an objective list mirrors some of the issues also faced by objective list welfarism. Recall that welfarists who argued for an objective list version of their metric were confronted with the difficulty that their preferred list might not track what really mattered to people. So it is potentially with Nussbaum's approach. Identifying ten capabilities is not exhaustive of what is good for people and may not capture what is important to the vast array of individuals and their life plans, even considered just as citizens. Far from guaranteeing pluralism, it may suppress it. The worry here is that by specifying ten capabilities and insisting that each individual should be provided with all of them so as to have a life with human dignity, she prescribes too thick a theory of the good. The first part of the objection regarding advancing an objective list of goods is faced by all objective list theories, although the definiteness of Nussbaum's list perhaps increases her vulnerability to it. More of an issue is her insistence that all the capabilities must be provided at a threshold level to people and that a life without any one of them falls short of a life lived with human dignity. This seems a strong claim in that one could imagine a life short on some capabilities but high on others and nonetheless an excellent and dignified life. For instance, lives of great worth and fulfillment might have had an incredible level of opportunity and achievement of engagement with community, loving relations, intellectual reward, and so on but were short on the opportunity for play. We might consider these very good lives, but they would fail Nussbaum's criteria. This is especially true given Nussbaum's insistence (as we see in Chapter 4) that putting the list forward in a global cross-cultural agreement raises the likelihood of disagreement even further.[100] In terms of providing not just a metric but a metric that can combine with distributive and democratic principles to form a plausible account of social justice, Nussbaum's approach has done more than the other approaches of capability theorists to fulfill this task. But her account remains troubled by the tension between her Aristotelianism and her commitment to Rawls's political conception of liberalism. Insisting that the ten capabilities are essential for a fully human life lived with dignity and then hoping that they can form the basis of an overlapping consensus potentially negates the legitimacy of such a consensus.

As we have seen, Sen weights capabilities differently: through arguing that a partial ordering is both philosophically preferable and practically workable. It is philosophically preferable because it respects and observes the fact of pluralism in conceptions of the good better than does Nussbaum's Aristotelian approach to weighting. This difference comes down to a different interpretation of how to respond to the demands of pluralism in modern societies. Nussbaum thinks that her approach, which respects pluralism by focusing on capabilities, allows individuals to choose their own level of functioning with respect to each capability. For Sen this is a necessary but not sufficient condition for respecting pluralism. What is needed is both a focus on capabilities and democratic selection and a partial ordering of the selected capabilities.[101]

There might be ways for someone committed to both the capability approach and a form of procedural liberalism to steer between Sen's ultrademocratic approach and Nussbaum's Aristotelianism. Instead of arguing that ten specific capabilities are required for a life of dignity, one might ask what is required for citizens to function in a modern democracy. The selection process might be limited by what is required to debate policies (education, knowledge of laws and obligations), to be healthy enough to engage in debate (access to health care, avoiding morbidity, bodily integrity) and other capabilities that may help further the democratic and individual good. Along these lines, Anderson suggests that which capabilities are provided should be determined by objective interests, specifically the interests of following rules of justice, and persons framing their own conceptions of the good of individuals considered as citizens rather than in terms of their subjective preferences for their own specific life choices.[102] Considering only their needs as citizens will greatly reduce the danger of a proliferation of idiosyncratic capabilities. Nussbaum also contends that her list is flexible given that it can be instituted in different ways in different places, thereby responding in a nonperfectionist way to local concerns. But this will not help with the selection of the list itself, nor will it solve the weighting problem, when all capabilities are required for a life lived with dignity. An objective list account such as hers avoids the excesses of subjective welfarism but does so at the cost of removing adequate participatory engagement. Surely what is needed for the approach is a way of providing a list that is objective and appropriately limited but maintains a measure of democratic decision making at the level of weighting *and* selection. This kind of requirement has not been forthcoming from adherents to the approach.

A similar problem might confront how we rank the list of capabilities once we have decided on them. Capabilities might conflict, or they might be hard to rank against each other. Nussbaum's answer to this issue is to nominate two capabilities – affiliation and practical reason – that "suffuse" all the others.

Hard cases, heterogeneity, and disrespect

One of the features of the capability approach that has made it attractive to philosophers and others is its claimed ability to deal with heterogeneities of various sorts. Sensitivity to the differences between people is perhaps the most important difference between resourcists and capability theorists. This is particularly the case with disability. We have seen why Sen and company have thought that resourcist theories fail to capture this difference and that it has profound consequences for their theories of justice. But focusing on disability raises as many important questions for the approach as it does for the other metrics. For a start, we need to be clear why people with a disability should be treated differently. On this point Pogge argues that some institutional types of discrimination against the disabled, such as lack of access to public buildings, will clearly be addressed by supporters of the other metrics. But this is a different question from whether people who have done badly in what Rawls calls the "natural lottery" should be compensated as a matter of justice. On the first point, Pogge claims that insofar as, for instance, people with a disability are discriminated against, they have a claim of justice to rectify such discrimination, which a resourcist conception would address. Pogge also claims that capability theorists believe that institutional schemes should be structured to equalize some natural inequality. This is a claim with which resourcists do not agree.[103]

A further and more troubling complaint made by Pogge is that capability theorists view human natural diversity in vertical terms; that is, they rank the different abilities and attributes people have and give them a value (often not a precise value). This introduces a moralized hierarchy that resourcists avoid by having a horizontal conception of human natural diversity, which by not ranking overall bundles of endowments thereby recognizes diversity. For Pogge this is a major difference, because it leads to patronizing and belittling attitudes toward the disadvantaged. It will involve stigmatizing the disadvantaged by notifying them of their natural inferior endowments and offering them compensation.[104] Pogge is also particularly critical of the inability of the capability approach to explain how compensation for lacking natural endowments is to be funded. He argues that when the capability approach is used as a metric within the theory of social justice, it needs to be able to explain how the demands of compensation can be met. For example, the person with a higher metabolism, and therefore higher nutritional requirements, has a claim of justice on the resources, held by others, that are needed to satisfy the additional nutritional requirement. So if additional labor is needed to produce the food that the hungry person needs, those who can provide the labor have a duty of justice to do so. While Pogge is at pains to point out that there might be all sorts of moral claims that require the satisfaction of this particular need, it is not a demand of justice.[105] Moreover, capability theorists might be committed to expending vast sums of money raising people with capability deficits up to the relevant level. This might not only be costly but also place unfair burdens on others.

Yet capability theorists can avoid much of the force of this objection. For instance, as Elizabeth Anderson observes in responding to Pogge's former objection, no such stigmatizing is implied by the metric, and arguing for a standard package of resources will not account for human difference, especially disability. Anderson, in fact, thinks that a provision of a standard bundle of resources shows a tension in the resourcist approach between a demand to have an "unbiased" standard of needs with a concern to take into account the full range of human diversity. It respects equality by treating everyone the same but by doing so does not respect human diversity.[106] She also claims that capability theorists understand a person's capabilities to be a product not only of their natural endowments but of their access to external resources in the social environment in which they live. If this is the case, then individuals experience discrimination because society does not value their particular natural endowments. Capability theorists might offer them a remedy in the form of changing their endowments. So in the case where persons are discriminated against because of their looks – perhaps they are disfigured – Anderson argues that a just society might provide the option of plastic surgery, not because it endorses the discriminatory views but because it realizes that this may be one way to avoid discrimination (changing society's views might be another).[107] Thus, according to Anderson, capability theorists endorse a horizontal view of endowments, not a vertical one. On the cost issue raised by Pogge, Anderson responds that capability theorists need not be committed to futile expenditures. For instance, where some individuals have health care needs that are not satisfied no matter what is spent on them, there is nothing implicit in the approach to say that such expenditures must be undertaken. Similarly, where large expenditures are required to make only a trivial or small difference to some people's capabilities, others can object to the expenditures on the grounds that they are an unfair burden on them.[108]

Pogge's response highlights some crucial issues for capability theorists, yet it is not clear whether they are committed to a "no limit" system of compensation for those with severe and expensive deficits. To some degree this is a problem for welfarist theories as well, insofar as people have costly preferences that have to be equally satisfied. It is certainly true that once you abandon a metric that has a "fixed" level of distribution, costs may vary in individual cases. It is also an issue for resourcists insofar as they are committed to making the background conditions fair, which may entail a large allocation of resources for the badly discriminated against. Two points on this objection: the background conditions that are an important part of resourcist metrics may also incur costs that are high in relation to specific individuals who are disadvantaged in some way. Access to a legal system for nonnative speakers or people with a disability may also siphon resources from the common pool. In relation to limiting the costs of bringing people with capability deficits up to a threshold or equal level, there is nothing to prevent capability theorists from insisting on other justice-based rules that limit such expenditure. A theory of justice that adopts a capability metric might also adopt rules recognizing that some of the cost of improvements in the capability of the very-worst-off might be better directed to increasing equality of the next-worst-off and so on.

2.7 Conclusion

The "equality of what?" debate continues to be fundamental to how egalitarians conceive of what an equal society would look like. It offers an insight into the character of the institutional and distributional structure that an egalitarian society would entail. More than that, it offers insights into more general concerns about well-being and development, as well as telling us much that is useful for political philosophy in general.

Specifically, there are several noteworthy features of the debate worth drawing attention to in closing. I have argued that in trying to assess the metrics at the most general level, we need to distinguish issues of genuine difference in the metrics. This requires us to eliminate disagreements that are at cross-purposes. Several issues stand out. First, which metric is more freedom-promoting seems often to be a debate that is at cross-purposes and misses the right focus. Sen is perhaps the most insistent that his capability metric is freedom-maximizing. But all the other metrics have strong claims to be called freedom-maximizing views. Rawlsians can surely point out that understanding equality in terms of a set of all-purpose means is just what individuals need to maximize their freedom. After all, being able to use a set of resources to pursue your own conception of the good is surely the sort of freedom that states should promote. Similarly, welfarists might claim that their metric maximizes freedom because it allows people the equal freedom to pursue their own set of preferences, which they have individually determined. It thereby respects the sense in which people can freely decide on their own conceptions of the good. This is not to say that all versions of these metrics are focused just on freedom understood as an opportunity to do something important. Many of the metrics' advocates argue that actual achievements should also be aimed at, not just opportunities. We need to distinguish, therefore, the different senses in which a metric might be said to advance or increase freedom. We might categorize these senses in terms, respectively, of increasing valuable opportunities and of allowing people freedom to choose for themselves the things they value and of enabling people to access opportunities (via increasing their resources or skills). We also need to assess these metrics in terms of *why* this freedom is so important. This is related to the previous point regarding the background assumptions of each of the advocates of the different metrics. In terms of why freedom is important, it could be because it is intrinsically important to be able to freely choose between options, as Sen stresses, or because whether individuals had the freedom to do something, which led to their being unequal, for instance, is relevant to the assessment of what compensation they are due.

The role of preferences, in versions of all three metrics, is also an example of where debate has sometimes been at cross-purposes. As we have seen, whereas both Sen and Dworkin reject welfarism, they nonetheless find a role for preferences in their theories that is substantial and important. Although welfarism is most closely associated with the importance of preferences, each type of metric has a version that incorporates preferences. Subjective welfarists, of course, argue that preferences themselves should be the currency of egalitarian justice. The other metrics dispute this exclusive focus on preferences. Nonetheless, they all make room for preferences in their metrics in different ways. For instance, Dworkin's resourcism relies on individuals having reliable capacities to form preferences so that everyone can decide on which bundle of resources to bid for in an initial auction. Similarly, Sen argues that capabilities may be selected via a democratic procedure that might just as well be described as selecting the capability one prefers. So when assessing the different responses to the relevance and importance of preferences for each metric, we need to observe precisely what role for preferences they endorse or object to. Further, arguments about preferences can be at cross-purposes because what appear to be criticisms of rival metrics are in fact criticisms of the specific theories of justice in which they are embedded. As we noted, a metric ought to be able to serve as a public criterion as part of a conception of justice. This is a very important criterion for an egalitarian theory. As we will see, foregrounding responsibility, as many of the metrics advocates do, is likely to shape the items that compose any metric. Likewise, there are reasons to suppose that where one stands on perfectionism, neutrality, and paternalism will also affect one's choice of metric.

The metric debate has also evolved to include, at least to refocus on, important disadvantages, like disability and a lack of respect, left out of or downplayed in earlier versions of the metrics. These are important developments and certainly better equip metrics to face challenges relevant for modern societies. Metrics must be able to account both for the range of relevant differences that exist between people and for disability. Whether or not the capability approach actually achieves these aims, Sen's work in particular has forced others to clarify how their versions of other metrics can account for these two problems. How they do so should also be able to serve as a component in a theory of justice in the ways we have elaborated. Acting as a public criterion for an identifiable constituency places special demands on a metric, demands not as apparent for metrics used in development or purely well-being contexts.

I am not suggesting that when we remove features of the debate that are at cross-purposes we will be able to see what are really only a few major differences between the positions. Major differences will remain, and advocates of the various metrics should pay attention to whether their theory works as part of a conception of justice. Nonetheless, there is, to borrow a phrase from climate debates, some degree of "contraction and convergence." Norman Daniels (even Rawls, to a degree) argues that resourcism and capability metrics are closer than they originally appeared.

In terms of the future of the "equality of what?" debate, two issues stand out as needing further attention: whether the metrics are substantive enough and whether there should be combined metrics. On the first issue politically, much about egalitarianism in the "equality of what?" debate reflects the dominant political mood of the last thirty years in many Western countries. It should come, then, as no surprise that some of the metrics are not as politically robust as they might have been in the preceding thirty years. Given the dominance of the political right in politics generally, it is to be expected (though not celebrated) that philosophical reflections on the kinds of things in terms of which we should be equal have had a more defensive character than they should have had. This is particularly disappointing with the increased need for a focus on inequality as basic inequalities become more extreme.[109] Some of this defensiveness no doubt stems from genuine worries about avoiding unwarranted perfectionism, yet it is hard to think that all of it comes down to this concern alone.

One of the elements of a more substantive egalitarianism is a concern with how people's lives actually go. On the this issue, Dworkin's concern with ex post rather than ex ante inequalities seems to be an insubstantial conclusion to an innovative theory, as does his heavy reliance on the market. Here not enough attention has been paid to the causes of inequality. Similarly, Sen's deliberately vague specification of a list of capabilities is not evidence of a willingness to address the kinds of severe disadvantage we have discussed here. Moreover, perhaps the fact that the context for the debate is located firmly within a family of liberalism that strongly favors opportunities over outcomes also increases the likelihood that a weaker form of egalitarianism might eventuate. Opting for just capabilities and not functionings in some crucial dimensions of a metric will limit its ability to achieve equal relations. But functionings can also be important, especially when certain functionings are necessary for other capabilities to occur, as may be the case with basic health levels. Metrics that are purely opportunity-focused run the risk of allowing people to get left behind if they do not make the most of opportunities or their luck turns sour. Unless there are considerable safeguards, pure opportunity views can exist side by side with considerable inequalities.[110]

On the issue of the potential of mixed or combined metrics, typically, advocates of one metric define their positions by rejecting one or more of their rivals.' Yet with the notable exception of Cohen's access to advantage view, there is little that explicitly combines features of the different metrics into a pluralist metric. It seems that if a metric is to serve as a part of a theory of justice, this is precisely what needs to happen. From our earlier discussion we can identify a number of points that steer us toward a pluralist metric. While a metric will have to be composed of objective elements that are independent of people's subjective preferences, if the criticisms we have considered above concerning endorsement are correct, the metric will need to have some connection (in the sense of endorsement) with those to whom it applies. Without endorsement a metric will not have the right kind of connection. Another sense in which metrics ought to be mixed is in their combination of outcomes and opportunities. We have seen that focusing just on opportunities may lead to a lack of substantiveness in a metric and that equalizing some outcomes will matter as well. That people are equal in terms of some key indicators is likely to be crucial in contributing to whether their lives go well. This is not to remove opportunities from the picture but merely to argue that they are only part of what constitutes a successful metric. The incorporation of outcomes will be one of the largest challenges for egalitarians because of the dominance of opportunity views. Yet advocates of some metrics already incorporate outcomes, often in a way that does not emphasize them, as we see with Nussbaum's list of capabilities, which includes an outcome such as achieving human dignity. Metrics are also likely to work best when they are a mixture of ends and means. Anderson is right to suggest that we should have a presumption in favor of metrics that endorse important ends, as these are ultimately what we are aiming to achieve. But it is unlikely that everything in a metric will be solely an end in the sense that there will likely be constituents of a metric that are means as well.

One further element to the debate that also has a large bearing on how the metrics are assessed is the degree to which we should tolerate people falling below an equal level. In this context, one important feature of the "equality of what?" debate is the role of responsibility, modeled through the chance/choice distinction. Many of the justifications for why one metric is better than another implicitly or explicitly has to do with whether it allows an appropriate role for individual responsibility in assessing the goodness of actions in the compensation that may accompany them. Dworkin's and Rawls's criticisms of welfarism, for instance, have much to do with the concern that welfarism is vulnerable to the expensive tastes objection. Similarly, dissatisfaction with Rawls is in part due to the belief that he did not properly incorporate an account of responsibility in *Theory*. Both Rawls and Dworkin thought that a reason to choose their metrics over others was that they accounted for the important role that responsibility should play within a metric. Dworkin insists that a metric should be guided by the thought that what happens to people should reflect their choices. Likewise, for Sen, responsibility certainly seems to be implicit in his metric – witness his doubts about whether the rich religious faster ought to receive assistance – but he addressed the issue of the role of responsibility less directly. For welfarists, a reason for favoring a preference theory was that it could model a concern for responsibility because preferences were (at least in the ideal case) chosen; hence we could tell whether someone had good or bad luck. Note that this is not the same as the issue of whether a principle of responsibility ought to trump equality but, rather, whether we ought to let a principle of responsibility shape the metric of equality.

In many of these cases, responsibility or the lack of it was a reason for choosing or rejecting a metric. But allocating such a decisive role to responsibility is itself controversial. Most egalitarians think it should play some role in deciding the nature and extent of redistribution. Nonetheless, if it is the case that responsibility plays this role, there is a question of whether the debate about "equality of what?" has been too focused on ensuring that the metrics are designed to incorporate this feature. Whether this is justified is a question we cannot fully answer until the next chapter, after we consider the luck egalitarian position. But the question is whether the issue of which metric is best is too focused on responding to the chance/choice distinction. Perhaps one of the reasons the chance/choice distinction plays such a role is that the discussion of metrics is too closely tied to a certain type of liberalism – one that values individual responsibility excessively. This is an issue to which we now turn.

3
Egalitarianism and Responsibility

3.1 Introduction

The connection between egalitarianism and responsibility has been the most controversial part of the recent debate about egalitarianism. The debate revolves around two positions that seek to capture the proper role for responsibility within a conception of egalitarian justice. On the one hand, many egalitarians have sought to defend a version of egalitarian justice that is motivated by the idea that it is fair for people to be compensated for those disadvantages that are the result of chance and not of choices for which the agent is responsible. The terms *luck egalitarianism*, *equality of fortune*, and *responsibility-sensitive egalitarianism* are used to describe those positions that defend a prominent role for responsibility within egalitarianism.[1] Relational egalitarians, in contrast, claim that the goal of egalitarian justice is to ensure that people stand in relations of equality with one another and not to ensure that justice models the distinction between chance and choice. At stake here are several important issues. One is the issue of just what role responsibility should play within egalitarian justice. But another broader question that has emerged out of this debate is what the proper goals of egalitarianism actually are.

Both relational and nonrelational positions cut across different metrics of equality and for several reasons provide one of the best insights into the current state of egalitarian thinking about justice. For one, the discussion more closely connects with overtly political debates about personal responsibility that are the staples of political life in Western democracies. The idea that it is fair that we should bear the costs of the decisions for which we are responsible and be compensated for bad luck for which we are not responsible is powerful and important. This kind of claim is common in public discussion about the allocation of government funding. Think, for instance, of attitudes toward costly treatments for illnesses for which we often hold people responsible: smokers who require treatment, those injured in extreme sports, or those who have lived too much of the good life without thinking of the consequences are all often thought to fall on the choice and not chance side of the divide. If they are responsible for their ill health, then it is easy to see how, all things being equal, many would argue that it is unfair that others pay for their disadvantage. There are, of course, many other ways in which this position could be defended – for example, because it respects the freedom of individuals to make their own choices.

Let us begin with luck egalitarianism. Luck egalitarians think that people ought to assume responsibility for their choices and the outcomes of those choices (all things being equal) but not for the bad effects of pure chance. Determining whether or not individuals are responsible for their actions and the outcomes that result is a way of distinguishing when inequalities are permissible and when they may require compensation. This applies to inequalities that result from making good choices – whether resulting in an increase in someone's resources or welfare or a decrease of it. For the most part, we will be focusing on losses in what follows. Luck egalitarianism thus also includes a claim about when inequalities that are a gain to an individual are permissible. Recall that Dworkin claimed that an egalitarian theory of distributive justice "should aim to improve the position of people who are physically handicapped or otherwise unable to earn a satisfactory income, for example – but should not aim to mitigate or compensate for differences in personality – for differences traceable to the fact that some people's tastes and ambitions are expensive and other people's are cheap."[2] Similarly, while relocating Dworkin's cut between responsibility and luck, G. A. Cohen claimed that the proper aim of egalitarianism is to "eliminate *involuntary disadvantage*, by which I (stipulatively) mean disadvantage for which the sufferer cannot be held responsible, since it does not appropriately reflect choices that he has made or is making or would make."[3]

These two very strong statements of the role of responsibility point to the distinction between actions that are a function of choice and those that are the result of chance, which roughly corresponds to the distinction between brute luck and option luck that underpins the luck egalitarian position. The statements by Dworkin and Cohen tell us not only about the role of the chance/choice distinction but also about the *goal* of egalitarianism, which is to eliminate the effects of bad brute luck. According to the simple outline here, luck egalitarianism tells us that a person who is responsible for his or her own inequality has no justice-based claim to compensation or assistance, or at most a severely diminished claim. So if someone gains as a result of his or her responsible actions (and not brute good luck), then that inequality is permissible. The inequality may be bad for that person and others, but it is not a concern of justice. What we can call "pure" luck egalitarianism would not compensate at all for bad option luck. In practice, as we will see, a range of compensatory schemes are proposed. One could, for instance, compensate or assist victims of bad option luck by giving them something for their loss but not something of equivalent value. For example, if only to encourage responsible behavior, one might assist those whose choices have caused their unemployment by giving them enough to live on but not the equivalent of a working wage.[4] We should note that luck egalitarians are not deaf to the claims of those who are discriminated against or who suffer oppression of some description, but according to this brief characterization, they think that the main goal of egalitarianism is to compensate for bad luck. What is distinctive about the luck egalitarian position is not that responsibility matters – almost all egalitarians think that it does – but that it should play a decisive and prominent role in determining the distribution of goods and in determining when inequalities are acceptable.

The focus on the distinction between choice and chance has important advantages. For one, it captures that type of concern, discussed at the beginning of the chapter, about the appeal of not compensating people for inequalities they have caused themselves, a point that is likely to appeal not only to many egalitarians but to nonegalitarians as well. Moreover, it captures an important dimension of equality by removing (or at least mitigating the effects of) those inequalities that are out of our hands, such as poor genetic endowments or accidents, while at the same time acknowledging that we are agents who make decisions about our lives for which we can be held accountable.

The other side of this debate, what I will call *relational egalitarianism*, holds that the goal of egalitarianism is to create a society of equals by placing people in relations of equality. Elizabeth Anderson's account of democratic equality is an example of such a position, as is the position developed by Samuel Scheffler.[5] The goal of relational egalitarianism is to enable people to function as equals in society, which might involve ensuring that everyone's culture or identity is properly acknowledged or accepted or by ensuring that everyone has the conditions of freedom secured, whether these are material goods and benefits or important opportunities generated by institutions. This is relational egalitarianism's positive aim. Relational egalitarianism's negative aim is to eliminate disadvantage caused by, for example, sexism, racism, or, indeed, excessive accumulations of wealth. Relational egalitarians claim that their conception is not primarily a distributive ideal. It aims principally not at distributing equal amounts of some good but at establishing relations of equality. So, for instance, Anderson claims that of most importance is whether or not people stand in relations of equality with one another and have a sufficient level of goods in a distributive sense. Anderson is sufficientarian in respect of the distribution of the constituents of her metric. So relational egalitarianism is compatible with a sufficientarian or prioritarian distributive principle.

For relational egalitarians, these latter types of disadvantage are the most important and should be a higher priority than eliminating the effects of brute bad luck. This is not to say that the latter is not important; rather, it is an issue of which kind of reason principally motivates a theory of justice. According to relational egalitarians, a key difference between their conception and that of the luck egalitarians is that theirs does not leave people destitute if they make bad choices. On a pure version of luck egalitarianism, individuals who foolishly lose all their resources or their health will not have a justice-based claim to assistance. By ensuring that everyone is able to function in relations of equality, relational egalitarianism claims to be motivated by a more plausible set of ideals and to be closer to the egalitarian tradition.

So much for the brief characterization. As we will see, the reality involves a great deal more complexity and overlap than this summary provides. In fact, on several key issues the two positions have more in common than first appears – for instance, on whether benefits of cooperation are conditional. On other issues, there is genuine disagreement, particularly regarding the role of outcomes over opportunities. But suffice to say that the contours of the recent debate revolve around these two positions with their different understandings of distributive justice and the broader motivations for egalitarian justice.

Different kinds of responsibilities

The sense of responsibility invoked in this debate is a particular kind of responsibility. When we talk of someone being responsible, we can mean different things. Someone can be responsible in the sense of having responsibility for someone else, such as when a parent has responsibility for the welfare of a child, it being his or her "job" to look after the child. Or responsibility can mean being responsible as an agent for an action. While there are many ways in which the concept of responsibility can be understood, for simplicity I will use Scanlon's distinction between responsibility as attributability and substantial responsibility.[6] According to this distinction, someone can be responsible in the sense that we can attribute responsibility to him or her. This is to say that the person's action is of a kind that makes it the subject of moral praise and blame. Typically this means that an agent has acted in a voluntary way and brought about the relevant action. Where such conditions exist, to use Scanlon's terminology, we can attribute responsibility to the agent who brought them about. Thus, according to this sense of responsibility agency can be identified without attaching sanctions to actions in all or some cases. We can morally assess a person's actions but not attach penalties to them. By contrast, consequential or substantive responsibility, as Scanlon calls it, entails accepting responsibility for the consequences of an action and the costs involved. What is relevant here is the question of when and whether someone who is responsible in an attributive sense is also substantively responsible for his or her actions. For instance, if everyone in society has equality of opportunity, then provided opportunities were equal in the right way, there can be no complaint in terms of egalitarian justice if we do not compensate for bad option luck. Note that this is not to say that we do not have reason to be concerned about people who suffer bad option luck, just that there is no reason in justice for our concern. Humanity or charity might motivate us to aid them but not justice.

People can suffer brute luck by being victims of circumstances in a number of ways. The most obvious way is to suffer an accident. Accidental injuries, natural disasters, and so on constitute different kinds of bad brute luck. But another way in which one's luck can be bad is by being unlucky in what Rawls has called the "natural lottery": receiving unmarketable talents, a low IQ, and so on. The clearest case of bad option luck, in contrast, is where someone makes a foolish decision and is disadvantaged in some way. Recklessly buying sports cars or holiday houses or engaging in physically risky activities without due care are all examples of such luck. But note that someone might also make a choice that though fully informed, prudent, and well thought out, might still create an inequality. For instance, training to be an engineer during a mining boom might seem like the right thing to do at the time but might turn out to be a bad choice if there were to be a prolonged slump, a drop in commodity prices, or the like. Bad option luck that originates from a good choice with unexpectedly bad consequences might also be something that does not attract egalitarian concern. Relatedly, Dworkin makes the point that failing to insure for bad brute luck is also something for which people could be held responsible.

Two roles for equality: Rawls and the luck egalitarians

One way of understanding the differences between these two accounts of responsibility is to trace them to two rival schools of thought about the role of responsibility and equality in Rawls's work. Several proponents of each position locate their view by reference to Rawls. Thinking about the debate in this way offers both a way to understand the role of responsibility and equality in Rawls's influential work and a way to appraise the debate independently of *A Theory of Justice*.

Two key discussions in Rawls's work give rise to the claims about luck egalitarianism. The first is his informal defense of the two principles in the second chapter of *A Theory of Justice*. Rawls's second principle of justice concerns the distribution of goods and the design of institutions. The principle states that "social and economic inequalities are to be arranged so that they are both: to the greatest benefit of the least advantaged."[7] Rawls also asserts a principle of equality of opportunity that can be interpreted in a number of ways and defends what he calls "democratic equality" from rival interpretations. On the first interpretation – a system of natural liberty – everyone has equal formal access to opportunities. So where jobs are open to the talented, provided we all have a chance to compete for those jobs, rewards would be distributed to those who are best qualified. Yet for Rawls, this ignores the fact that some have been lucky in the natural lottery and have been given marketable talents, a high IQ, and so on. So if we are concerned about the moral arbitrariness of the distribution of these advantages, then we should also be concerned about the rewards these advantages accrue. The injustice of the system of natural liberty is that it allows these morally arbitrary factors to influence distributive shares. What Rawls calls the liberal interpretation of equality of opportunity corrects the unfairness of the first interpretation by adding the further condition of "fair equality of opportunity." The liberal interpretation requires not only the removal of formal barriers but that everyone should have the same chance to attain opportunities by, for instance, putting in place measures that can even out class and other barriers.[8] For instance, those with the same abilities and talents should not be held back by social or cultural barriers. Yet this position is also flawed because even if we eliminate social barriers, some people will be born with more talents than others, and that is still arbitrary from a moral point of view. So Rawls insists that the moral arbitrariness of both talents and social position should not prove decisive in the allocation of certain goods and opportunities – a point that neither the system of natural liberty nor fair equality of opportunity captures. Rawls's solution is to combine the principle of fair equality of opportunity with his difference principle so as to remove influences that might make some more able to use their talent and consequently the advantages that might accumulate. The other dimension of Rawls's work that is said to have motivated luck egalitarians is his commentary on primary goods. As we saw in Chapter 2, Rawls's account of primary goods is the basis of interpersonal comparison between people in a just society. The primary goods are what people can legitimately expect as part of being in a just society. What is relevant here for our purposes is how Rawls deals with the expensive tastes objection, which maintains that if some individuals have tastes that are costly to satisfy while others have cheap tastes, an equal distribution of primary goods will not satisfy everyone equally. Rawls responds that citizens can be assumed to be responsible for their ends. He writes, "The use of primary goods, however, relies on a capacity to assume responsibility for our ends,"[9] and "those with less expensive tastes have presumably adjusted their likes and dislikes over the course of their lives to the income and wealth they could reasonably expect; and it is regarded as unfair that they now should have less in order to spare others from the consequences of their lack of foresight or self-discipline."[10] Responsibility here looks to be playing the kind of role in a distribution of goods that luck egalitarians think it should – that is, as an arbiter of when inequalities are unjust.

3.2 Motivating luck egalitarianism

Detractors typically claim that, at best, luck egalitarians have lost sight of what egalitarianism means, which is that it should place people in relations of equality and not attempt to model a metaphysical distinction between chance and choice. At worst, its detractors claim, it has gone too far in adopting the language and arguments of the political right, with disastrous consequences for egalitarians. Others suggest modern versions of egalitarianism stand for very little that is recognizably egalitarian, and so what was once a robust set of views is now empty of meaningful content. Or worse still, where luck egalitarians do advance content, it should trouble even those on the left because it embodies fundamentally disrespectful values. These claims involve several discrete objections, which I will call the *disastrous consequences, disrespectful treatment, information constraints, indeterminateness of the distinction,* and *opportunities versus outcomes* objections, and the more general claims that luck egalitarianism has the wrong goals. The most important of these objections is that luck egalitarianism misses the point of egalitarianism and what it means to be committed to equality.

The harshness objection and lack of respect

By far the most influential discussion of these issues is Elizabeth Anderson's article "What Is the Point of Equality?" which I will use to discuss several important types of objections. Although several other authors had questioned the focus on responsibility, it was Anderson's article that sparked a prolonged debate about responsibility's proper role and about the broader goals appropriate to luck egalitarianism. Anderson coined the term *luck egalitarianism* and provides by far the most trenchant criticism of responsibility-type views. Her claim is that luck egalitarians have lost sight of the goals of egalitarianism, which is not to compensate for bad brute luck but to end oppression and to create a community in which people stand in relations of equality. Anderson claims that luck egalitarianism fails the test of what a true egalitarian theory should be because it would have us fail to treat people with equal concern and respect. It does this for three reasons. First, people who accept it wrongly exclude citizens from the "social conditions of freedom" (potentially their welfare entitlements or health benefits) when they are to blame for their loss, and in trying to rectify this, they descend into paternalism. Second, people who accept its principles express "contemptuous pity" for many of the people they believe should be assisted. Finally, in attempting to make people responsible for their choices, people who accept it make "demeaning and intrusive judgements" of the ability of individuals and their choices.[11] She argues that what luck egalitarians end up with is an unattractive hybrid of capitalism and the welfare state. According to Anderson, luck egalitarians treat the victims of both option luck and brute luck badly.

On the first point, citizens can lose the conditions of their freedom if they have to pay for disastrous consequences. Under luck egalitarianism the victims of bad option luck fare particularly badly, according to Anderson, because they prescribe rugged individualism. She presents a series of cases that highlight the harshness of the doctrine, according to her. For instance, she claims that negligent drivers who injure themselves in car collisions would be liable (all things being equal) for the costs of initial emergency care and subsequent care if their actions were a result of option luck. Similar examples point to how luck egalitarianism abandons the prudent when their luck turns sour. For example, if someone chooses to live in a geographic location occasionally afflicted by cyclones, then the state would not be obligated to give them disaster relief if the worst happened. Similarly, workers who choose risky occupations might also not be compensated by the state should they suffer an accident at work. A luck egalitarian position fails to treat people with respect because a society that allows people to sink to such depths does not respect them.

Anderson claims that luck egalitarians also fail to treat the victims of bad brute luck with the respect and concern they deserve. In particular, a luck egalitarian fails to properly identify who is worst off. For instance, she claims that Dworkin's scheme to compensate people who insure against disability is discriminatory against people who fail to insure against rare diseases that they could not foresee contracting. For people that luck egalitarians do aid, the principle is deeply disrespectful. Toward people who are disabled, talentless, or socially awkward, Anderson claims that luck egalitarians would make judgments about their disadvantage in order to compensate them, effectively raising *"private disdain to the status of officially recognised truth,"* thereby reproducing the stigmatizing approach of the Poor Laws.[12] Such bases for compensation express pity, and pity is not a good basis on which to compensate because it is incompatible with the dignity of others. In addition, requiring that people demonstrate that a disadvantage was not their fault might require what Wolff has called "shameful revelation." For instance, if at a time of low unemployment a person cannot get a job through no fault of his or her own, on a luck egalitarian understanding, to access benefits an unemployed person is required to admit that he or she lacks talents and has failed to get a job not through bad choices but simply through not being good enough. This sort of shameful revelation is demeaning and may undermine self-respect if the person is forced to admit that he or she is actually not good enough to get a job.[13]

Limiting the role of chance and choice

Many of these points underscore the general claim about the unattractiveness and role of the chance/choice distinction. At a very abstract level, the claim that people ought not to have to suffer inequalities from bad brute luck and also ought not to have to ask others to pay for the inequalities they have brought on themselves has prima facie plausibility. Many people might think that such a view is both obvious and attractive, yet its substantive versions might invoke less support. Anderson's examples are intended to tease out the consequences of observing the distinction. For those who suffer bad option luck, the consequences might be dire or even life-threatening, and for those who suffer bad brute luck, they can provoke responses that are patronizing. It might thus depend on the circumstances whether one supported the use of the distinction. While we might agree in general that such a distinction is useful, not all cases where inequalities arise as a result of choice should be compensated as a matter of justice. In addition, we might think that inequalities that were freely chosen – for example where someone chose to enter into voluntary slavery – should be seen as permissible.[14] Similarly, not all cases where someone suffers bad luck might be compensatable either.[15] So while the abstract principle might draw much support, its substantive versions might not.

One concern for luck egalitarians is that relying on a distinction between chance and choice to determine when inequalities are permissible will be limited by the likely information constraints. To give an example: individuals who are unemployed might be so because either they are genuinely unable to find work or their own choices might have contributed to their situation. It can be difficult to determine responsibility for unemployment accurately and on a large scale, as is typically required. Except in cases where a person either admits that he or she is not trying to get a job or is caught perpetrating a fraud, it is often an imprecise process. A range of factors might play a role here. For an assessment to be complete, an assessor might have to consider a person's past responsibility in acquiring marketable skills, the person's efforts at finding jobs, the nature of the job market, and, importantly, the person's motivation. All these things produce a complex picture from which governments and their representatives must make decisions about personal responsibility. Similarly, in regions that are remote from populous centers and lacking in sustainable employment, it might be difficult to determine all the factors that could influence an assessment of a person's responsibility for unemployment. It is easy to imagine that where a person has attachments and commitments to a location, it might be possible for someone to leave but be very costly to do so. These examples illustrate that it is often hard to determine responsibility for being unemployed in a straightforward way. But it is also very important to get it right because the consequences for the individuals whose eligibility for welfare benefits is being assessed are often extraordinarily severe. A loss of income leaves the unemployed without access to all but the most basic goods. But there are other obvious consequences as well, such as loss of self-esteem, loss of opportunities to function in valuable ways, and being subject to social stigma.

This kind of example tells us that we might also find it difficult to keep chance and choice separate. For instance, at the level of moral theory, responsibility for actions might be vitally important, but it might be impossible to sort through all the causal chains that were involved in a specific outcome. That someone chose to pursue a risky business venture that failed might, on the face of it, look like an act of choice, but that person's upbringing, perhaps social conditions that promote risk, easy lending from banks, and similar factors might have contributed to the person's taking the risks he or she did. As we have seen, this objection has sometimes been met by the "endorsement" argument made by Dworkin and others.[16]

A related point is that sometimes "private responsibility" is not as distinct from circumstances as it might seem. Susan Hurley argues that assumptions about individual responsibility play an important role in deciding when and how governments can intervene in society to influence citizens' behavior to prevent harms. For instance, often a criterion for when not to intervene in others' lives is that even though they may be harming themselves, they not harming anyone else. Governments should not attempt to influence them because their acts (let us assume) are responsible ones.[17] Traditional liberalism assumes the "priority of private responsibility." Yet Hurley suggests a naturalistic challenge to this model of using responsibility as a limit to government intervention by exploring the sense in which responsibility is not prior to the public realm. Private responsibility has a "public ecology" to which governments and others typically contribute. For instance, an agent may assimilate traits and beliefs from his or her social environment that have a role in how the agent decides to act, such as when people of certain races or cultures are portrayed in negative ways that affect how others respond to them. Thinking of an agent as built around a rational core that provides capacities for responsible decision making leaves out the role that a public environment plays in forming the basis of people's action. Such situated rationality and its public origins ought to factor into our thinking about how responsible agents really are. If agents act in a certain way because they are influenced by things they are not aware of and may not have liked to have been influenced by, then we may have grounds for intervening to counter this manipulation of the private sphere of responsibility. Setting aside the issue of when it is legitimate to intervene, we might see these kinds of concerns about the public ecology of responsibility as further grounds for objecting to the usefulness of the distinction between chance and choice.

Others have also made the point that a conception of justice dominated by a concern to model chance and choice in a prominent way is too focused on ensuring that opportunities are equal and ignores the possibility of overall outcomes that exhibit gross instances of hierarchy, misery, and inequality of outcome. "Conservative egalitarians," as Fleurbaey calls them, focus excessively on *ex ante* allocations of equality of opportunity, whereas we should also be concerned with the content of opportunities, especially those that lead to people having the resources to live decent, fulfilling lives.[18] As we will see, however, this charge could also be leveled at Anderson.

We can divide the preceding criticisms into two broad groups. The first-order objections concern the goals that luck egalitarianism is said to have and how they are in fact the wrong goals for egalitarianism. These kinds of objections are at the heart of the dispute between the two positions. The second-order objections focus on the difficulties of implementing luck egalitarianism – its information constraints, harshness, and so on. Each offers a challenge to the plausibility of luck egalitarianism.

3.3   Relational egalitarianism

Equality as equal standing

The claim that most distinguishes luck egalitarians from their opponents is that their conception of equality appeals to the wrong ideal of equality – a narrow distributive conception that is not connected to a more fundamental notion of equality as a social and political ideal. While this point is not limited to discussions of Rawls's work, proponents of this ideal seem to understand justice as fairness as providing the prototype of such an alternative view to luck egalitarianism. Recall that Rawls understands his principles of justice as being designed for people conceived of as free and equal citizens. He writes, "How is it possible that there may exist over time a stable and just society of free and equal citizens profoundly divided by reasonable though incompatible religious, philosophical, and moral doctrines?"[19] His question is how to design a set of institutions and principles that answers these questions. According to relational egalitarians, what is of importance here is the way in which a principle of equality is fundamental to regulating questions of distribution.[20] The basic conception of equality is one, not of which distribution is the best, but of how we can get people to stand in relations of equality with one another. Unless other principles governing distribution reflect this, they will lose their appeal. Luck egalitarians fail to connect their principles of distribution, governed as they are by the chance/choice distinction, with this broader ideal and so are unconvincing. One clear indication of Rawls's view, highlighted in particular by Daniels, is that Rawls proposes a division of labor regarding responsibility. For Rawls, to guarantee that citizens can stand in relations of equality with each other, society ought to take responsibility for ensuring that everyone is provided with the equal basic liberties, fair equality of opportunity, and primary goods, while individuals take responsibility for adjusting their ends in light of what they can expect from this provision.[21] So if Daniels and others are correct, then responsibility is important for a theory of justice but only after everyone has been made equal in important respects.

The importance of acknowledging a broader conception of equality is illustrated in Anderson's account of democratic equality, where the fundamental goal is to place people in relations of equality with one another. That is the positive aim of her conception of democratic equality. For her, placing people in relations of equality is a different aim than establishing patterns of equal distribution. Those patterns are important but are informed by this broader egalitarian goal. Scheffler makes a similar point when he writes, "Any form of distributive egalitarianism, if it is to be at all plausible, must be anchored in some more general conception of equality as a moral value or normative ideal."[22] Such an account has a number of implications. For instance, according to Anderson, some goods might be held equally but others only up to a level sufficient to ensure that relations of equality are maintained. Importantly, these relations are meant to hold over an entire life, so democratic equality is not a starting-gate theory, where the conditions can be lost through, for instance, bad option luck. Its negative aim is to abolish oppression. As such, it is different, she claims, to luck egalitarianism, whose primary aim is to abolish the effects of bad brute luck.

Relational egalitarians do, nonetheless, emphasize that responsibility plays an important role. Anderson stresses that egalitarians need to face up to the issue of irresponsibility, if only to not bankrupt the state. There are two ways of doing this. The first is the luck egalitarian way in which individuals can be deprived of goods using the chance/choice distinction as a deciding criterion. The second is by using a different distinction between goods that citizens require to function as equals and those that are not necessary to do so. Democratic equality favors the latter. Anderson's view also promotes responsibility by guaranteeing the conditions for the exercise of responsible agency. So responsibility certainly features in her sketch, but its role is fundamentally different from that in luck egalitarianism. The goal of democratic equality is not to embody a distinction between chance and choice but to place people in relations of equality. Notice that the differences between the two positions do not reduce to the issue of whether one position has a role for chance/choice and the other does not. They both have a role, and the difference is how each type of position employs the distinction. For luck egalitarians the chance/choice distinction is fundamental, in the sense that it motivates or grounds their discussion of distributive equality. Distributive equality should be designed to reflect the impact of chance and choice. For democratic egalitarians, on the other hand, chance/choice is important but does not motivate their egalitarianism. Their egalitarianism is motivated by the ideal of, for example, placing people in relations of equality.

3.4   Luck egalitarian responses

Critics of luck egalitarianism argue that they have attached too much significance to the distinction between chance and choice. The most extreme form of the criticism asserts that there is no compensation or assistance due to those who suffer because of bad option luck. But it is important to note that several consequences could follow from observing this distinction. Luck egalitarians can claim that their view does not have to be as harsh as a pure version of luck egalitarianism would appear to be. There are at least three ways in which they might interpret the consequences of observing the chance/choice distinction. They could concur with Anderson that those who are unequal because of bad option luck deserve no assistance whatsoever. Alternatively, they could claim that the point of the distinction is to indicate who has priority in the distribution of resources. When faced with the choice of whom to assist first, a public authority could be guided by whether the inequality was the result of option or brute luck. This does not mean that no assistance should be given to those whose disadvantage is their own fault. Also, they could maintain the fundamental importance of observing the distinction between chance and choice but make allowances for citizens who fell so low through their own bad decisions that their lives were threatened or they could no longer function as citizens. Compulsory insurance or welfare schemes might fill the funding gap required to keep people at an appropriate level. Moreover, they might claim that their views are not as harsh as they are being portrayed because while there might not be a duty of justice to make good the lives of the irresponsible, there might be humanitarian duties to do so. So in practice as in theory, luck egalitarianism would be less harsh.[23] Similarly, Tan argues that the domain of luck egalitarianism should be seen as being distributive justice, which he defines as the allocation of benefits and burdens *after* basic needs have been met.[24]

Acknowledging the force of some of the criticisms but denying that they apply in the way that relational egalitarians assert has been one response to criticisms of luck egalitarianism. This is particularly true of the responses to the informational and disastrous-consequences objections. Luck egalitarians claim that it is certainly true that a theory such as theirs, when applied on a national scale, will encounter all sorts of information constraints concerning the real causes of inequality in particular cases. Yet acknowledging this point does not diminish the importance of the moral theory of luck egalitarianism, which is a set of abstract moral principles and not a theory of the best way to apply such principles. Luck egalitarians may claim that some of these criticisms are just criticisms of bad applications of a good theory. Where restrictions apply to the gathering of information, luck egalitarians might adopt a second-best approximation of their theory. In short, criticisms of the failings of likely luck egalitarian institutions are criticisms of nonideal luck egalitarian institutions and not ideal luck egalitarian theory.[25]

One issue that the humanitarian approach to assistance does raise is whether having a humanitarian claim to assistance is a strong enough claim. If it is a claim of charity, which cannot be enforced as a justice-type claim can be, the outcome for the disadvantaged is very different. Observing a difference between justice and charity claims does make the luck egalitarian position more likely to result in harsh consequences. If, in contrast, the humanitarian claim is one that allows the disadvantaged to insist on some form of aid, then it does raise questions of how it might differ from a justice claim and why we wouldn't be better thinking of it in those terms.

Pure luck egalitarians might respond to the disastrous-consequences objection in the same way that some "intrinsic" egalitarians respond to the leveling-down objection – by admitting that it is a consequence of their view but an extremely unlikely one. While society might deny medical care to the victims of bad option luck, it is likely that other values will override considerations of responsibility. While this is one response, it still makes luck egalitarianism an unattractive position. A better approach is to argue, as Dworkin and others do, that any theory of justice that endorses luck egalitarian–type views is not only compatible with but likely to be paired with one that, for instance, endorses compulsory insurance for the imprudent.[26]

A further set of differences – which also involves some overlap – concerns the role that luck egalitarian ideals play in their theories of justice. This is the most important objection that Anderson and Scheffler make against luck egalitarians – that they have either the wrong ideal or, worse, no ideal at all. This objection can be divided into three different but related objections. The first is that luck egalitarianism is unregulated by any broader ideal. However, this does not seem to be true of most luck egalitarian positions. Dworkin insists that his position is an articulation of the more fundamental ideal of treating everyone with equal concern and respect. Similarly, Arneson describes his later position of responsibility-catering prioritarianism as motivated by a concern to increase well-being but also to allow for substantive responsibility. Scheffler's claim can more accurately be described as being about the narrowness of the ideal – that luck egalitarianism is too focused on distributive issues at the expense of broader social and political ideals. But at the very least, luck egalitarians, such as Dworkin, can claim that they are trying to model more fundamental ideals.

A more accurate rendering of this objection is that luck egalitarians refer to broader ideals but fail to live up to them in their theories of justice. For instance, if Anderson's argument that luck egalitarians deny citizens the conditions of their freedom or demean them with paternalist intrusions into their private lives is correct, then they fail to live up to the ideals of treating everyone with equal concern and respect. This objection turns on the issue of whether and to what extent luck egalitarian conceptions are likely to be guilty of these consequences. As we saw earlier, if they can avoid the harshness objection, for instance, by incorporating insurance schemes, then they will not be likely to deny people the conditions of their freedom. This objection to luck egalitarianism is partly one of implementation, which is not as fundamental as it appears.

Of most concern for luck egalitarians is the claim that their theories do refer to a broader ideal but that it is the wrong one. Recall that the relational egalitarians argue that designing a theory of justice so as to model a distinction between chance and choice is a distorted version of egalitarianism. Moreover, it makes egalitarianism into a distributive ideal that ignores relational concerns. (I return to this second issue later.) On the former issue, luck egalitarians can respond that, at the very least, the chance/choice distinction is a fundamental ideal that deserves to be prominent in any conception of egalitarian justice. Indeed, as we saw previously, it also has a role in relational conceptions, just not such a prominent one. It can also be combined with an ideal of treating everyone with equal concern and respect or of increasing well-being. This is Arneson's strategy in arguing that his responsibility-catering prioritarianism is egalitarian because it favors the worst-off, whose condition is judged good or bad not in comparison with others but by objective standards of well-being.[27] Because this is a view that does not compare states of well-being interpersonally, it should not be thought of as invoking pity and envy.

One response that is open to luck egalitarians is to claim that it is not that they do not refer to broader moral ideals; just that they draw different conclusions from them. This point gains some support from Scheffler's comments on the lack of broader ideals for luck egalitarians; they are worth quoting at length:

> Human relations must be conducted on the basis of an assumption that everyone's life is equally important, and that all members of a society have equal standing. As Anderson insists, in defending a version of this ideal, equality so understood is opposed not to luck but to oppression, to heritable hierarchies of social status, to ideas of caste, to class privilege and to the rigid stratification of classes and to the undemocratic distribution of power. In contrast to the inward-looking focus of luck egalitarianism, it emphasizes the irrelevance of individual differences for fundamental social and political purposes. As a moral ideal it asserts that all people are of equal worth and that there are some claims that people are entitled to make on one another simply by virtue of their status as persons.[28]

As described previously, the difference is not plausibly between different broad moral and political concepts but in what conceptions best capture these concepts. Luck egalitarians claim that modeling chance and choice is an important part of any conception because it captures part of what it means to treat people with equal respect. As we have seen, a pure luck egalitarian doctrine can moderate its harshness by building in a safety net. Relational egalitarians, too, modify their claims to equal standing because they make them conditional on satisfying obligations that are reasonable in a political sense. This is an important point to note. Both Anderson and Scheffler stress that what a person needs to function as a citizen is not just a shopping list of goods and relations that the state must provide, but also the obligations that come with being part of a polity.[29]

The point about ideals both raises a further difference and involves some overlap between the conceptions. Relational egalitarians accuse luck egalitarians of misconstruing the point of equality because they see it as a fundamentally distributive ideal. If for luck egalitarians the point of equality is to compensate for the effects of bad brute luck through a distributive arrangement, then they have misunderstood what egalitarianism should stand for. Relational egalitarians argue that equality is better understood as a moral or political ideal that aims to place people in relations of equality and is not, as such, fundamentally distributive. However, this assessment seems too swift. What relational egalitarians are concerned about is that luck egalitarian theories of distribution are not guided by the right kind of ideal, as we saw previously. This is not equivalent to saying that their view is merely distributive. As we have seen, luck egalitarians do refer to ideals, but relational egalitarians think they are the wrong ones or ideals poorly applied. In fact, it is more accurate to say that both positions have distributive implications that result from their different ideals. As Scheffler notes, the distributive implications will be very different depending on the ideal to which they refer.[30] Luck egalitarians will distribute resources based on their commitment to the chance/choice distinction, whereas relational egalitarians refer to the ideal of placing people in relations of equal standing. Both will distribute resources as a result, albeit in different ways.[31] But there is also a question of what is required by the goal of standing in relations of equality with one another. There are minimalist and maximalist versions of this goal. At times it seems as if relational egalitarianism would demand a high level of redistribution and institutional reform to guarantee that people stand in relations of equality with each other. A focus on oppression would seem to require ensuring the elimination of barriers, including discrimination in the workplace, recognition and proper wages for undervalued work such as dependent carers, and the proper recognition of marginalized groups in society. These are the traditional aims of recent social movements and an important dimension of egalitarian commitments. They are also far more strongly represented in relational egalitarian writing than luck egalitarian contributions.

Yet in other respects relational egalitarians seem to propose that only minimal standards or none at all apply to other traditionally important areas of egalitarian concern. For instance, Anderson proposes that citizens be raised to a level sufficient to function as equals in a society. One concern with her view is that she proposes only a sufficient level of resources be provided to people. She claims that the state does not owe people resources such as obtaining PhDs in literature for them to be equal, but it does owe them a decent education. This is no doubt correct. It makes it sound as though the level of sufficiency will be set quite high. But at other points it appears that the level is quite low or even nonexistent, especially when she discusses what is owed to those who do not meet the requirements of reciprocity. This is the problem for sufficiency theorists. As we saw in Chapter 1, if the threshold is set too low, we can easily meet it, but justice will not be done; if it is set too high, it will be difficult for all or many people to meet it. A further difficulty is that depending on what this sufficient level is, it may allow large inequalities. This is potentially a troubling outcome for many egalitarians. If income and wealth are very unequally distributed, then some will be able to have very good lives – go on holidays, purchase luxury items, spend extra on their families, and so on – and others will not. Where there are flow-on effects, they may include having greater access to a whole range of effects in terms of education and political power. This is precisely why egalitarians have been so concerned with metrics of equality: having the right distribution of the constituents of the metric matters a great deal. Achieving equality of status without patterns of equality with key elements of the metrics seems a difficult goal. Relational egalitarians can object that if large increases in wealth affect broader relations of equality, then they would prevent or curtail them. But if this is so, why not stipulate that these issues are prima facie subject to principles of equality in the first place? If placing people in relations of equal standing is inconsistent with large inequalities of wealth, then this outcome is unlikely to be the case – but this is not clear from the writings of relational egalitarians to date. This is not simply a case of these being details that can be worked out at the policy phase, because it is possible in principle to articulate what kinds of inequalities are permissible and desirable for egalitarians.

3.5   Conclusion: assessing the debate

Assessing what is at stake in this debate can be divided into two broad tasks: determining whether any differences are a result of confusion or disputes that are at cross-purposes and determining what differences stem from genuine disagreements over substantial matters. A great deal of the debate is a response to the issues that Anderson and others have raised about the priority of responsibility, the broader goals of egalitarianism, and the necessity of ensuring that people do not fall below a threshold. To some extent, the gulf that separates the two camps has lessened, at least on certain topics. One effect of Anderson's criticism has been to elicit from luck egalitarians an account of how they would deal with those who are destitute as a result of their own imprudence. Similarly, in response to the charge they lack a proper ideal (or any), many luck egalitarians have pointed to the strong role ideals of equality do play in their theories. Nonetheless, significant differences remain in the ideals that both positions assert as fundamental to the egalitarian project. Despite some overlap, the two positions appear to disagree substantially on the need for a role in three areas: responsibility, the function of ideals, and whether equality is relational.

On the first issue, it may seem as though relational egalitarians leave little or no room for a conception of responsibility in their accounts of justice. But this is not the case; *both* relational egalitarians and luck egalitarians give an important role to responsibility. Relational egalitarians are committed to a potentially high-impact account of responsibility because they presuppose an ideal of reciprocity.[32] Democratic egalitarians assume that only those arrangements that all can reasonably accept can be imposed on other members of a democracy. Crucially, Anderson's conception makes benefits conditional on fulfilling obligations to other citizens. Persons who fail to look for work responsibly or who do not use their talents to obtain employable skills would be denied proper access to divisible resources, with all the consequences for their access to the social conditions of freedom that this may entail. Thus, citizens do not owe other citizens "the real freedom to function as beach bums. Most able-bodied citizens, then, will get access to the divisible resources they need to function by earning a wage or some equivalent compensation due to them on account of their filling some role in the division of labor."[33] Anderson's criticism of luck egalitarianism was that it denied citizens the conditions of their freedom by making intrusive and often paternalistic judgments concerning whether or not their actions are responsible. But relational egalitarians nonetheless have grounds for limiting or restricting access to goods even if they are not paternalist. Democratic equality guarantees access to goods, but that access is conditional in some cases on the effort (for which they are responsible) of citizens. Access to jobs requires that people take them if they can. If they do not, then access to the goods provided by work is not guaranteed.[34] So access to goods is conditional, in this case, on choosing to work or not. People still have to obtain training, choose the right career path, and so on. But providing the conditions of freedom also provides the resources to exercise agency in a responsible way, further enabling people to act responsibly.[35] Now, it may be for Anderson that a minimum welfare payment may still be provided in the case of beach bums, but to decide whether someone is willing to work, we need to make precisely the kind of judgment that relational egalitarians think is intrusive. Conditionality does allow responsibility to play a role in the distribution of resources. Relational egalitarians appear to be "conditional egalitarians" as well. Anderson also argues that personal responsibility must play a role in egalitarian justice "if only to avoid bankrupting the state."

What differentiates relational accounts from luck accounts is not that one disavows responsibility but that relational egalitarians, at least to some degree, claim to disengage their interest in responsibility from talk of sanctions and punishments. They seek to provide conditions whereby agents can be responsible in an attributive sense, but they leave aside the substantive sense (in Scanlon's usage), which on the face of it is more important for luck egalitarians. If this is the view of relational egalitarians, the difference between their position and that of luck egalitarians is in the role that responsibility plays, not in its value per se. This is still a large difference but perhaps not as large as it might at first appear. Interestingly, Tan claims that luck egalitarians are more likely to be able to extend their egalitarianism to the global sphere. He notes that it is no coincidence that many democratic egalitarians are skeptical of global justice. If this is true, then for the motivations of democratic equality to apply globally, democratic egalitarians will have to demonstrate that an ideal of reciprocity applies globally, which may be hard to do.[36] Luck egalitarians, in contrast, can argue for redistributions on a simpler basis. Because they are motivated by the importance of arbitrary factors on the outcomes of people's lives – where they were born, for instance – they have a more robust basis for establishing a principle of global equality.[37]

The distance between the two camps also depends on which of the conclusions are drawn from accepting the chance/choice distinction. If as Anderson seems to suggest, it is the first and most extreme conclusion – that no assistance is owed to those who are disadvantaged because of bad option luck – then there is a large difference between the aims of the two positions. But if either of the other conclusions is in fact what luck egalitarians hold (that we should give priority to the victims of bad brute luck or that we assist them but not as a matter of justice), then in practice the positions are unlikely to be very far apart. As we noted, much depends on what kinds of claims the unequal have when their claims are not justice-based.

Despite their differences, relational egalitarians and luck egalitarians are closer than they think on the issue of responsibility. Each camp has been able to modify its claim to address some of the more pressing objections raised by the other camp. Yet regardless of whether one side of the debate has accurately represented the other, the overall significance of the debate lies in its being an important correction to the overemphasis on responsibility by egalitarians. Egalitarians have devoted too much time and space to the issue of when disadvantage is a matter of choice and when a matter of chance. One of the reasons it has been an overemphasis is that the most important causes of inequality are likely to lie elsewhere. If we had to identify the major causes of inequality, they would more likely be drawn from causes such as unfair trade and labor practices, inadequate access to education and health, and discrimination between groups and genders. These are causes that have led to great inequalities both nationally and locally. In such a case, it does not seem appropriate for egalitarians to give so central a place to considerations of responsibility when there are so many other more important factors to take into account. Placing responsibility at the center of egalitarian theories of justice is mistaken in this context, and on that issue the relational egalitarians have come closer to the truth. Again, it is reasonable to suppose that part of the rationale for this reluctance is a defensiveness in relation to arguments that might promote outcomes. As with the metric debate, it is also legitimate to ask whether enough attention has been paid to the most important causes of inequality. As a consequence, future egalitarian debate in this area should be directed not to the challenges of irresponsible hikers or welfare cheats but to the kinds of problems that are posed by achieving better outcomes and the challenges this raises in respect of perfectionism and paternalism. This direction for the debate will also run up against explicitly right-wing objections. But egalitarians should be undeterred by these objections.

The most important part of the concern raised by other egalitarians was that luck egalitarian theory left potentially large numbers of people to their fate, whether that was destitution or lack of assistance, not being able to overcome oppression, or being stuck in a range of disrespectful social practices. Even allowing for the kind of mitigation to the harshness objection that luck egalitarians might provide, the extent to which a revised position would allow large inequalities for crucial indicators is still not clear. Allowing people "just enough" to ensure their survival, whether for incentive reasons or otherwise, will leave society a very unequal place. This criticism applies particularly to relational egalitarians. Those whose benefits are conditional may be entitled to sufficient means to sustain themselves, but that may be very far from equality. Not having a job and living on (presumably low) benefits might be far removed from examples of the kind that started the debate, but it is also a long way from an egalitarian society, certainly in a distributive sense. What we need is a clearer understanding of the appropriate kinds of mitigation (in the case of luck egalitarians) and a better understanding of the impact of conditionality on eligibility for benefits.

So if what we are left with is a set of positions – which may differ in important respects – that still allow a range of very bad outcomes, then more needs to be said about reframing egalitarian theories so as to diminish the likelihood of such outcomes. In terms of future directions for the debate, one thing that appears desirable is not to renew hostilities over the place of responsibility but to focus instead on the need for ensuring equal outcomes across a range of key indicators. We need not suppose that this will be the result for most or even many goods or relations. But for some fundamental types – adequate material means, education, self-respect, bodily integrity – achieving outcomes that entail substantial equality will be where we should direct our attention. More attention should be given to whether achieving such outcomes trumps the instantiation of a principle of responsibility within egalitarian justice.[38]

4
Global Egalitarianism

4.1 Introduction

Extending egalitarian justice from a domestic to a global setting poses special challenges for egalitarians. This chapter looks at several interrelated problems that arise from the attempt to make egalitarianism global. The first problem concerns the kind of justifications that can be made for this extension. Understanding how to justify global egalitarianism is necessary before we can see what kind of distributive principle might apply globally. This is a natural extension of egalitarianism for several reasons. Egalitarians are committed to the political goal of there being substantial equality between people as a matter of justice. Egalitarians, together with many nonegalitarians, are also commonly committed to claims about the equal moral status of individuals. The central idea of cosmopolitanism is that it is individuals who are the ultimate units of moral concern and that this status extends to everyone equally, not just one's compatriots.[1] The combination of these two sets of ideas poses a challenge for egalitarians to determine whether and for what reason principles of egalitarian justice should apply to all people, not just fellow nationals. If we are committed to egalitarianism in a substantive sense and to cosmopolitan claims about equal individual moral worth, we need to ask why egalitarian justice is not global.

The other motivation for global egalitarianism is the sheer scale and severity of the inequalities that exist globally. The reasons for why we should be interested in global egalitarianism is perhaps even more compelling than those for domestic egalitarianism. The inequalities that exist between people globally are more alarming than many intrastate inequalities. According to a recent UNICEF report the top 20 percent of the global population enjoys more than 70 percent of total income and 30 percent of total wealth.[2] More is spent on European cows than on many children, with each European cow attracting a subsidy of over US$2 a day, greater than the daily income of half the world's population. These subsidies cost the European Union (EU) taxpayer about $2.5 billion a year. Half of this money is spent on export subsidies, which damage local markets in low-income countries.[3] According to Milanovic "The richest people earn in about 48 hours as much as the poorest people earn in a year."[4]

In what follows we explore the arguments for principles of *justice* of the kind that we have examined to this point, not the kind of commitments that arise from humanitarianism, assistance, aid, or charity. Many who are egalitarians at a domestic level support global duties only on these other kinds of grounds. There are a great many interpretations of what the difference is between justice and humanitarianism (for present purposes I consider duties of charity, assistance, and so forth to mean the same thing). I do not attempt to repeat them all here but make some brief points to outline a basic contrast. To begin with the concept of justice, we need to distinguish definitional issues from substantive ones. We will see that for many, global justice must focus on institutions, not on interactions in the form of individual actions. Kok-Chor Tan claims, for instance, that "a theory of global *ethics* has an interactional focus while a theory of global *justice* has an institutional focus."[5] It is also said that justice is to apply only to those who are in the right kind of association or should entail only negative duties.[6] These issues in particular are best seen not as part of the definition of justice but as substantive interpretations of what the site of justice entails. A further thing to note about justice is how it differs from humanism. Again, there are many versions of this distinction. A useful one is provided by David Miller, who identifies three differences. Humanitarian duties are "less weighty" than duties of justice; while we can have reason to perform them, we are not required to do so. Duties of justice are enforceable by third parties. Finally, duties of justice arise only when someone is not responsible for his or her own disadvantage. Humanitarian duties, not duties of justice, may still arise where a person has squandered his or her resources.[7] But the first two capture something important about the contrast between humanism and justice, which is that justice invokes an urgency that ethics does not. Claims of justice are plausibly seen as picking out a domain of claims we can make on other people and enforcing those claims when they are not met. Whether the precise basis of these demands is associational or a function of moral personality is a further question.[8]

The types of justifications for egalitarian global justice divide broadly into two.[9] On the one hand, there are relational justifications. Relational egalitarians hold that the justification for the principles of distributive justice is determined by the types of practices they regulate. So, for instance, some relationalists hold that there must be the right kind of shared social and political institutions that involve cooperation or reciprocity in order for distributive justice to apply. Others claim that duties of global justice are triggered when institutions have a "pervasive impact" on the higher-order interests of others. Different again is the claim that the legitimate exercise of coercion is required to trigger duties of global justice. As we will see, much depends on what is meant by the "right type" of shared institutions. Relational views also hold that the kinds of practices that exist between people might also determine the value and type of certain sorts of goods that form part of the distributed outcome. Goods such as working conditions or relations with family might gain part of their value from the importance and meaning a culture places on them. I examine three types of arguments that seek to limit global egalitarianism (GE) and consider the objection that each of them contains internal reasons to support GE.

Nonrelationalists, on the other hand, argue that it is not the relations people find themselves in that matter but that there are basic features of moral personhood that ground global distributive principles of equality. So if everyone in the world shares morally relevant properties and we ought to treat everyone as mattering to the same degree, we ought also to extend our distributive concerns globally.[10] Nonrelationalists also sometimes appeal to the idea of the moral arbitrariness of being born in one country rather than another to ground claims of global distributive justice. In the same way that egalitarians in wealthy countries should not be denied equal access to goods because of their skin color or location, the fact that one person was so unlucky as to be born into a desperately poor country with no resources and high mortality is simply morally arbitrary and should not determine the kind of life he or she has.

The second important question concerns the type of equality that egalitarians should adopt if they think that global egalitarianism is justified. Here we discuss several issues. First, we consider the claim that a specific type of good ought to be equalized – namely, natural resources. Resources are neither a product of cultures nor created by anyone's labor and were arbitrarily distributed. One particular set of resources that nicely illustrates the egalitarian distributional challenge is the resource associated with the climate, which we consider in the last section of this chapter.

4.2   Justice as association: the basic structure

Relational egalitarians claim that for duties of justice to arise, there must be the right kinds of relations between individuals. I look at a version of this argument that claims that the relation in question is the basic structure, which I call the *global basic structure argument*. According to Rawls, the primary subject of justice is the basic structure of society. In a well-known passage he writes, "The basic structure of society is the way in which the main political and social institutions of society fit together into one system of social cooperation, and the way they assign basic rights and duties and regulate the division of advantages that arises from social cooperation over time."[11] The kinds of activities and institutions that characterize cooperation are familiar ones consisting of the political constitution that assigns rights to persons, the structure of government, and economic rights, the division of goods, and the structure of the economy itself, as well as various social arrangements, including the role of the family.[12] The significance of this type of argument for GE revolves around whether the *site* of justice is coextensive with the *scope* of justice. For Rawls, identifying the basic structure as the subject of justice tells us what the site of justice is (what kind of things justice is about). The scope of justice, in comparison, is concerned with those to whom these principles of justice apply. Thus, in the Rawlsian framework, if the basic structure is global, justice will also be global.

Importantly for Rawls, the basic structure is conceived of as a cooperative arrangement where society is organized for the purpose of cooperating for mutual benefit. The idea of cooperation also includes the fair terms of cooperation, which in turn implies a notion of reciprocity, wherein all those who do their part can expect to benefit from what is produced by society. Reciprocity – or mutuality, as it is also called – is important because it gives us a special reason why obligations are directed toward compatriots and not noncompatriots. It is also crucially one of the things that sets cooperation apart from mere interaction. As Rawls puts it, "Social cooperation is guided by publicly recognized rules and procedures which those cooperating accept as appropriate to regulate their conduct."[13] This kind of ongoing scheme of cooperation exists as a closed system; as a "self-contained national community," it applies to domestic societies only and does not exist on a global scale.[14] Understanding the basic structure in this way has predictable appeal. Requiring that justice apply to fairly distributing the benefits of social cooperation distinguishes justice from mere interaction. This is important to the associational argument for global egalitarianism because reciprocity is what generates the claims on others and justifies the imposition of authority. The thought is that we owe special duties to those who, as part of a cooperative scheme, provide us with the kind of extensive goods that are necessary to allow a good life. The provision of security, stable legal institutions, markets, and the other elements of the basic structure gives a special weight to the duties we owe to those who provide them and is fundamentally different from the relationship that we have to outsiders, to whom we do not owe these special duties. This is not to say that we have no duties to outsiders or that such duties cannot emerge, but they will be different in kind if there is no basic structure. According to the basic structure argument, it is only with the kinds of functions that the basic structure provides that justice claims can emerge. Notwithstanding the obvious global interdependence that currently exists, we might still be concerned that this kind of interdependence is not cooperation of the right kind to generate duties of justice. In a similar vein, Brian Barry argues that trade between countries, in particular, is merely what he calls justice as requital and not justice as fair play. Justice as requital is concerned with getting the right value for whatever is traded – a fair return – but it does not generate the kinds of duties that fair play does.[15] Justice as fair play arises from the provision of public goods that are collectively enjoyed or from insurance schemes.

While Rawls is not the only one to argue for the importance of cooperation in generating claims of justice, his argument usefully illustrates the kinds of assumptions such arguments make: to wit, the importance of cooperation and its implications for when principles of justice can be generated.[16] This position has obvious affinity with the kind of constitutive egalitarianism encountered in the previous chapter. Democratic egalitarians argued that equality was part of an account of justice that saw access to goods as being tempered by a claim about reciprocity. Citizens need to be able to put forward principles of justice other citizens can accept so that when they engage in activities for mutual benefit, they can claim access to the goods flowing from such activities. Anderson makes clear that egalitarians do not just advocate a system whereby everyone has a right to receive goods without anyone having an obligation to produce them. Participating in a system of cooperative production involves reciprocity and accepting a principle of interpersonal justification.[17] A further reason for interest in this type of argument is that an influential first wave of theorists of global justice argued that Rawls's theory of justice ought to have a global scope. Globalizing Rawlsians such as Beitz and Pogge were instrumental in setting the terms of the debate. Basic structure arguments continue to be influential. Here I address three different understandings of why the basic structure is important: because it involves cooperation and reciprocity between members, because it has a profound impact on people's lives, and because it involves coercion.

Arguments about the necessity of the basic structure for principles of global justice to apply have both a normative and an empirical premise. The normative premise says that some kind of basic structure needs to exist for duties of global justice to exist; the empirical premise concerns whether the requisite type of basic structure actually does exist globally. As we will see, those who support global egalitarianism attack one premise or both. If the normative premise concerning reciprocity holds but there is simply not a sense in which cooperation extends beyond society's borders, then they will be, at best, domestic egalitarians.[18] If, in contrast, there is a plausible case for arguing that there is some kind of basic structure, then duties of egalitarian justice may be global.[19] This is not to say such duties cannot be limited by other domestic associational duties, such as the ones we might have to states or families. But note that this is a separate question from the earlier one. What interests us here are the arguments for GE that establish prima facie duties of justice. These duties could be modified by other duties or by feasibility constraints, but those issues are not discussed here.

4.3   Assessing the cooperation/reciprocity argument

Reciprocity

There is obviously no direct global equivalent of the domestic basic structure in Rawls's sense. Despite increasing interaction between states, there are no overarching political structures that resemble the institutions of government and the courts present within states. In this sense, a global scheme of cooperation does not exist. One response to this issue is to affirm the importance of associations but deny that great weight should be put on the kind of cooperation that Rawls and others have in mind. As Beitz notes, a slave-owning society might be cooperative even though the slaves do not cooperate willingly or benefit. An alternate way of understanding cooperation is by thinking of justice as applying to institutions and practices where benefits and burdens are produced that would not have existed without such practices.[20] Beitz argues that international interdependence involves "a complex and substantial pattern of social interaction, which produces benefits and burdens that would not exist if national economies were autarkic."[21] The account is still focused on institutions but does not require the presence of the same degree of cooperation to generate duties of justice. What we might call the "global interdependence thesis" asserts that a significant degree of economic production is, in fact, global and could not take place without global interaction. This kind of production certainly produces benefits and burdens, is interactive, has an enormous impact on our significant interests, and could be subject to rules. According to Beitz, these points underscore that cooperation need not include a voluntariness condition that underpins the importance of reciprocity and the significance of social interaction. Moellendorf makes a similar point when he claims that duties of justice are generated by associations but associations do not have to be voluntary to generate duties of justice. Moellendorf writes that "the existence of duties of justice is a function of the justificatory demands of equal respect in an association of the requisite kind."[22] By "requisite" he means an association that is strong, enduring, and governed by institutional norms and that affects the higher-order interests of others. So understood, the basic structure need not involve cooperation and thus need not be organized for reciprocity in order for justice to apply.

These kinds of claims affirm the importance of association – but not association understood as the kind of cooperative arrangement Rawls originally had in mind when he described the basic structure. It is an association that is in part nonvoluntary and is produced not just by the coordinated actions of governments but by economic activity and inter-dependence. Yet it satisfies at least some of the kinds of things Rawls had in mind. For instance, global economic arrangements have legally recognized rules and ownership rights that attach to transactions and property. This is not the same as within-state rules and rights, but it is enough, according to relational egalitarians, to assert that where such relations exist, they generate duties of justice – with all that implies for their future regulation by principles of justice where possible. We need to be clear that claiming that there is a global basic structure is a more limited claim than that there is a global society. As Tan notes, defenders of the former claim do not say that there is a global political culture with a shared set of norms or practices. While that would be a sufficient condition to generate justice claims, it is not a necessary one.[23]

A further concern for this limiting of egalitarianism to domestic associations is that it runs the risk of privileging the status quo. Several authors have made the point that simply because a desirable feature of social interaction *does* not exist does not imply that it *should* not exist.[24]

Claiming, for instance, that duties of justice can exist only if there is *already* a basic structure that regulates the terms of cooperation in a fair way is unfairly biased toward the status quo. Returning to Rawls's conception of the importance of the basic structure, he makes clear that the basic structure is the best way of realizing the ideal of the fair terms of social cooperation. But as Abizadeh puts it, it is an instrumental condition for realizing justice.[25] This is a claim not so much about what features of the world must exist for there to be demands of justice as about specifying what features of social interaction must be realized for justice to occur. If this is correct, justice need not rely on cooperation or even reciprocity for claims to arise, merely on certain types of interaction that require the right kind of regulation to make them fair. In other words, for interactions to be just, there needs to be a basic structure, not that there is only justice once a basic structure exists. Even so, such an argument might still be vulnerable to a constraint about feasibility. If no kind of institution could exist such that it would make the right kind of cooperation possible, then the argument will be limited in an important sense. But observing that we might have feasibility constraints is nonetheless very different from stating that cooperation must already exist.[26]

Pervasive impact

Another way of understanding the basic structure's importance is as having a profound and pervasive impact on important human interests.[27] This is part of what Rawls refers to when he describes the basic structure, and it is a plausible way of interpreting why the basic structure is the site of justice. Yet a focus on this way of understanding the basic structure makes global egalitarianism arguably more plausible. Whereas we might debate what kind of cooperation is necessary for some set of practices to constitute a basic structure, there can be no such debate about the pervasive impact of political and economic institutions in some countries on the lives of those beyond national borders. Indeed, it is arguable that features of globalization have a more profound impact on the lives of the poor than do many of the decisions and institutions of their own countries. Of all versions of the basic structure argument, this one seems the least defensible against the claims of global egalitarianism.

Coercion

A final approach to understanding the basic structure is to claim that what triggers duties of egalitarian justice is the presence of coercion and its effects on autonomy. Blake argues that all individuals, no matter what institution they are associated with, ought to have the conditions of autonomy.[28] Yet what those without autonomy ought to be provided with according to Blake is not an egalitarian distribution but a sufficient level of resources. An egalitarian distribution only applies within states. Where they redistribute wealth, states coerce citizens through either the criminal law or taxation, and owe a special kind of justification to those subject to such coercion, even where it is beneficial. Blake claims that even though coercion by the state might be necessary to guarantee the conditions of citizens' lives and the ability to lead them autonomously, coercion is an imposition on autonomy and thus in need of justification. Blake claims that we need a form of hypothetical consent where citizens could not reasonably reject being subject to the coercion of the state. This justification comes in the form of whether or not resources are distributed; how this is done provides a reason to accept or reject the coercion used to achieve it. Crucially, this criterion must come with an egalitarian regard for relative deprivation between citizens because the liberal state, deeming that the autonomy of all its citizens matters, must justify any coercive redistribution to everyone equally. On this account, what generates a concern for material equality is the need to justify coercion. If the kind of coercion associated with the laws of the state did not exist, there would be no reason to be concerned with material equality.

Thomas Nagel also emphasizes that coercion is a necessary condition for claims of egalitarian justice to arise. Mere cooperation is not, by itself, enough to generate duties. So while there is obviously much international cooperation and economic interaction, justice requires the right to impose collective decisions by force.[29] There are, of course, laws produced in one country that have a profound impact on those outside its borders. Crucially for Nagel, what differentiates such laws is that they are not made in the name of those affected. Nagel writes, "The laws are not imposed in their name, nor are they asked to accept and uphold those laws. Since no acceptance is demanded of them, no justification is required ... "[30] It is this feature of making laws in someone's name, not the fact that there might be externalities for noncompatriots, that marks a crucial difference for Nagel between domestic coercion and global coercion.

If the coercion account of the reasons to be concerned with material equality is correct, then the concern will not exist in the global sphere. Blake acknowledges that while kinds of coercion do exist globally, they are not equivalent to the within-state kind that generates a concern for material equality. To be clear, these accounts are not claiming that just because there are few ways of enforcing justice globally (perhaps because there is no world government), justice therefore does not exist. It is not simply a point about feasibility. Rather, the coercion argument contends that there is no global egalitarian justice because without the context of a cooperative order that can coercively impose itself on people, duties of justice do not even occur.

How does this argument hold up against the other basic structure accounts? Despite the insistence on the presence of coercion to justify our concern with material equality, the account is a mixed one that needs a combination of coercion's presence, reciprocity, and impact. This can be seen when we look at why domestic coercion is supposedly different from global or international coercion. For Blake, coercion is important because it is such a profound threat to autonomy. Coercing someone into unfair taxation arrangements or ordering that he or she be incarcerated, restrained, or deprived of some liberty is clearly, in turn, a significant impact on an individual; hence the need for justification, which generates the need for the kinds of material equality we saw earlier. States do this through a system of laws that apply sanctions to such activities. On the whole, there does not exist anything nearly so complicated as a global equivalent of a domestic legal system. Yet as we have seen, the mere absence of an elaborate legal system does not mean that the kind of coercion occurring in the global arena does not have enormous and often deadly effects on noncompatriots. There is a clear threat to people's autonomy and their general well-being as a direct result of law-governed coercion. Moreover, these kinds of laws and their effects are not one-offs; they are part of well-established and ongoing legal arrangements that have a profound effect on people's lives. If this is so and if coercion arrangements are in need of justification because of their effects on autonomy and other important values, then the legal coercion that exists globally also needs justification in the way it invokes material equality. Nor does this argument from coercion tell why no duties of justice are not associational.[31] Thus, Nagel's point about coercive laws needing to be made in one's name so that someone can demand a justification seems to ignore an obvious point: those disadvantaged by laws that they did not devise but to which they are subject are entitled to at least some justification. This seems especially true given the kind of disadvantage being suffered here.[32] If coercion implemented in someone's name is not necessary for claims of justice to arise, it becomes harder for coercion theorists to maintain that the only proper form of distribution is sufficientarian.

Each of the three arguments against global egalitarianism has difficulty confining duties of justice to the domestic realm. According to the objections considered here, reasons internal to the basic structure argument give us grounds to extend egalitarianism globally. The reciprocity argument seems to focus on a feature sufficient but not necessary for claims of justice to arise. In terms of the normative premise of this type of argument, requiring that there be cooperation and reciprocity in the same way as for a state seems unnecessary for claims of justice to occur. Once the normative premise is relaxed, the empirical premise is satisfied given the high degree of activity and cooperation that currently exists. The pervasive impact account of association seems even weaker given how significant the impact of the actions of institutions of wealthy countries on the lives of those in poor countries is. Finally, the coercion argument relies on an overly voluntary account of the generation of coercive laws. Common to the counterarguments to the three kinds of anti–global egalitarian arguments are strong emphases on the empirical details of global association and the generation of duties that derive from nonvoluntary dimensions of associations. The first point is surely well made given the now pervasive interdependence of much of the world's economy and culture. Moreover, as we will see, very strong arguments can be derived from our interdependence on the climate and other key resources. A point made by all responses to the three interpretations of the basic structure argument is that the existence of something like a global state is not necessary for duties of justice to arise. The normative conditions required by plausible versions of each of the three interpretations are satisfied.

4.4 Moral personality

Given the extent of globalization and of the pervasive institutions that support it, relationalists have strong grounds for extending egalitarianism from the domestic to the global sphere. But focusing on any kind of relation to establish duties of justice encounters a problem. Those who live in very remote places, who have little contact of the requisite type with the rest of the world, or who are not significantly impacted do not fall under the scope of relational justice. If such people are desperately poor and outsiders could easily do something to help, on the relationalist account there is no justice-based duty to assist. Other duties might exist, but they are not justice-based. This problem may not actually seem especially severe. After all, if globalization is as extensive as has been claimed, cases of those who are not affected will be relatively rare. Yet even were only some were affected by associations, this is not really the point. What is at issue is the basis of duties of justice. However, it does highlight the potential harshness of the relational view. A more pressing problem concerns how the associational account may not properly identify the most plausible basis of GE.

Moral persons

Nonrelational accounts of GE proceed differently. They claim that the justification for global justice is based on features of our moral personality. Arguments from moral personality typically proceed in two stages. First, they identify relevant features of our moral personality – interests, autonomy, sense of justice – that everyone has reason to value and that are the basis of entitlement to considerations of justice. Second, they invoke the principle of moral cosmopolitanism, which claims that people are the ultimate units of moral concern and that there is a prima facie reason to treat everyone equally. So whereas relationalists would not have duties of justice to those they do not interact with, have no impact upon, or cooperate with, nonrelationalists would accept that as other people have moral properties of the requisite kind, they too are entitled to considerations of justice. On this account, to base entitlements on where a person is born is to introduce morally arbitrary or discriminatory reasons. While the cosmopolitan principle does not generate a distributive principle by itself, when combined with the claims of the first type it provides the basis of a prima facie reason in favor of such a principle.

Several authors have sought to extend Rawls's work in this way. In a change from his earlier views, Beitz argues that a contract approach to justice should not assume that what matters is membership in an actually existing cooperative scheme but whether people have the two moral powers.[33] He claims that having a capacity for a sense of justice and the ability to form and revise a conception of the good should be the criteria of membership in a global original position. Because people have these powers irrespective of what country they are born into, national borders should not confine the scope of justice. Just as much of what makes life go well is arbitrary to some degree – for instance, our talents or the race or class we happen to be born into – the arbitrariness of our country of birth should also not be decisive for determining our entitlements.[34] As we saw previously, for Beitz this view is still subject to a feasibility constraint, but it bases global egalitarianism on features of individual moral personality. (Later we address the criticism that the valuation of the two moral powers might be culturally specific, but for now it is important to note that the defense of global egalitarianism proceeds in a nonrelational way.)[35] Similarly, Nussbaum maintains that personality features can generate global principles of justice. As we saw in Chapter 2, she thinks that while her list of capabilities can be the focus of an over-lapping consensus, it is not a product of one. She advocates a "thick and broad" list of human personality features that she thinks can form the basis of constitutional claims concerning global human goods. In turn, Hillel Steiner claims that because people can be said to be self-owner of their own body, justice vests them with the ownership of their labor where they have not otherwise contracted it away, providing a basis for claims of justice.[36]

Beitz's argument is one of several that attempts to globalize the basic Rawlsian framework. Simon Caney argues that not only contractarian but also several other justifications for domestic theories of justice should be seen as providing the basis for justifying global justice in a nonrelational way if we look closely at the assumptions internal to a domestic theory of justice. He claims that justifications of domestic justice "entail that there are cosmopolitan principles of distributive justice."[37] He argues that contractualist positions such as Beitz's are not the only ones leading to a cosmopolitan conception of justice; common consequentialist positions do so as well. A consequentialist such as Singer argues that we have a duty to aid those in dire need where we can and where doing so does not involve undue sacrifice. For Singer, duties are generated by an appeal to features of moral personality we hold in common, not the fact of association or lack of it.[38]

One problem for these accounts concerns what we might call perverse implications. It has been said of the moral personality account of global justice that it extends our moral concern too far and in ways that are wildly implausible. So, for instance, Moellendorf worries that unless we endorse the associational account, we will in principle be committed to duties of justice to intelligent beings on other planets with whom we have no contact. While we may have broader moral duties not to harm such beings, we do not have duties of justice.[39] His interplanetary example is far-fetched, but it draws attention to a realistic situation we are more likely to confront: duties to the many others in the world with whom we do not interact. If associations of the right kind do not exist, duties of justice are confined to those with whom we have associations. How might someone committed to the moral personality account respond to this objection? One interesting response has been to disentangle the objection's different elements. For a start, the issue of whether we have duties to intelligent nonhuman beings is separate from whether we have duties to those outside an association. One possible source of the implausibility is that it might simply not be feasible to aid such beings at a reasonable cost. While important, this issue is a separate consideration. To eliminate such issues, Caney proposes, instead of the dual planet example, that we consider a case where a sea channel separates two peoples. There exists no association, nor do we harm the other people, but they are badly off. In contrast, being very well off, we could help them at a reasonable cost.[40] What the modified example in fact draws attention to is the moral arbitrariness of being born on the poor side of the channel. A situation caused by morally arbitrary circumstances, then, does not exclude us from our duties of justice to assist the disadvantaged.

Several points should be noted about this response. For a start, arguments from moral personality typically establish a prima facie claim about global egalitarianism. They do not imply that this claim cannot be limited in various ways by special ties or feasibility constraints. Nonrelational principles might be limited in specific applications, such as where fulfilling a duty is unreasonably costly. It is also not the case that the argument from moral personality is incompatible with all relational accounts. One could argue that the primary justification for global egalitarianism is our moral personality but also claim that some egalitarian duties are generated by global associations as well. More generally, some kinds of duties of justice might arise only in associational contexts. Some of the reasons we have for being concerned about inequality are indeed generated in specific associational contexts. In Chapter 1 we listed several classes of inequalities, such as disrespectful treatment and discrimination in the workplace, as typical examples of important inequalities. These, having an associational origin, are different from the bad brute luck that afflicts the disadvantaged islanders across the channel.

A relational opponent of the idea that there are duties of justice based on nonrelational criteria could agree on the strong moral force of these duties but simply deny that they are duties of justice. Several authors argue that we have moral duties distinct from justice to help the global poor, but they are humanitarian duties.[41] The distinction between duties of humanity and duties of justice is often invoked in these contexts, yet very different things can be meant by it. Tan uses it to refer to the difference between institutional and interactional contexts.[42] Others, such as David Miller, think duties of justice are enforceable, are weightier, and apply only where someone is not responsible for the disadvantage. As we saw with the associational accounts of global justice, duties of justice are also thought to track cooperation, coercion, and impact. Whatever the precise nature of the distinction, it cannot be correct to define justice simply by reference to one's preferred substantive conception of what justice entails. For instance, claiming that justice pertains only to institutional situations seems too narrow for a *definition*. True, there might be good reasons to support this particular interpretation of justice as giving people their due, but it is not the same as a definition because it admits of interpretations both interactional and institutional. What is at stake in this debate is the basis of our duties of justice to others – whether relational or nonrelational – and we should avoid ruling out some accounts of either type simply by definition.

Both the relational and nonrelational accounts of GE offer powerful reasons to extend egalitarianism from the domestic to the global sphere. They each claim to take ideas central to egalitarian justice and demonstrate that there are good reasons to extend them globally. Each account of why egalitarianism should be extended yields a strong reason in favor of GE, but the accounts do not converge even though they may have similar conclusions. Each account of the motivations of GE draws on important but different intuitions about distributive justice. Relationalists variously draw on the idea that relations of a specific type, such as cooperation, coercion, or impact, generate justice. In terms of the primary reason for extending egalitarianism globally, this kind of motivation seems close to traditional egalitarian commitments to ending oppression and domination that claim that these ideas are the most fundamental in generating duties of justice. Nonrelationalists, in contrast, place greater emphasis on the fact that justice should not disadvantage people because of reasons, such as nationality, that are arbitrary from a moral point of view and on a claim about important features of moral personality being justice-generating. This account of the reason to extend egalitarianism also draws on something fundamental to the egalitarian tradition. So even though both types of justification agree with the cosmopolitan moral claim, they combine this claim with different assumptions about what is important about generating duties of global egalitarian justice. This does not mean that there is no overlap between the two positions. There is no conceptual barrier to having an account of justice that assumes nonrelational motivations and also emphasizes how important certain types of interaction are for claims of justice. Nonrelationalists can also be motivated by claims of injustice from traditional egalitarian origins, such as oppression; nonetheless, it is important to note the different parts of justice on which they draw for extending egalitarian justice globally. Another point worth noting is that plausible versions of both accounts seem to downplay the necessity of voluntariness for duties of justice to arise. Nonrelationalists do this most clearly: they assume we can owe one another duties even if we have not consented to be part of a state or distributive scheme. Relationalists might seem to rely on some degree of voluntariness that depends on the type of cooperation deemed important. Cooperation understood as interdependence does not require consent to generate duties of justice, whereas cooperation as fair reciprocity is more likely to.

The versions of the basic structure argument we have considered might seem to offer a very strong case for extending egalitarianism globally – and indeed they do. But it is important to be clear on what this depends. If interdependence between people or its impact on them is not extensive or pervasive, the case for extending equality becomes weaker, too. This is important because it tells us something about whether the accounts converge. In a sense they do converge if globalization is as extensive as it seems. Both relationalists and nonrelationalists will claim there is a case for GE. Yet given the dependence of relational GE on the facts of globalization, it is easy to see that the bases of the two accounts remain importantly different.

4.5 Equality of natural resources

If it is important to achieve equality globally as well as domestically, we should also consider what form equality will take. Which of the metrics we considered in Chapter 2 is best suited to this task? An equally interesting exercise is to consider some more concrete applications of a principle of equality, those that themselves employ certain of the metrics. The two separate but related discussions of a principle of equality to be considered here are the claims made in support of global equality of resources (GER) and how equality relates to the global emissions budget.

A very specific and important application of the principle of global equality is in its relation to natural resources. In many ways, resources seem ideal candidates for the application of a principle of equality. In tending to be arbitrarily allocated and contested, resources are the product of luck. Consider a comparison between resources and natural talents. Rawls and others have argued that the distribution of talents among people is arbitrary from a moral point of view. Whether or not someone has a particular sporting or musical ability is a matter of good luck. Of course, a talent can be developed through hard work, but the fact of someone's being born with it is not a matter of effort. Nor is the fact that some talents might be extremely valuable to other people at certain times whereas others are not. The distribution is thus arbitrary from a moral point of view. We might not think it unjust that people have the rewards of such talents. As we saw in Chapter 3, it can be hard to estimate what part of a talent is down to hard work and what to brute luck – or are talents perhaps just part of who we are and thus not in need of the kind of justification that other windfalls require?

Natural resources are importantly different from personal talents in a way that makes them morally more arbitrary. For a start, resources are not part of a person's character as the ability to sing is part of a singer's personality. The distribution across the earth of an important resource such as iron ore cannot be said to have been caused by any particular individuals or nations. Similarly, any claims we have on a resource such as the atmosphere are not based on the input of our labor in the way that claims about owning the outputs of manufacturing or farming are. Our labor did not create the atmosphere, and so the justification for its use cannot be claimed on such a basis, which might warrant unequal distribution.[43] If these points are correct, then there is a plausible case that the distribution of resources should also be viewed as morally arbitrary and a plausible candidate for a principle of GER.[44]

Another reason why there might be equal claims on resources stems from their crucial role in determining how societies develop and maintain high standards of well-being. On an individual level, people need access to the benefits that resources bring. Even a minimally good life requires that we consume and use basic resources. Any modern country's economy will use significant amounts of resources to maintain its standard of living, establish trade, build infrastructure, and generate energy. The need for resources is most obvious where countries are so poor they lack even basic necessities. But the need for equitable division of resources will be even greater if we adopt broader egalitarian goals. Take the example of equal opportunity. The shift of resources required to achieve equal opportunities for people in poor countries will presumably be far greater than that needed just to achieve subsistence. In the case of climate change, countries that need to develop will require a greater share of the emissions budget than developed countries and possibly other assistance, such as clean development technologies, to assist in the transition to a low-carbon future. Countries that have an abundance of natural resources often have a tremendous advantage over those that do not. This is not to say that countries with resources will necessarily be prosperous or that those without abundant resources cannot maintain a high standard of living. Nigeria and its oil wealth is an example of the former, while Japan, with few natural resources, is an example of the latter. But generally speaking, a resource-rich country will have advantages over a resource-poor country.

We need to be clear about what we mean by resources. The most obvious kinds are raw materials such as oil, gas, valuable metals, and water that we extract and use. Resources also include features of the planet that are not commodities but are nonetheless crucial – the atmosphere, sunlight, the oceans. This resource class is more like a natural system than a commodity; it includes things that are not in themselves exhaustible yet access to which is unevenly distributed. Sunlight, for instance, while nonrivalrous, is differently distributed, with consequences for how countries generate power or grow food. Finally, some authors include land itself in the list of resources that ought to be distributed. Steiner, for instance, thinks that the value of land ought to form the basis of what is divided according to a global distributive principle.[45]

Not distributing resources fairly could also exacerbate existing global inequalities. As Barry notes, the problem here is not just that we are uneasy with undeserved windfall gains.[46] Rather, the immense wealth concentrated in some resource-rich nations might lead to the kinds of increased inequalities globally or regionally with which we are familiar domestically. Countries with excessive wealth can influence trade treaties, buy influence, and threaten other countries by withholding resources or increasing their price. Those without resources may find it difficult to overcome such practices. Getting the distribution right is all the more important now as many resources collectively needed are being degraded or becoming scarce.

A global egalitarian distribution of resources (GER) would likely have a significant impact on resource-poor countries and on how resource-rich countries, as well as resource companies, use resources. In contrast to the current system of primarily state control of internal resources, a GER principle would endorse a system of distribution of the benefits of natural resources that takes into account the fact of some form of common ownership or common rights to benefit from the exploitation of resources. Different schemes have been proposed for how a distribution might work and the level of access or claim that individuals or countries might have under a principle of GER. Rather than consider all such global schemes, we focus on those that have egalitarian considerations at some level. This might entail a strong claim that all are entitled to an equal share of resources or a weaker claim that all should have an equal opportunity to use resources to satisfy basic needs.

The combination of claims about the arbitrary distribution of resources with the crucial role that resources play in the fulfillment of well-being in all societies provides several possible justifications for saying that everyone should have an equal prima facie claim to resources. Whether this results in an equal distribution of resources themselves depends on how the claim is interpreted. Several rights-based theorists argue that what is held equally is a right to something important, such as subsistence or security; this in turn generates the claim to resources. Rights such as these require that we have enough of an important resource to allow us to exercise a right. For instance, in the case of climate, what could be required is enough access to a safe climate to allow everyone a decent standard of living. This does not require that everyone have equal access to the climate per se.[47] Henry Shue makes the point that people have rights to subsistence and so each national community should be able to obtain the natural resources it needs for it to be self-determining.[48] Similarly, Beitz argues that we can entertain departures from this fundamental entitlement to equality of resources because we can apply a global difference principle.[49]

Some rights theorists, however, argue for an equal claim to resources. As part of a more elaborate conception of rights, Hillel Steiner proposes that everyone is entitled to an equal share of the earth's resources. He claims that equality is a default norm at a fundamental level. Where it applies is in the initial equalization of the rights we have over our bodies and its extension to natural resources. Rights over our bodies require access to things external to our bodies because such things – resources in this case – are necessary conditions for any activity.[50] Rights in respect of resources are to acquire an equal share in them. All have prior rights over their own body, which in turn requires that others have negative duties not to constrain this initial ownership.[51] Where some have acquired a greater than equal share of initially unowned resources, they have undertaken a redistribution. Those with less than an equal share are entitled to reclaim a fair share via some form of compensation. To distribute the entitlements to natural resources, Steiner proposes taxing the market value of the untransformed resources as a kind of pool of brute luck in resources. All the revenue accumulating from this tax is collected in a global fund. People with less than an equal share have a claim on the fund, and those with more than their share owe a debt. The details of the global fund are complex, but the central idea is that everyone is entitled to an equal share calculated on the worth of the sites.[52] He writes, "Each person's initial domain includes a right to the quotient: a right to an equal portion of the aggregate global value of territorial sites."[53] The equal share is a kind of basic income. The rights to an equal share of resources are claims of justice, not humanity.

They are not based on whether an individual has a particular need for assistance.

Leaving aside questions concerning the impact of multiple generations and the valuation of resources, Steiner's proposed global fund raises a number of interesting issues for egalitarians. A resourcist conception of equality, is based on what we are owed rather than what we need to fulfill our conceptions of the good. His proposal amounts, in effect, to a pooling of the value of the brute luck of resource distribution. That it does not take account of the different circumstances or needs of individuals might make it vulnerable to some familiar criticisms. Supporters of other metrics of equality will argue that it does not aim at the right goals because it is not connected with people's welfare (welfarist egalitarians). Others will claim that it does not fully address the difficult and different circumstances in which the poor find themselves (capability theorists) because as a libertarian proposal that tries to allocate a fair share of resources, it is not concerned directly with alleviating poverty. In contrast, giving everyone their share might be less good than creating public goods, for instance. Some critics charge that while there is scope to employ a principle of equality for establishing the justifications of claims to resources, the allocation requires a different principle. Those, such as Beitz, who attempt to extend Rawls's difference principle from a domestic to a global context will favor allocating resources according to a difference principle that would function in international society as it does in domestic society[54] (I will not repeat the arguments for sufficientarianism or prioritarianism.). Distributing resources in this way may also not promote equality of opportunity and may focus unduly on applying a principle of equality to the wrong set of things. For instance, Caney objects that applying a principle of equality to the resources themselves employs equality in the wrong way. Instead, we should apply it to equalizing appropriate opportunities and distribute resources in ways that will aid equalizing opportunities.[55] Likewise, David Miller objects to the application of a principle of equality to resources because it does not take into account the sense in which the value of sites is determined by the rules and practices of the people in the countries themselves. For a start, it will make a difference to the value of a site whether it is public or private or whether in general what makes the site productive is allowed to be fully utilized. If a country has land that is particularly well suited to growing valuable export crops but that land is slated for a nature reserve or a public park, problems for how it is to be valued will arise. To extend this example, even if the land was open to agricultural development, the people in the country would have to have the skills to farm it, improve their infrastructure enough to get the goods to ports or across the border, and so on. The country might be too poor to undertake these kind of improvements or perhaps chooses not to invest in the education of its citizens.[56] The upshot of these points is that the value of land, even unimproved land, is likely to be in large part a function of choices that people in the relevant countries make about their own development, and there is no clear way of distinguishing these kind of factors from the raw resources (This claim is familiar from Chapter 3.). How we distinguish between the effects of good brute luck and the advantages that stem from good choices and effort is thus problematic. Defenders of an ownership model might respond that many of these objections miss their mark in assuming that distributive arrangements must focus on outcomes, not on the justice of initial allocations. Moreover, critics underestimate the degree to which equalizing resources in this way really changes the lives of many, especially the poor, for the good. After unpacking historical injustices that have accrued to the wealthy and powerful, redistribution would leave countless people much better off and significantly reduce inequalities.

A more general response to GER has been to argue that resources are simply not as important for a country's flourishing as has been made out and that no special distributive principle is necessary. Rawls comments that the crucial determinant for how a country fares is its political culture, not the level of resources it enjoys.[57] If this is the case, then there is less need for a distributive principle focusing specifically on resources. Another claim that highlights the problems for countries with resources, although in a different way, is the phenomenon of the "resource curse." Leif Wenar outlines how the presence of valuable resources within a country's territories can sometimes make the situation of the poor worse. Where a country is ruled by an oppressive regime, the availability of the revenue from a resource such as oil might strengthen that regime's ability to oppress its people. Civil conflict may also result from armed competition for resources or in increased incentives for military coups. For this and other reasons a resources curse may strike because lower growth can also sometimes be linked to dependency on resources.[58] According to Wenar, these points call less for a redefinition of ownership than for a renewed commitment to the implied rules of property and international trade. He proposes a series of measures for ensuring that the sale of a country's resources occurs only with proper consent; where that does not occur, sanctions should be considered.

A response that takes into account the importance of resources but does not make egalitarian commitments is Pogge's "global resource dividend" (GRD). The GRD does not assume the kind of stringent egalitarian ownership justifications that are typical of Steiner's view. Pogge claims that states should not have full libertarian rights over the resources present in their territories. Instead, they should have to share a small part of the value of those resources they develop or sell; the proceeds could then be used to ensure that all people can "defend and realize" their basic interests.[59] The justification for the GRD is presented in terms of how citizens and governments in the developed world are imposing an unjust situation on others. This violation of a negative duty generates the urgent moral reason to impose the GRD. Injustice can be understood as stemming from any of three causes: the effects of shared social institutions such as trade practices, exclusion from the use of natural resources, or the effects of a violent common history, such as that associated with colonialism. Pogge's strategy is ecumenical: he claims that all these accounts would argue that radical inequality is unjust and all could agree that something like the GRD would be a step in the right direction. Elsewhere Pogge seems to argue that there is also a sense in which humankind has a "minority stake" in resources that entitles it to some of the benefits of the resources.[60]

4.6   Equality and the carbon budget

The case of resources offers a unique set of reasons for our having an interest in equality. One particular resource offers an even more specific context in which to consider applying a principle of equality to the global sphere. The distribution of the benefits and burdens associated with adapting and mitigating climate change has involved significant discussion of how to fairly approach this important and complex issue. Egalitarians' reasons to be interested in problems associated with climate change range from how current decisions affect future generations to whether climate solutions should refer to broader egalitarian conceptions of how society ought to be organized. The discussion that is particularly relevant here concerns what we can call the carbon budget problem. This problem concerns how we allocate emissions given that the amount of Green House Gases (GHG). we can put into the atmosphere before we trigger dangerous climate change is finite. If this is to be avoided, we need to immediately and drastically reduce worldwide total GHG emissions. We have already emitted a significant amount, and these emissions, together with what we are allowed to safely emit, make up our emissions budget. But how is this budget to be distributed among countries and people? Getting the allocation right is incredibly important because transitioning to a low-carbon future will impose significant costs. This is not to suggest that for well-off countries the task will be easy or inexpensive. Nonetheless, we need to put the cost in perspective. For instance, Nicholas Stern estimates that to achieve a reduction to 500 ppm might cost 2 percent of global GDP – around US$1 trillion per annum.[61] To take one example, it is estimated that the cost to transition Australian stationary energy generation to a zero carbon level will be around AU$300 billion over ten years.[62] While no one pretends that this is a trivial amount, it is a small percentage of GDP and will lead to significant cost savings over time because renewable energy generation typically has free or low-cost fuel sources. The claims that people have to emit GHGs constitute an important problem of global distributive justice for a now very limited and important resource.

It is useful to consider some of the figures and likely timelines associated with the problem to get a sense of how and why egalitarian considerations should apply. The consequences of the global mean temperature rising by or beyond two degrees Celsius have been extensively discussed. Our focus here is on the distributive issues associated with limiting global carbon dioxide and equivalent emissions so as to achieve a high probability of avoiding such a temperature increase. As far as the science goes, it is clear that only a limited amount of GHG can be permitted if temperature rises are to be kept to less than two degrees.[63] Determining the quantity of allowable emissions means working out, until the year 2050, a global carbon budget compatible with avoiding the two-degree rise. Following the scientific literature, we can assume that the period in which to "spend" the emissions budget is now between 2014 and 2050.[64] According to some estimates, to have a 67 percent chance of avoiding a two-degree temperature rise, global emissions cannot exceed 750 gigatons (Gt) for the period 2010–2050.[65] After 2050 only a very small amount of GHGs can be emitted. If the probability of staying within the two-degree guardrail were increased to 75 percent, the budget would reduce to 600 Gt. Moreover, to avoid having to reduce emissions at an unrealistic rate, reductions must begin immediately, with peaks in the period 2011–2020. For instance, a peak in 2011 would result in an annual reduction rate of 3.7 percent, a peak in 2015, 5.3 percent, and in 2020, 9.0 percent.[66] Raising the probability of avoiding the temperature rise would obviously increase these targets.[67]

As these figures show, the situation is bad now and getting worse with every year in which no overall agreement to reduce emissions is reached. Moreover, many countries are busy spending their carbon budgets and may well be in deficit in the near future. (Some of the ways we can divide the global carbon budget are discussed later.) For purposes of illustration, assume we allocate emissions on a per capita basis, with 2010 as the reference year for population data. On the basis of this scenario, we divide the carbon budget by the world's population, estimate an annual emissions rate, and allocate emissions rights to countries. The United States would be allocated 0.85 Gt per year (it currently emits 6.1 Gt); at present rates it would spend its budget in six years. China, on the other hand, would have twenty-four years; this is obviously better but still well above the required emission rates. Looking globally at individual emission budgets, each person would be allocated around 2.7 tons of GHGs per year for forty years.[68] This is around 25 percent of what New Zealanders spend every year (8.6 tons per year), which is better than Australians (17.3) and much better than the world's leading emitters, the Qataris (60).[69]

While there are of course many other ways to distribute emissions, this example illustrates both the magnitude of the task of reducing emissions and the importance of getting the distribution right according to a defensible criterion. This brings us back to the distributive question, which centers on how we are to allocate emission entitlements and ensure access to a safe climate in a just way. Outlining a framework involves identifying justifications for dividing emissions, understanding what kind of distributive schemes are consistent with these justifications, and, finally, determining whether the framework can provide guidance in a real-world setting. In what follows, we assume that emissions are distributed at a country level and determined by population, with a baseline year to set relevant population levels.

Equality is by no means the only value relevant here. For the purposes of this discussion, we do not consider the important role of allocating responsibility for historical emissions and their relevance for future carbon budgets. Rather, we focus on an ideal distribution as a first step in working out how to divide the carbon budget. We can allow that responsibility is relevant but not the main consideration for distributing emissions. Thus, this discussion does not preclude modifying an equal distribution because of some other value. Nonetheless, using equality as a baseline for distribution tells us something important about how we should distribute emissions.

The atmosphere and equal shares

A number of broadly cosmopolitan positions defend a prima facie claim to equal rights to use and benefit from a safe climate. One way of construing this claim is that each of us has an equal human right to emit GHGs, similar to the right to food, shelter, liberties of various kinds, and other goods. But understanding emissions rights in the same sense as other fundamental rights is problematic. Emissions rights, while significant, gain importance through their instrumental value to other goods. Having a right to emit stems from the essential role emissions play in contributing to basic well-being. Given the current dependence on fossil fuels, it might be impossible to generate any acceptable level of well-being without having access to emission rights. If this is why emissions are important, then it is better to understand the fundamental right as concerning food or shelter, for example, and emissions as simply being one of the things we need in order to fulfill such a right.

A different justification underpins the appeal to the "equal per capita" (EPC) approach. Baer argues that everyone has a prima facie claim to a share of the earth's resources because it is a kind of global commons: "The central argument for equal per capita rights is that the atmosphere is a global commons, whose use and preservation are essential to human well being. Therefore ... all people should hold both decision-making rights and use rights equally unless there is a compelling higher principle."[70]

As with the argument from fundamental rights, equality here is also a kind of default position guiding distribution. Functioning as a common good, the global commons is not or should not be anybody's to own. As we saw, Beitz argues that while departures could be justified, each person has an equal prima facie claim to available world resources.[71] In a similar vein, Singer writes, "Why should anyone have a greater claim to part of the atmospheric sink than any other?"[72] He conceives of this as a plausible starting point for discussion about dividing up rights to emit.

Given the nature of the atmosphere and emissions, it is easy to see why these types of claims are appropriate. The atmosphere, while not a finite resource in the same way as oil or coal, is nonetheless limited. It has a limited capacity to absorb what we put into it without causing widespread changes to our climate. In this case, each time one of us emits something, the possibility for others to emit is thereby reduced. Moreover, as we saw earlier, what claims we have on the atmosphere are not based on the input of our labor.[73] A healthy climate and its constituents also plays a pivotal role in guaranteeing our access to broader goods. As a functioning atmosphere is part of the background condition that enables decent lives, rapid deterioration of the atmosphere will obviously cause significant harms for large numbers of people, many of whom, in addition, will bear little or no moral responsibility.[74]

A further reason for the relevance of equality may have nothing at all to do with ownership. Justifications for equal emissions entitlements may stem simply from their usefulness in reducing emissions themselves. Giving everyone equal access might be the best way, politically and environmentally, to make emission reductions clear, effective, and fair; besides, it would have the virtue of simplicity. Advocates of the position known as "contraction and convergence" make this clear, as do advocates of the greenhouse development rights (GDR) framework. Although they say that equal emissions is a human right, they claim that the motivation is pragmatic because it is the only approach with any chance of success.[75]

The EPC approach to dividing emissions draws on several justifications, particularly rights and pragmatic justifications. This approach is worth examining in more detail because it seems to be the target of several objections to egalitarianism in the climate space generally. The EPC approach simply divides the amount of carbon dioxide we can emit by the number of people in the world (usually adjusted to reflect a population baseline year), which gives the number of tons of carbon dioxide–equivalent gases a person can emit as a baseline for allocating emissions entitlements. On this account, our GHG emissions ought to contract to a safe level over time, after which all should be able to emit an equal fraction of a safe quantity of GHGs.[76] The approach is simple – fair in an intuitive sense – and offers the prospect of evening out some of the existing inequalities between the emissions rights of the world's poor and those of the world's rich. It does not, for instance, grant industrialized countries rights to emit based on their previous appropriation of the atmosphere – "grandfathering," as it is known. As it also offers hope that emissions will be stabilized by setting a clear target and perhaps giving people a stake in meeting the target, it may have the virtue of efficiency. On some versions of the scheme, people could also trade their emissions. On the most favorable interpretation, this might allow people in poorer countries to earn income by trading their surplus emissions, which richer countries could then use to ease their transition to a low-carbon economy.

It should be noted that arriving at a baseline figure is no barrier to adjusting the per capita figure in various ways to take account of historical emissions, changing populations, or compensation for past wrongs. For instance, several authors have proposed an EPC account that is then adjusted to reflect the previous emissions of high-emitting countries.[77] To meet the objection that allocating per capita emissions would give countries an incentive to increase population and thereby increase their emission allowance, it has been proposed to measure a country's population from a certain past year (say, 1990).[78] We could also, as Vanderheiden and Shue suggest, divide emissions into those necessary for subsistence and luxury emissions, with only the latter being distributed equally.[79]

Assessing the equal per capita approach

However, the EPC emissions approach faces a number of more serious objections than those touched on here. If we consider mitigation more broadly as both reducing GHG emissions and utilizing GHG sinks, then we should have a distributive principle that encompasses both these elements, not just emissions. Similarly, if person A emits the same amount as person B but also promotes or contributes to the transfer of green energy technology, this contribution to mitigation should also be part of the equation. We might call this the *incomplete response* objection.[80]

A focus on emissions rights is also only one (resourcist) interpretation of equality – a problematic one at that. Focusing on emissions might fetishize goods at the expense of what those goods allow us to do; we should be more concerned about having an equal ability to pursue various goals.[81] A related point is that focusing on goods ignores the different needs people have in relation to emissions. For example, they might live in a cold area that requires (emission-intensive) heating, or perhaps they have to travel to work. They may have different levels of access to renewable energy and hence have to emit more to do basic tasks.[82] Call these the *differential uptake* objections.

Other responses to carbon egalitarianism claim that the EPC approach does not fit equality of welfare, resources, or capabilities or any other recognized larger theory of distributive equality. For instance, welfare egalitarians will be reluctant to construe access to the atmosphere in terms of equal rights to emit because they favor equalizing preferences, fulfillment, or satisfaction, and sets of preferences may require different quantities of emissions to satisfy.[83] Capability theorists will not endorse equal per capita approaches for similar reasons. They will require that emissions be distributed so as to achieve equal capabilities, which, when adjusted for disabilities and human differences, will lead to differential claims to emissions. The metric that the equal per capita approach most closely resembles is the resourcist metric. Yet even here there may not be support for the position. Resourcists typically think of resources in terms of a broader set of goods, such as background conditions, and Dworkin, for instance, require that bundles of goods be envy free rather than just distributed according to the strict equality the EPC approach endorses. These are *general metric* objections.[84]

A further approach to the problem of how to fairly divide emissions is to understand it as a matter of burden sharing. David Miller argues that rather than see individuals or countries as having a human right to some resource, we should see the problem as one of fairly dividing a burden – the burden of avoiding dangerous climate change. Miller would have emissions allocated to countries, which in turn allocate them to citizens according to their own principles. Countries receive emission quotas based on their level of poverty. Invoking a version of Marx's distributive principle, Miller argues that poor counties receive emission quotas based on need and rich countries make sacrifices based on ability to pay. Miller's approach is based not on ownership or claim rights but on the recognition of a burden that needs to be fairly distributed.[85] The burden is how to reduce the risk of dangerous climate change by undertaking the sacrifices necessary to reduce emissions. His criticisms of the EPC approach center on its inability to account for the different emissions levels countries may need due to their different levels of development. A simple equality metric will not be able to accommodate these differences and so will fail to reflect an important principle of global justice.

The greatest difficulty with applying a principle of equality to emissions is that it treats this one good in isolation from a broader set of concerns and from the "package of goods that metrics usually consist of. How might supporters of the EPC approach respond to this concern?

They might argue, for instance, that where a resource is scarce, highly valued, contested, and crucial to the fulfillment of other goods, equality seems a perfectly reasonable basis for dividing the good. To take a simple example, imagine that people value hiking in a national park because they find it wild and beautiful but that, unfortunately, a lot more people want to hike than there are parks available to accommodate them. In this case it seems plausible to divide the ability to hike in the park equally, giving access to hikers via some agreed-upon method because everyone has a claim, no one has private ownership rights, and so on. There are, of course, other reasons that might help us determine park use, such as who will use it best or appreciate it most (perhaps botany students) or where someone is fulfilling a dying wish. However, these considerations do not rule out our arguing that there are good reasons for dividing access equally, only that other reasons may override equality or modify it in some way on some occasions. The case of the claim to emit seems very like the park case in that it is an important and scare resource that people need to use in order to fulfill other important goals. Here the claim that people have the right to emit is based on the moral claims that people have to a resource necessary for the enjoyment of other goods. They have this claim right because there is an issue of the most appropriate way of dividing up a scarce and useful resource. That it is not by itself valuable does not preclude our invoking equality in order to regulate its distribution, even if this is modified by other overriding principles in some cases.

This leads us to a response to another of the objections to the equal division of emissions. Miller seems also to suggest that we have only shallow reasons (based on simple fairness) to distribute emissions equally; he offers objections to what he calls "deep" reasons (e.g., that the inequality would be disrespectful). He claims that one type of deep reason for dividing things equally is that not doing so shows disrespect. Denying someone the vote in national elections is an obvious instance of an inequality that is unjust because it is disrespectful. Having one fewer vote in a country the size of the United States makes little difference to political outcomes, but it is deeply disrespectful to the person from whom the right is taken. It is true that emissions do not have the status of votes. But we can imagine countries complaining bitterly that they are being denied important opportunities for development and being treated disrespectfully because other (more powerful, perhaps colonial) countries are determined to gain more rights to emit for themselves. The unfairness of such an approach could go far beyond a lack of consideration for the status of a country. It could lead to the oppression of one country by another because denying it emission rights of the right kind is also denying it the right to develop in what is a carbon-constrained world. Indeed, this is exactly what many claim has been occurring in the current rounds of climate negotiations. Deeper reasons thus enter into calculation of why equal claims matter in this case.[86]

4.6   Conclusion

In the context of increasing scarcity of global resources and the continuing plight of the global poor, there is good reason to think that the kinds of disputes over resources that we are seeing – over water, the atmosphere, the oceans – demand of us not only ways of negotiating but of devising a principled basis on which to divide resources. Each of the approaches we have considered for extending egalitarianism globally has provided strong reasons for thinking that the egalitarian tradition itself can provide them. Relational egalitarians are able to demonstrate that the kinds of relations that they consider necessary for the generation of duties of justice are present globally. Nonrelationalists have a strong case for claiming that it is arbitrary not to extend duties of justice globally. One of the notable issues about the discussion of global egalitarianism is the relevance of nonvoluntary impacts and institutions in generating duties of justice. In the case of the pervasive impact argument, for instance, it is not relevant for institutions that have an impact to gain the consent of those affected. This is also true of the coercion and reciprocity accounts of the basic structure. That associations be in some way voluntary has been overemphasized in this debate. This fact tells us something important about how our obligations ought to be generated.

There are also compelling egalitarian reasons why there ought to be some level of control or ownership of global resources. The arguments that resources are distributed in a morally arbitrary way, are essential for even basic flourishing, and are likely to be necessary to lessen or remove severe global inequality are important types of egalitarian arguments familiar from other debates. But the important issue for GER is whether there is a distinct principle that equally divides resources or whether resources are divided in order to fulfill other egalitarian claims. The answer to this question partly depends on other commitments that are held. Steiner's libertarian theory of ownership requires an equal division as a matter of rights, but for those who are committed to other goals, such as achieving a range of capabilities, most resources will be divided in a way that achieves an equal division of some other good.

As far as the content of the principle of global equality is concerned, our discussion has canvassed a range of perceived barriers to how to conceive such a principle and the relevance of applying it to important contexts. Miller's claim that there are only shallow pragmatic reasons for equality is also not borne out by his other claims. He argues, for instance, that two deep reasons for valuing something equally occur when it is disrespectful to allow an inequality and when a resource is scarce and there are reasons of fairness not to permit inequalities. Either of these reasons could plausibly apply in the emissions case. Countries might think they and their citizens are suffering disrespect by unequal division, for instance. Emissions are also arguably precisely the type of scarce resource that needs equal division. One of the interesting points to note concerning egalitarian approaches to the distribution of resources is that it indicates how egalitarian principles are appropriately applied to situations that lack a clear overarching political authority. The issue of resources and climate raises an interesting new argument for egalitarians; it illustrates the kind of claim we explored in connection with associational arguments that there did not have to be consent-based interaction for duties of justice to arise. This type of example substantially expands the scope of global egalitarianism. Moreover, the discussion of the emissions budget alerts us to the importance of an issue encountered in Chapter 2, one relating to the importance of applying a principle of equality to the right domain. We have seen that applying equality just to GHG emissions fixates on one small dimension of environmental justice – the ability to emit – and applies the principle of equality to this dimension alone, whereas what should interest us is whether we have equal access to a whole package of goods.[87] For instance, just as we do not have a separate distributive principle for the allocation of iron ore or rare earths, we should not have one for emissions. Emissions gain their importance from the contribution they make to other goods, and it is those goods to which we should apply a principle of equality.

Conclusion: Assessing the Prospects for Egalitarianism

This book has sought to reassess the contemporary debate concerning egalitarianism. I hope to have been able to clarify some of the major disputes and some overlapping themes of the recent debate. What I have also tried to demonstrate is that achieving substantive equality continues to be an important and meaningful goal. However, I have also tried to show that there remain difficult issues for egalitarians to confront. Chief among these is whether egalitarianism has identified the most important sources of inequality and whether the positions that have been advanced are substantial enough to achieve significant types of equality between people.

I will not repeat all of the arguments about the direction of egalitarianism, but in what remains I make some comments on the major themes I have identified. I begin by emphasizing that there continues to be a powerful set of reasons why achieving equality is desirable. The fact that there are such compelling examples of the disadvantages caused by inequality is one of the main reasons why egalitarianism remains an important position in political philosophy. Yet the framework that some egalitarians have used to assess the value of equality has not always proved adequate. The debate has been stuck between thinking of equality in purely instrumental terms and an unrealistic conception of intrinsic value. This has been particularly true since Parfit's criticisms of the value of equality. As we have seen, conceiving of equality's value as constitutive allows us to escape what I have called Parfit's straitjacket and provide a more nuanced understanding of how the value of equality ought to be conceived. The many ways in which equality helps combat important disadvantages, together with the constitutive sense in which equality is valuable, should leave us confident that the value of this key concept is placed on a securer footing. Moreover, thinking of its value in a constituent way allows us to reemphasize the link between equality and a conception of justice and to see how the leveling-down objection in particular is misguided. Ultimately, equality is valuable because achieving it in key areas is part of what it is to live in a just society.

A large part of the answer to what it is to live in an egalitarian society has been addressed in the debate about metrics of equality. What the plateau challenge demonstrated was that having a commitment to equality of *any* type was not equivalent to being an egalitarian. Yet there has been a trend to put forward conceptions of equality of condition that have not been substantive in important senses. This is nowhere more true than in the debate about the currency of egalitarian justice. Many of the metrics we have encountered predominantly focus on providing people with opportunities to do valuable things. The capability approach is not called the functioning or achievement view because its focus is on providing opportunities. Similarly, providing people with opportunities to purchase key goods in an auction is also seen by Dworkin as focusing on opportunities in the right way. Opportunities are a valuable part of any metric. Not everyone will choose the same things given the same set of options, and we clearly need to incorporate a conception of opportunity into egalitarian justice. But there is also a sense in which an overemphasis on opportunities can be too defensive.

If this is true, then what egalitarian metrics should also not ignore is the sense in which just societies may depend on there being outcomes of a certain sort for people to be truly equal. It should not seem implausible for egalitarians to argue that *some* important outcomes matter. We might think that while it is a restriction on freedom to compel people to get an education (and to compel the necessary taxation arrangements), it is fundamental to improving an individual's life chances and to having a society in which people can understand, debate, and decide on important matters collectively. Key outcomes might have to be achieved – not just have the option of being achieved – if this is to occur. The discussion of egalitarianism and the problem of climate change provide an illustration of this point. We should aim for the opportunity not merely to enjoy a safe and functioning climate but to provide a safer climate to everyone, as best we can. Similarly, allowing opportunity conceptions to dominate thinking about equality of condition and the goals of egalitarianism can lead to situations in which too many people are left without the means for a decent life.

Stressing the need for having a substantive metric should also not ignore the important sense in which an egalitarian metric ought to have legitimacy in the sense we have discussed. We have already noted how, in many parts of the egalitarian debate, the role of preferences in particular and endorsement in general has been a persistent but often unrecognized feature. This is perhaps the area which is least discussed in the debate. The role of preferences in the metric of equality is one of the many places in which the issue arises. While a more nuanced understanding of the role of preferences and choice would arguably be helpful in this particular debate, the more general problem is the role of democratic endorsement of egalitarian principles. While authors do not put forward their metrics, for instance, as things that must be adopted no matter what, there is on the whole a reluctance to weigh the value of what we have been calling legitimacy against the justification of the particular principles. The reliance on preferences also indicates that the metrics are not as diametrically opposed as their adherents sometimes claim they are. This is not to say that egalitarians are headed to a point of unity on the metric question anytime soon but are just not aware of it. Yet it does show the persistence of the attachment egalitarians have to the concept and a greater need to fully appreciate the role that it plays.

The discussion of responsibility is the most politically charged dimension of the debate. It is also the one where the opposing sides appear farthest apart. Yet as we have seen, the divide is not so huge as it might at first appear. Both relational and nonrelational egalitarians have a role for responsibility. But the overall significance of the debate lies in whether egalitarians place too much emphasis on responsibility. It seems clear that there has been too much attention given to responsibility when, as we noted, the biggest barriers to equality do not seem to be whether people make responsible choices. More important is to focus on eliminating inequalities generated by unfair trade and labor practices, inadequate access to education and health, discrimination involving groups and genders, and other causes. As a consequence, future egalitarian debate in this area would be better directed not to the challenges of irresponsible hikers or welfare cheats but to problems posed by achieving better outcomes and the challenges thus raised in respect of perfectionism and paternalism.

A further important feature highlighted by the recent debate is the importance of the connection of the value of equality to justice. Part of the reassessment of egalitarianism offered here has involved examining the link between equality and justice as a way of understanding how several of the debates have gone astray. One example is Derek Parfit's discussion of the value of equality. One notable thing about Parfit's discussion was how many responses to it attempted to reconnect equality with justice as a way of answering his leveling-down objection. Understanding equality as a demand of justice and not a general moral value opened up the possibility of a more nuanced response. We have seen that the debate has to some extent been polarized, viewing equality as either instrumentally or intrinsically valuable. But more recent responses to this issue have tried to give an account of equality's value that links it to other values connected to accounts of justice. This third type of approach opens up a productive way of accounting for equality's value by reconnecting it with egalitarian concerns for just states of affairs and circumventing what I have called Parfit's straightjacket. Similarly, in the discussion of global egalitarianism we observed that there were several strong valuations of a global principle of equality that saw global equality as a demand of justice, not an ancillary moral principle.

A challenge for the immediate future is the extent to which egalitarianism can embrace a global set of issues. We have noted that a substantive conception of equality will focus on outcomes and opportunities across a range of important indicators. Many causes of inequality have a global dimension. This is nowhere better seen than in the climate change debate. Egalitarianism can offer insights into the kinds of values appropriate for dealing with both a fair division of climate burdens and other crucial issues and the resources needed for adaptation. It is also incumbent on egalitarians to challenge their own accounts of justice so that they reflect the importance of the debate's global dimension. Not only should egalitarianism reflect the importance of global issues; it should transfer insights, such as the desirability of achieving important outcomes. Again, we can appreciate the importance of this in the climate debate when we reflect on the need to achieve a stabilization of the climate and curtail lifestyles and freedoms that lead to excessive emissions of GHGs.

I have argued that egalitarianism continues to offer a meaningful and powerful set of resources for understanding the claims of justice. The reassessment offered here hopefully adds to the plausibility of understanding how egalitarianism can fulfill the demands of living in a just society. This is now more necessary than ever given the crises and challenges facing modern societies. If egalitarianism is to continue to be a viable way of approaching the challenges of justice, then it needs to offer a vision and a set of implementable principles that can form the basis for achieving a more equal set of relations in the face of the kinds of prevalent disadvantages many people face. To do this we need to clarify the kinds of debates that concern egalitarians and ensure that debate is headed in the right direction. As we have noted, the complexity of the debate about egalitarianism, its substantial overlap of issues and agendas, has led to some of the key issues becoming unclear. Disentangling these threads has been one of the tasks of this book.

Notes

Introduction

1. Amartya Sen, "Equality of What?," in I. S. M. McMurrin (ed.), *The Tanner Lectures on Human Values* (Cambridge: Cambridge University Press, 1979); John Rawls, *Political Liberalism* (New York: Columbia University Press, 1993).
2. Harry Frankfurt, "Equality as a Moral Ideal," *Ethics* 98 (1987), 21–42.
3. Cited in Martha Nussbaum, *Women and Human Development* (Cambridge: Cambridge University Press, 2000), 139.
4. Martha Nussbaum, *Frontiers of Justice* (Cambridge, MA: Harvard University Press, 2007), 115ff.
5. Anderson, "What Is the Point of Equality?"; Samuel Scheffler, "What Is Egalitarianism?," *Philosophy and Public Affairs* 31 (2003), 5–39.
6. Charles Beitz, "Cosmopolitan Ideals and National Sentiment," *Journal of Philosophy* 80 (10) (1983); Abizedeh, "Cooperation, Pervasive Impact and Coercion: On the Scope (Not Site) of Distributive Justice," *Philosophy and Public Affairs* 35 (4) (2007); Tan, *Justice without Borders*, 33.
7. Michael Blake, "Distributive Justice, State Coercion and Autonomy," *Philosophy and Public Affairs* 30 (2001).
8. Simon Caney, *Justice beyond Borders: A Global Political Theory* (Oxford: Oxford University Press, 2005), 265.
9. Darryl Moellendorf, *Cosmopolitan Justice* (Boulder, CO: Westview Press, 2002), 31.
10. P. Casal, "Progressive Environmental Taxation: A Defence," *Political Studies* (2012).
11. Hillel Steiner, "Left Libertarianism and the Ownership of Natural Resources," *Public Reason* 1 (1) (2009).
12. P. Singer, *One World* (Melbourne: Text Publishing, 2002), 39.
13. S. Caney, "Justice and the Distribution of Greenhouse Gas Emissions," *Journal of Global Ethics* 5 (2) (2009), 130.

1 The Value of Equality

1. There are not, in fact, many explicit defenses of why equality matters in political philosophy that argue that it matters no matter what else does. Opponents of intrinsic egalitarianism have articulated what such a position would look like. See Joseph Raz, *The Morality of Freedom* (Oxford: Oxford University Press, 1986), ch. 9.
2. Roger Crisp, "Equality, Priority and Compassion," *Ethics* 13 (2003), 745–763; Harry Frankfurt, "Equality as a Moral Ideal," *Ethics* 98 (1987), 21–42. For a

144

response, see Larry Temkin, "Egalitarianism Defended," *Ethics* 113 (2003), 764–782.

3. We should also note that concern for equality is not confined to issues of justice limited to the state. This issue is discussed more fully in Ch. 5, but for now we should not assume that egalitarians could not be concerned with practices that avoided stigmatizing individuals in other countries or creating conditions that undermined their self-respect.

4. Jean-Jacques Rousseau, "The Social Contract," in *The Social Contract and Discourses*, trans. G. D. H. Cole Cress (London: Dent, 1983).

5. Darwall, "Two Kinds of Respect," *Ethics* 88 (1) (1977), 36–49. This should be contrasted with appraisal respect, which involves the positive appraisal of a person or his or her particular characteristics.

6. Elizabeth Anderson, "What Is the Point of Equality?," *Ethics* 109 (2) (1999), 288. See also Timothy Hinton, "Must Egalitarians Choose between Fairness and Respect?," *Philosophy & Public Affairs* 30 (1) (2001), 72–87.

7. Anderson, "What Is the Point of Equality?," 305.

8. John Rawls, *A Theory of Justice* (Oxford: Oxford University Press, 1999), 544; John Rawls, *Justice as Fairness: A Restatement* (Cambridge, MA: Harvard University Press, 2001), 131.

9. "Levellers" refers to a seventeenth-century English movement whose political program included demands for equal manhood suffrage and the abolition of the tithe. For a discussion, see Henry Phelps Brown, *Egalitarianism and the Generation of Inequality* (Oxford: Oxford University Press, 1988), 111ff.

10. Ibid.

11. Ibid.; see also the feminist discussion in Iris Young, "Five Faces of Oppression," in M. Adams (ed.), *Readings for Diversity and Social Justice* (New York: Routledge, 2000), 35–49.

12. Rawls, *Justice as Fairness*, 131.

13. Ibid.

14. Rousseau, "The Social Contract," 204.

15. Richard Wilkinson, *The Impact of Inequality* (New York: New Press, 2005), 48. He also reports that more than fifty studies have shown a correlation between income inequality and homicide rates.

16. Ichiro Kawachi and Bruce P. Kennedy, "The Relationship of Income Inequality to Mortality: Does the Choice of Indicator Matter?," *Social Science and Medicine* 45 (1997), 1121–1127. For general discussion of these issues, see Wilkinson, *The Impact of Inequality*, chs. 2–4.

17. Wilkinson, *The Impact of Inequality*; Richard Wilkinson and Kate Pickett, *The Spirit Level: Why More Equal Societies Almost Always Do Better* (London: Penguin Books, 2009); Sudhir Anand, Fabienne Peter, and Amartya Sen (eds), *Public Health, Ethics, and Equity* (Oxford: Oxford University Press, 2004).

18. Michael Marmot, "Social Causes of Social Inequalities in Health," in Sudhir Anand, Fabienne Peter, and Amartya Sen (eds), *Public Health, Ethics, and Equity* (Oxford: Oxford University Press, 2004).

19. Wilkinson and Pickett, *The Spirit Level*, ch. 4.

20. Wilkinson, *The Impact of Inequality*, 54. See also T. Nagel, "Equality, Priority and the Levelling Down Objection," in Matthew Clayton and Andrew Williams (eds), *The Ideal of Equality* (Basingstoke: Palgrave Macmillan, 2002).

A similar theme is developed by Robert Putnam in *Bowling Alone*, which reports that US states with lower levels of inequality were less likely to be socially cohesive. See Robert D. Putnam, *Bowling Alone: The Collapse and Revival of American Community* (New York: Simon and Schuster, 2000).

21. R. Dworkin, *Sovereign Virtue: The Theory and Practice of Equality* (London: Harvard University Press, 2000), 1.

22. Scanlon, "The Diversity of Objections to Inequality," in Matthew Clayton and Andrew Williams (eds), *The Ideal of Equality* (Basingstoke: Palgrave Macmillan, 2002), 46.

23. Ibid., 44.

24. Frankfurt, "Equality as a Moral Ideal," 21. For other discussions of sufficiency, see Frankfurt, "Equality and Respect," *Social Research* 64 (1997), 3–15; Frankfurt, "The Moral Irrelevance of Equality," *Public Affairs Quarterly* 14 (2000), 87–103; Paula Casal, "Why Sufficiency Is Not Enough," *Ethics* 117 (2007), 296–326; Yitzhak Benbaji, "Sufficiency or Priority," *European Journal of Philosophy* 14 (3) (2006), 327–348; Brown, "Priority, Sufficiency...or Both?," *Economics and Philosophy* 21 (2) (2005), 199–220. Crisp, "Equality, Priority, and Compassion"; Roger Crisp, "Egalitarianism and Compassion," *Ethics* 114 (2003), 119–126; David Wiggins, "Claims of Need," in *Needs, Values, Truth* (Oxford: Blackwell, 1991), 1–58; David Miller, "Justice and Global Inequality," in Andrew Hurrell and Ngaire Woods (eds), *Inequality, Globalization, and World Politics* (Oxford: Oxford University Press, 1999), 187–201; David Miller, "National Responsibility and International Justice," in Deen Chatterjee (ed.), *The Ethics of Assistance: Morality and the Distant Needy* (Cambridge: Cambridge University Press, 2004), 123–147; Debra Satz, "International Economic Justice," in Hugh LaFollette (ed.), *Oxford Handbook of Practical Ethics* (Oxford: Oxford University Press, 2002), 620–642.

25. Frankfurt, "Equality as a Moral Ideal," 21; emphasis in original.

26. Ibid., 23.

27. Ibid., 31. Emphasis in original.

28. Nagel, "Equality."

29. As Casal notes in "Why Sufficiency Is Not Enough," it is also a challenge to desert principles that may lead to some not having enough if they do not deserve it. Nussbaum also seems to endorse a version of the sufficientarian view in her *Frontiers of Justice* (Cambridge, MA: Belknap Press, 2006). She advocates a mixed sufficiency/equality view. She writes, "Some capabilities must be secured to citizens on a basis of equality, or equal dignity has not been respected. Others, however, do not seem to have this intrinsic relationship to dignity; with these, the capabilities approach supplies a threshold of adequacy" (295).

30. Casal, "Why Sufficiency Is Not Enough."

31. For a full critical discussion of the difficulties of sufficiency views, see ibid.; Richard Arneson, "Egalitarianism and Responsibility," *Journal of Ethics* 3 (1999), 225–247. See also R. E. Goodin, "Egalitarianism, Fetishistic and Otherwise," *Ethics* 98 (1987); 44–49; Jonathan Wolff and Avner de-Shalit, *Disadvantage* (Oxford: Oxford University Press, 2007).

32. Casal, "Why Sufficiency Is Not Enough," 307.

33. Mason, "Egalitarianism and the Levelling Down Objection," *Analysis* 61 (2001), 246–254.

34. Frankfurt, "Equality as a Moral Ideal," 38.
35. Wolff and de-Shalit, *Disadvantage*, 92–93.
36. Crisp, "Equality, Priority and Compassion."
37. See Arneson, "Egalitarianism and Responsibility"; also Richard Arneson, "Perfectionism and Politics," *Ethics* 111 (2000), 37–63, at 57, for a discussion of how Martha Nussbaum's capability approach faces related threshold problems. Wolff and de-Shalit, *Disadvantage*, 92–93, also discuss this issue in relation to the capability approach. A further objection to Frankfurt's account is that it primarily attacks equality of money and does not account for other egalitarian metrics, such as welfare, which share many of the same concerns as Frankfurt does about fetishizing money. See Goodin, "Egalitarianism, Fetishistic and Otherwise."
38. As Susan Hurley notes, priority views still involve comparisons in the sense that a person's well-being (where they are badly off) is compared to a different state of well-being (where they could be better off). So instead of being interpersonally comparative, priority views involve counterfactual comparisons. Elizabeth Hurley, "The 'What' and the 'How' of Distributive Justice and Health," in Nils Holtung and Kasper Lippert-Rasmussen (eds), *Egalitarianism: New Essays on the Nature and Value of Equality* (New York: Oxford University Press, 2007). Other prominent discussions of prioritarianism include Nagel, "Equality"; Arneson, "Egalitarianism and Responsibility"; Richard Arneson, "Luck Egalitarianism and Prioritarianism," *Ethics* 110 (2) (2000), 339; Crisp, "Equality, Priority and Compassion"; Derek Parfit, "Equality or Priority," *Ratio* 10 (3) (1997), 202–222. For some recent criticisms see Michael Otsuka and Alex Voorhoeve, "Why It Matters That Some Are Worse Off Than Others: An Argument against the Priority View," *Philosophy and Public Affairs* 37 (2) (2009), 171–199.
39. Parfit, "Equality or Priority," 204.
40. Ibid., 98.
41. Ibid., 104.
42. Rawls, *A Theory of Justice*, 302.
43. Parfit notes that if Rawls allows only inequalities that benefit the least-well-off, then his view is not strictly speaking a version of the priority view. Where an inequality benefits some but does not make the least-well-off better off or worse off, then prioritarians will nonetheless endorse it (Parfit, "Equality or Priority," 166ff.).
44. Rawls, *A Theory of Justice*, 83.
45. Ibid., 67.
46. Rawls thinks of justice as fairness as egalitarian and cites several reasons why equality matters in itself. See Rawls, *Justice as Fairness*, 131ff. I do not go into the issue of which justification is best. For a brief discussion, see Matthew Clayton and Andrew Williams, "Some Questions for Egalitarians," in Matthew Clayton and Andrew Williams (eds), *The Ideal of Equality* (Basingstoke: Palgrave Macmillan, 2002), 1.
47. Arneson, "Egalitarianism and Responsibility."
48. Ibid., 237.
49. Larry Temkin, "Equality, Priority and the Levelling Down Objection," in Matthew Clayton and Andrew Williams (eds), *The Ideal of Equality* (Basingstoke: Palgrave Macmillan, 2002), 155.

50. Ibid., 136.
51. For an extended discussion of this issue, see Larry Temkin, *Inequality* (Oxford: Oxford University Press, 1996), ch. 9.
52. Temkin, "Equality, Priority, and the Levelling Down Objection," 139.
53. Egalitarians might also admit that the leveling-down objection applies but contend that it also applies to prioritarianism. Ingmar Persson adopts this line: Ingmar Persson, "Why Levelling Down Could Be Worse for Prioritarianism Than for Egalitarianism," *Ethical Theory and Moral Practice* 11 (2008), 295–303.
54. Hurley, "The 'What' and the 'How' of Distributive Justice and Health," 331ff.
55. A general point about leveling down that might count in its favor is that we do, in fact, level down all the time. If in an election someone has more votes than others, we would level down as a matter of course, because it is the inequality that contributes to a harm, in this case the harm of having more impact in a democracy or the disrespect that having extra votes may show to someone or some group. If an unequal division of some good does cause disrespect of this kind, then it is a reason to level down.
56. Broome's approach to this issue is importantly different from Temkin's. Broome thinks that the harm to the saints in the saints and sinners example is a personal and not an impersonal harm. He argues that suffering an injustice is bad for someone. John Broome, *Weighing Goods* (Oxford: Basil Blackwell, 1995), 165; for a response, see Temkin, "Equality, Priority, and the Levelling Down Objection," 146ff.
57. Broome, *Weighing Goods*, 197. Another fairness-related argument for equality's value is provided by left libertarians. An example of the left libertarian fairness argument for equality is provided by Michael Otsuka. For Otsuka, the conflict between the libertarian right of self-ownership and an egalitarian support for equality is largely an illusion. Otsuka's argument is that it is possible to distribute initial unowned resources in a way that achieves equality of opportunity for welfare that is also consistent with a robust right of self-ownership. He argues that both can be combined in a way that will guarantee a minimum amount of resources even for the disabled. His approach combines two features: a libertarian insistence on a right of ownership over one's own body and labor together with what he terms the "egalitarian proviso." The proviso states, "You may acquire previously unowned worldly resources if and only if you leave enough so that everyone else can acquire an equally advantageous share of unowned worldly resources" (Michael Otsuka, *Libertarianism without Inequality* [Oxford: Oxford University Press, 2003], 24). What underpins the proviso is a claim about fairness. Nozick's account of ownership and acquisition is unfair because it condemns many to poverty and unfairly advantages the person who first grabs the land. Otsuka's egalitarian proviso removes this unfairness by stipulating that everyone should be allowed to claim their fair share, which is a share equal to everyone else's. The equality of condition that Otsuka favors is part of what it is to observe a claim about fairness: Otsuka, *Libertarianism without Inequality*, 236. Other left libertarian discussions of this topic include Hillel Steiner, "How Equality Matters," *Social Philosophy & Policy* 19 (2002), 342–356, and Peter Vallentyne, "Equality, Efficiency and the Priority of the Worst Off," *Economics and Philosophy* 16 (2000), 1–19.

58. Dennis McKerlie, "Equality," *Ethics* 106 (1996), 274–296. There are also arguments for equality that relate to its importance for procedural fairness. I do not specially address these types of arguments for equality. See A. J. Julius, "Basic Structure and the Value of Equality," *Philosophy and Public Affairs* 31 (2003), 321–355.

59. Martin O'Neill, "What Should Egalitarians Believe?," *Philosophy and Public Affairs* 36 (2008), 119–156, at 124.

60. Ibid., 130. While he is surely correct to point out that Parfit's distinction is too narrow to capture the other (in O'Neill's terms) nonintrinsic versions of egalitarianism, Parfit's distinction between telic and deontic relies on two further distinctions: (1) the outcome/genesis distinction and (2) the intrinsic/nonintrinsic distinction. While admittedly not always clear in Parfit's work, the former distinction separates egalitarians according to whether the badness of inequality is a product of a faulty genesis or because the wrong state of affairs obtains. The latter distinction categorizes egalitarians as intrinsic if they value equality in virtue of its intrinsic properties or as nonintrinsic if equality is valued for some other reason. While overlapping, these distinctions do not neatly fit together. Telic egalitarians value equal outcomes and for intrinsic reasons according to Parfit. For deontic egalitarians the case is not so clear-cut. They value equality because it is connected to some other moral value, but it is not clear where this leaves them in relation to the intrinsic/nonintrinsic distinction. For a fuller discussion, see Jeremy Moss, "Egalitarianism and the Value of Equality," *Journal of Ethics and Social Philosophy* 2 (2009), 1–6.

61. Scanlon, "The Diversity of Objections to Inequality."

62. On the distinction between telic and deontic egalitarianism, see Kasper Lippert-Rasmussen, "The Insignificance of the Distinction between Telic and Deontic Egalitarianism," in Nils Holtung and Kasper Lippert-Rasmussen (eds), *Egalitarianism: New Essays on the Nature and Value of Equality* (New York: Oxford University Press, 2007).

63. O'Neill, "What Should Egalitarians Believe?," 134.

64. Brighouse and Swift, "Equality, Priority, and Positional Goods," *Ethics* 116 (3) (2006), 471–497, at 476.

65. Scanlon, "The Diversity of Objections to Inequality."

66. This is the strategy adopted by Thomas Christiano. Christiano argues that a necessary condition for equality mattering is that "the thing being equalized is such that more is better than less" (Thomas Christiano, *The Constitution of Equality: Democratic Authority and Its Limits* [New York: Oxford University Press, 2008], 34). To take his example, if we were dividing bread between people and there was much more than was required, giving everyone more beyond a certain point does not matter. Equal amounts of bread in this case would be a matter of indifference. Whereas if we had enough only for all to avoid starvation but not to satisfy them, it would be important to provide an equal distribution. We care about the distribution in the second case because more bread is better than less. Christiano argues that the leveling-down objection tells us that because something is lost when there is inequality, any egalitarian state must be better than any nonegalitarian state in one respect. But he argues that the inference to the claim that we should not prefer a Pareto superior state is not warranted. All the egalitarian is committed to saying is

that the nonegalitarian state is unjust, not that it is better. Where we have a Pareto superior state that increases everyone's well-being albeit unequally, it would still be better if well-being was increased for all but in an equal way. The unequal state of affairs is better but not as good as it should be.

67. J. L. Ackrill also uses the term *constituent* to describe how good A can be for the sake of B without it being a means to B when he discusses Aristotle's account of eudaimonia in the *Nicomachean Ethics*. J. L. Acrill, "Aristotle on Eudaimonia," in *Essays on Plato and Aristotle* (Oxford: Clarendon Press, 1997). See also Stefan Gosepath, "Equality," *The Stanford Encyclopedia of Philosophy*, http://plato.stanford.edu/; Daniel Halliday, "Holism about Value: Some Help for Invariabilists," *Philosophical Studies*, forthcoming; Christine Korsgaard, "Two Distinctions in Goodness," *Philosophical Review* 92 (1983), 169–195; Moss, "Egalitarianism and the Value of Equality."

68. Raz, *The Morality of Freedom*, 200ff.

69. How deontic conceptions value equality is a complex issue. Most of the discussions of the valuations of equality discuss versions of telic egalitarianism. This is partly because for Parfit, deontic conceptions avoid the leveling-down problem and so have not generated as much controversy. But this does not tell us how they fare according to the intrinsic/nonintrinsic distinction. Deontic conceptions are, according to Parfit, valued for some other moral reason. This might appear to mean that equality is valued instrumentally. However, deontic constitutive conceptions of equality's value need not be committed to this nonintrinsic valuation.

2   Equality of What?

1. Thomas Pogge, "A Critique of the Capability Approach," in Harry Brighouse and Ingrid Robeyns (eds), *Measuring Justice: Primary Goods and Capabilities* (Cambridge: Cambridge University Press, 2010), 17–60.

2. Pogge, "A Critique of the Capability Approach."

3. Elizabeth Anderson, "Justifying the Capabilities Approach to Justice," in Harry Brighouse and Ingrid Robeyns (eds), *Measuring Justice: Primary Goods and Capabilities* (Cambridge: Cambridge University Press, 2010), 81.

4. John Rawls, *Political Liberalism* (New York: Columbia University Press, 1993), 66.

5. See, e.g., Michael Otsuka, *Liberalism without Inequality* (Oxford: Oxford University Press, 2003).

6. Robert Nozick, *Anarchy, State, and Utopia* (Oxford: Blackwell, 1975).

7. Patrick Boleyn-Fitzgerald, "Misfortune, Welfare Reform and Right Wing Egalitarianism," *Critical Review* 13 (1999), 141.

8. See Tim Scanlon, "The Diversity of Objections to Inequality," in Mathew Clayton and Andrew Williams (eds), *The Ideal of Equality* (London: Palgrave Macmillan, 2002), 46ff.; Anderson, "What Is the Point of Equality?," *Ethics* 109 (2) (1999), 287–337.

9. Following standard usage in the egalitarian literature, here I use the term *welfarism* as shorthand for the position that equates the currency of egalitarian justice with either conscious states or preference satisfaction. It has other meanings in philosophy, such as the view that morality is chiefly

concerned with advancing people's individual welfare. See L. W. Sumner, *Welfare, Happiness and Ethics* (Oxford: Clarendon Press, 1996); Simon Keller, "Welfare as Success," *Nous* 43 (4) (2009), 656–683. Perhaps the most comprehensive modern account is to be found in James Griffin, *Well-Being: Its Meaning, Measurement and Importance* (Oxford: Clarendon Press, 1986); Amartya Sen, "Rational Fools: A Critique of the Behavioral Foundations of Economic Theory," *Philosophy and Public Affairs* 6 (4) (1977), 317–344.

10. Sumner, *Welfare, Happiness and Ethics*; Sen, "Rational Fools."

11. For useful discussions of welfarism that have been influential in this debate, see Griffin, *Well-Being*; Sumner, *Welfare, Happiness and Ethics*; Serena Olsaretti, *Justice and Desert* (Oxford: Oxford University Press, 2003); Keller, "Welfare as Success"; Richard J. Arneson, "Human Flourishing versus Desire Satisfaction," *Social Philosophy and Policy* 16(1) (1999), 113–142; Tim Scanlon, *What We Owe to Each Other* (Cambridge, MA: Harvard University Press, 1998), ch. 3.

12. R. M. Dworkin, *Sovereign Virtue: The Theory and Practice of Equality* (London: Harvard University Press, 2000), 43.

13. Griffin, *Well-Being*, 8.

14. Derek Parfit, *Reasons and Persons* (Oxford: Oxford University Press, 1984), 493.

15. See Griffin, *Well-Being*.

16. The concept of revealed preference has been very influential in economics and social science. A preference is said to be revealed by, e.g., choices that consumers make in the marketplace. But the link between preferences and choices is often a weak one. My choosing one alternative over another does not mean I prefer either; only that between these alternatives one is better than the other. I may have a preference for an entirely different option or set of options. See Sen, "Rational Fools"; Sumner, *Welfare, Happiness and Ethics*, ch. 5.

17. Sumner, *Welfare, Happiness and Ethics*, 123.

18. John Elster, "Sour Grapes – Utilitarianism and the Genesis of Wants," in Amartya Sen and Bernard Williams (eds), *Utilitarianism and Beyond* (Cambridge: Cambridge University Press, 1982), 219–238.

19. On this and related points, see Cass Sunstein, *Free Markets and Social Justice* (New York: Oxford University Press, 1997), ch. 1.

20. Following Parfit, *Reasons and Persons*, 494. Dworkin's use of the term *success theory* to describe equality of personal success is narrower than the sense of success with which we began.

21. Dworkin, *Sovereign Virtue*, 17.

22. Ibid., 38.

23. John Rawls, "Social Unity and Primary Goods," in Amartya Sen and Bernard Williams (eds), *Collected Papers* (Cambridge, MA: Harvard University Press, 1999), 159–185.

24. Ibid., 185.

25. Other objective list theories are advanced by John Harsanyi, "Morality and the Theory of Rational Behaviour," in *Utilitarianism and Beyond*, eds. Amartya Sen and Bernard Williams (Cambridge: Cambridge University Press, 1982), 39–62. John Finnis, *Natural Law and Natural Rights* (Oxford: Oxford University Press, 1980); Martha Nussbaum, *Frontiers of Justice* (Cambridge, MA: Harvard University Press, 2007); David Brink, *Moral Realism and the Foundations of Ethics* (Cambridge: Cambridge University Press, 1989).

26. Richard Arneson, "Welfare Should Be the Currency of Justice," *Canadian Journal of Philosophy* 30 (4) (2000), 497–524.
27. Ibid., 515. Note that Arneson is not claiming that only opportunities matter for judging people's welfare. In several papers he claims that his earlier view regarding welfare as opportunity should now be seen as only partly opportunity-based and partly outcome-based. See Richard Arneson, "Equal Opportunity for Welfare Defended and Recanted," *Journal of Political Philosophy* 7 (4) (1999), 488; Arneson, "Distributive Justice and Basic Capability Equality: 'Good Enough' Is Not Good Enough," in Alexander Kaufman (ed.), *Capabilities Equality: Basic Issues and Problems* (London: Routledge, 2005), 17; Arneson, "Cracked Foundations of Liberal Equality," in Justine Burley (ed.), *Ronald Dworkin and His Critics* (Oxford: Basil Blackwell, 2005), 79–98.
28. Arneson, "Welfare Should Be the Currency of Justice," 516.
29. For a different objectivist position, see Tim Scanlon, "Preference and Urgency," *Journal of Philosophy* 72 (19) (1975), 655–669, where he argues for using objective criteria to compare people's well-being based on certain general categories of things that are of value as part of normal lives.
30. Arneson, "Cracked Foundations of Liberal Equality," 94–95. Versions of welfarism also seem to be strongly influenced by the chance/choice distinction. Arneson directly argues that his account, is valuable because it can respond to the importance of modeling this distinction in the metric. More generally, one reason to support welfarism is that focusing on preferences is an ideal way of seeing which outcomes and disadvantages are down to chance and which are the product of choice.
31. See also Arneson, "Human Flourishing." For others in this category, see Griffin, *Well-Being*.
32. See Martha Nussbaum, *Women and Human Development* (Cambridge: Cambridge University Press, 2001); Amartya Sen, *Inequality Reexamined* (Oxford: Oxford University Press, 1992).
33. Philippe Van Parijs (ed.), *Arguing for Basic Income* (London: Verso, 1992); Van Parijs, "Why Surfers Should Be Fed," *Philosophy and Public Affairs* 20 (2) (1991), 101–131; Van Parijs, *Real Freedom for All* (Oxford: Oxford University Press, 1995); Bruce Ackerman and Anne Alstott, *The Stakeholder Society* (New Haven, CT: Yale University Press, 1999).
34. Rawls, *Political Liberalism*, 4.
35. Ibid., 181.
36. Ibid., 172.
37. Sen, "Equality of What?," 215–216.
38. Ibid., 219.
39. See Nussbaum, *Frontiers of Justice*, 115–116.
40. Rawls, *Justice as Fairness*, 169. Rawls defines the two moral powers as; the capacity for a sense of justice and the capacity for a conception of the good. Ibid., 19.
41. Ibid., 169–170.
42. Ibid., 176.
43. Both Sen and Nussbaum disagree with this claim. Sen claims that his approach does not endorse any such conception because the capability approach reflects people's freedom to choose between different combinations of capabilities (Sen, *Inequality Reexamined*, 82). For Nussbaum, the case is more complex. She does

not endorse any comprehensive view but does have a view of human nature, which she claims is thin enough to avoid the charge of comprehensiveness.

44. Daniels, "On Liberty and Equality," 132.
45. Ibid., 322–323.
46. For a discussion of this point, see Will Kymlicka, *Contemporary Political Philosophy: An Introduction* (Oxford: Oxford University Press, 2001), 79–83. For an alternative, see Matt Matravers, *Responsibility and Justice* (Cambridge: Polity Press, 2007); Matt Matravers "Responsibility, Luck and the 'Equality of What Debate?,'" *Political Studies* 50 (3) (2002).
47. Dworkin, *Sovereign Virtue*, 6.
48. Ibid., 67.
49. Dworkin rejects the idea that his theory on the equality of resources is a starting gate theory of justice. Crucially, he claims that it is ambition sensitive, that "it reflects the cost to others of the choices people make" (Dworkin, *Sovereign Virtue*, 89). But it also recognizes that the distribution of resources must be endowment sensitive; i.e., we recognize that people have different abilities, which will produce different incomes in a market economy.
50. Ibid., see also Matravers, "Responsibility, Luck and the 'Equality of What Debate?.'"
51. For an interesting discussion of the evolution and coherence of Dworkin's distinction, see Matravers, "Responsibility, Luck and the 'Equality of What Debate?.'"
52. Ibid., 77.
53. Ibid., 78.
54. Ibid., 80.
55. Ibid., 81.
56. See ibid., 82. His scheme also has a hypothetical insurance market for talents that the tax and welfare system can model, which I do not discuss here. What Dworkin proposes is the following: imagine a situation in which before the initial auction had started we fed information about people's talents, raw materials, and available technology into a computer. The computer will then predict the number of people in each income level and the income structure. Further, people do not know where they will be in that structure. Insurance can be offered to compensate people in case they do not occupy an acceptable place in the income structure (Dworkin, *Sovereign Virtue*, 94). Dworkin proposes that a tax system be devised to replicate this insurance model for differential talents.
57. G. A. Cohen, "On the Currency of Egalitarian Justice," *Ethics* 99 (4) (1989), 906–944, 918.
58. Ibid., 919.
59. Ibid., 920.
60. Macleod, *Liberalism, Justice and Markets*, 27.
61. Ibid., 40.
62. Dworkin does later briefly elaborate what he calls a principle of authenticity of preference formation, but it is not adequately developed to respond to this objection. See Dworkin, *Sovereign Virtue*, 158–161.
63. See Kymlicka, *Contemporary Political Philosophy*. Some also object that Dworkin's proposal does not adequately allow for certain sorts of social disadvantages and hence is not really envy free. Imagine an unemployed person

who has received compensation from an incredibly successful sports star because the former's talents were simply not marketable. The unemployed person might still envy the life of the athlete even though due compensation has been obtained. For this and similar criticisms, see Philippe Van Parijs, "Equality of Resources versus Undominated Diversity," in Justine Burley (ed.), *Dworkin and His Critics with a Reply by Dworkin* (Malden, MA: Blackwell, 2006). For a different view on compensation for talents, especially looks, see Thomas Pogge, "A Critique of the Capability Approach".

64. For statements of Sen's approach and commentaries, see Amartya Sen, "Equality of What?," in I. S. M. McMurrin (ed.), *The Tanner Lectures on Human Values* (Cambridge: Cambridge University Press, 1979), 215–216; "Well-Being, Agency and Freedom," *Journal of Philosophy* 82 (4) (1985), 201; "Capabilities, Lists, and Public Reason: Continuing the Conversation," *Feminist Economics* 10 (3) (2004), 78; "Capability and Well-being," in Martha Nussbaum and Amartya Sen (eds), *The Quality of Life* (Oxford: Clarendon Press, 1993); *Inequality Reexamined*; *Development as Freedom* (Oxford: Oxford University Press, 1999); *The Idea of Justice* (London: Penguin, 2009). For recent critical commentary, see Harry Brighouse and Ingrid Robeyns (eds), *Measuring Justice: Primary Goods and Capabilities* (Cambridge: Cambridge University Press, 2010); Alexander Kaufman (ed.), *Capabilities Equality: Basic Issues and Problems* (New York: Routledge, 2006).

65. For a list of some applications of the approach, see UNDP, "Human Development Reports," *United Nations Development Program* (Oxford: Oxford University Press, 1990–2007).

66. Sen, "Capability and Well-being," 30. Sen's original discussion of equality in Sen, "Equality of What?," called his approach "basic capability equality." I refer chiefly to the later, more sophisticated development of that fundamental idea in his subsequent writings, notably "Capability and Well-being."

67. Sen, "Well-Being, Agency and Freedom," 201.

68. Curiously, both Sen and Nussbaum pay relatively little attention to the role responsibility should play in assessments of capability deficits. In places Sen identifies himself with the general distinction observed earlier between choices that are under our control and those that are not. Here the importance of distinguishing between freedom and achievements becomes apparent. As seen earlier, for the capability approach it is more appropriate to see the claims of individuals on society in terms of the freedom to achieve rather than actual functioning (Sen, *Inequality Reexamined*, 148). In addition, one of the advantages of the capability approach is that it allows us more information on whether a person had opportunities to achieve various important functionings. Not only does the addition of freedom here provide more information, but he seems to suggest that this information should be used to determine the justice or otherwise of inequalities. He writes that where a person is able to exercise freedom yet wastes his or her opportunities such that an inequality results, plausibly, no injustice has occurred (Sen, *Development as Freedom*, 283–289; "Capability and Well-being," 38). Redescribed in terms of the starving/fasting example discussed previously, the rich and religious faster is clearly responsible for his malnutrition, whereas the starving person is not. If, as suggested, freedom should be a factor in our political analysis, then the addition of responsibility will often be decisive in concluding that

some capability deficits will not be the responsibility of the state. Of course, incorporating responsibility might be done in a number of ways. One could use it as a criterion only when basic capabilities were not in danger, such as when a person jeopardized not his health but only his wealth. Alternatively, one could follow the example of some theorists of equality and argue that even consequences of choices that led to severe disadvantage should be borne by the agent. I am not suggesting that either of these approaches are what Sen would opt for, merely that to rule out either approach we need further arguments about the role and scope of responsibility. See also Jeremy Moss, "Justice and Capabilities: Does Personal Responsibility for Capabilities Matter?," *Ethics and Economics* 2 (2) (2005), 1–18.

69. Sen, "Capability and Well-being," 36. For discussion, see Nussbaum, *Creating Capabilities: The Human Development Approach* (Cambridge, MA : Harvard University Press, 2011), 197ff.
70. Sen, *The Idea of Justice*, 233.
71. Sen, "Capability and Well-Being," 36. He notes that a procedure similar to that used by Scanlon in "Preference and Urgency," might be used to rank capabilities in Sen, "Well-Being, Agency and Freedom," 198.
72. Sen, "Capabilities, Lists, and Public Reason," 78.
73. For discussion, see Nussbaum, "Capabilities as Fundamental Entitlements: Sen and Social Justice," in A. Kaufman (ed.), *Capabilities Equality: Basic Issues and Problems* (New York: Routledge, 2006), 44; Sen, "Capability and Well-Being."
74. For other versions of the approach, see Jonathan Wolff and Avner de-Shalit, *Disadvantage* (Oxford: Oxford University Press, 2007).
75. Nussbaum's version of the approach has gone through a number of iterations. For an extensive list of her works in this area, see *Creating Capabilities*. For the most relevant, see Martha Nussbaum, *Women and Human Development* (Cambridge: Cambridge University Press, 2000; "Aristotle, Politics, and Human Capabilities: A Response to Antony, Arneson, Charlesworth, and Mulgan," *Ethics* 111 (1) (2000), 102–140; "Capabilities as Fundamental Entitlements: Sen and Social Justice"; *Frontiers of Justice: Disability, Nationality, Species Membership* (Cambridge, MA: Harvard University Press, 2006).
76. Nussbaum, *Frontiers of Justice*, 70.
77. Ibid., 292.
78. Ibid., 81.
79. Ibid., 163.
80. Nussbaum, *Women and Human Development*, 76.
81. Sen, *Inequality Reexamined*, 48
82. Ibid., 76. For an interesting analysis of the problem, see Wolff and de-Shalit, *Disadvantage*, ch. 5. Wolff and de-Shalit propose adding (11) "doing good to others," (12) "living in a law abiding fashion," (13) "understanding the law," and (14) "verbal independence: being able to communicate in the dominant language for yourself" to this list.
83. Sen, *The Idea of Justice*, 234–235.
84. On this point, see Anderson, "Justifying the Capabilities Approach," 88. Pogge objects that if this is a benefit of the capability approach, it is in fact an argument for welfarism insofar as people's preferences are their ends (Pogge, "Can the Capability Approach Be Justified?," in Martha Nussbaum and Chad

Flanders [eds], "Global Inequalities," special issue, *Philosophical Topics* 30 [2], 167–228, 91).

85. Nussbaum, *Frontiers of Justice*, 78. Pogge objects that the capability approach is just as vulnerable to this objection from welfarists.
86. Thomas Pogge, "A Critique of the Capability Approach."
87. Nussbaum has both a primary and a secondary argument for why capabilities and not functionings should be the focus of justice; they are an inversion of Sen's reasons for preferring opportunities. Her primary argument is that we fail to show people respect when we do not give them a choice about how to live their lives and, therefore, which functionings to choose between. This is partly in response to a concern about paternalism. There is a subsidiary argument: that some capabilities do not have the same worth if they are not freely chosen. For instance, the ability to play is not as worthwhile if it is coercively enforced. For Nussbaum, these types of considerations push us in the direction of a Rawlsian political liberalism, which leaves people with spaces for choice and does not "dragoon" people into choosing certain sorts of functioning.
88. Nussbaum lists six reasons why she thinks her approach respects pluralism. See Nussbaum, *Frontiers of Justice*, 78–80.
89. She also claims that health has value in itself and this gives an additional reason why we shouldn't let people become unhealthy. *Women and Human Development*, 91.
90. Ibid.
91. Rawls, *Political Liberalism*, 139. Rawls is of course talking not just of autonomy but of the values that compose political liberalism. Yet if health and to some extent dignity can be promoted as functionings because of their benefit to an individual's ability to lead a good life and be a good citizen, then analogously, autonomy should be promoted as a functioning because it is a democratically important function.
92. Arneson also makes the point that more freedom might often be bad for a person if it leads him or her to make bad choices. See Richard Arneson, "Two Cheers for Capabilities," in Harry Brighouse and Ingrid Robeyns (eds), *Measuring Justice: Primary Goods and Capabilities* (Cambridge: Cambridge University Press, 2010), 17–60.
93. See Beitz, "Amartya Sen's Resources, Values and Development," *Economics and Philosophy* 2 (1986), 282–291; Arneson, "Two Cheers for Capabilities."
94. Arneson, "Equality," 91.
95. Dworkin claims that the most plausible way of interpreting what the capability approach means is not to reduce it to welfarism but to outline another version of a quality of resources expressed in different language. See Dworkin, *Sovereign Virtue*, 303.
96. Sen has several responses to Dworkin's criticism, including that one crucial difference between the two approaches is that capabilities are goals in the sense that resources are not and that Dworkin's approach exhibits "transcendental" tendencies that Sen's theory does not. See Sen, *The Idea of Justice*, 264–268.
97. Sen, "Capabilities, Lists, and Public," 78.
98. E.g., see his comments on the importance of freedom in "Capability and Well-being."

99. Sen, *The Idea of Justice*, pt. III.
100. Nussbaum, *Creating Capabilities*, ch. 5.
101. For an objection to partial ordering, see Pogge, "A Critique of the Capability Approach," 17–60.
102. Anderson herself advocates a sufficientist standard of capability provision. Capabilities are to be provided at a sufficient level to allow citizens to stand in relations of equality. See Anderson, "Justifying the Capabilities Approach," 86.
103. Pogge, "A Critique of the Capability Approach," 33.
104. Ibid., 48.
105. Ibid., 52.
106. Anderson, "Justifying the Capabilities Approach," 92.
107. Ibid., 96.
108. Ibid., 97.
109. Joseph Stieglitz, *Inequality* (New York: Norton, 2012).position that
110. Although a guarantee opportunities even if earlier opportunities are squandered would be much better than one that did not, such as some versions of luck egalitarianism; see Chapter 3.

3 Egalitarianism and Responsibility

1. For prominent statements of luck egalitarianism, see Richard Arneson, "Luck Egalitarianism and Prioritarianism," *Ethics* 110 (2) (2000), 339–349; Gerald Cohen, "The Currency of Egalitarian Justice," *Ethics* 99 (4) (1989), 906–943; R. Arneson, "Luck Egalitarianism: A Primer," in Carl Knight and Zofia Stemplowska (eds), *Responsibility and Distributive Justice* (Oxford: Oxford University Press, 2010); Will Kymlicka, "Liberal Equality," in *Contemporary Political Philosophy: An Introduction* (Oxford: Oxford University Press, 2002).
2. Ronald Dworkin, *Sovereign Virtue: The Theory and Practice of Equality* (Cambridge, MA: Harvard University Press, 2000), 286. Although Dworkin rejects the label "luck egalitarian."
3. Cohen, "Currency of Egalitarian Justice," 916.
4. On this point, see Gerald Lang, "Luck Egalitarianism, Permissible Inequalities and Moral Hazard," *Journal of Moral Philosophy* 6 (2009).
5. For statements of versions of this position, see Marc Fleurbaey, "Equal Opportunity or Equal Social Outcome?" *Economics and Philosophy* 11 (1995), 22–55; Fleurbaey, "Egalitarian Opportunities," *Law and Philosophy* 20 (5) (2001), 527–528; Samuel Scheffler, "What Is Egalitarianism?" *Philosophy and Public Affairs* 31 (1) (2003), 5–39; Jonathan Wolff, "Fairness, Respect, and the Egalitarian Ethos," *Philosophy and Public Affairs* 27 (1998), 97–122; Hurley, "The Public Ecology of Responsibility," in Carl Knight and Zofia Stemplowska (eds), *Responsibility and Distributive Justice* (Oxford: Oxford University Press, 2010), 188–189; Elizabeth Anderson, "What Is the Point of Equality?" *Ethics* 109 (1999), 287–337; Scheffler, "What Is Egalitarianism?"; Scheffler, "Choice, Circumstance, and the Value of Equality," *Philosophy, Politics, and Economics* 4 (2005), 5–28; Susan Hurley, *Justice, Luck, and Knowledge* (Cambridge, MA: Harvard University Press,

2003); Seana Valentine Shiffrin, "Paternalism, Unconscionability Doctrine, and Accommodation," *Philosophy and Public Affairs* 29 (2000), 205–250; Shiffrin, "Egalitarianism, Choice-Sensitivity, and Accommodation," In R. J. Wallace, P. Pettit, S. Scheffler, and M. Smith (eds), *Reason and Value: Themes from the Moral Philosophy of Joseph Raz* (Oxford: Oxford University Press, 2004); Matt Matravers, *Responsibility and Justice* (Malden, MA: Polity, 2007); Norman Daniels, in Carl Knight and Zofia Stemplowska (eds), *Responsibility and Distributive Justice* (Oxford: Oxford University Press, 2010).

6. For Scanlon, see *What We Owe to Each Other* (Cambridge, MA: Harvard University Press, 1998), ch. 6. See also H. L. A. Hart, "Postscript: Responsibility and Retribution," in Hart, *Punishment and Responsibility* (Oxford: Oxford University Press, 1968).

7. John Rawls, *A Theory of Justice* (Oxford: Oxford University Press, 1971), 302.

8. Ibid., 71–75.

9. Rawls, "Social Unity," in *Collected Papers*, 369.

10. Ibid., 369–370.

11. Anderson, "What Is the Point of Equality?" 289.

12. Ibid., 306; emphasis in original.

13. Wolff, "Fairness, Respect and the Egalitarian Ethos," 114–115. For a view that argues that Wolff's concern can be accommodated while still preserving a role for responsibility, see Timothy Hinton, "Must Egalitarians Choose between Fairness and Respect?" *Philosophy and Public Affairs* 30 (1) (2001), 72–87. This conclusion does not prohibit all moral evaluation of the agents in the negligent driver and similar cases. We might see the point in terms of two different conceptions of responsibility commonly discussed in this context. Thomas Scanlon distinguishes between responsibility and attributability, where an action "can be attributed to an agent in the way that is required in order for it to be the basis for moral appraisal"; Hinton, "Must Egalitarians Choose between Fairness and Respect?" 80.

14. Ibid.

15. See Scheffler, "Choice Circumstance and the Value of Equality," 10.

16. Dworkin, *Sovereign Virtue*, ch. 7.

17. Hurley, "The Public Ecology of Responsibility," 188–189.

18. Fleurbaey, "Egalitarian Opportunities," 527–528.

19. Rawls, *Political Liberalism*, xviii.

20. Will Kymlicka argues that Rawls's difference principle embodies a commitment to the chance/choice distinction yet one that places too much emphasis on the impact of natural inequalities and not enough on the impact of our choices (Kymlicka, *Contemporary Political Philosophy*, 73–74). In contrast, Samuel Scheffler thinks the best understanding of why Rawls's theory does not respect the chance/choice distinction is that Rawls is not trying to respect it because, for him, it does not have the kind of fundamental importance it has for luck egalitarians. Recall that for many luck egalitarians the goal of egalitarianism is to remove or compensate for the effects of bad brute luck. But this is not Rawls's goal. His principle of redress does aim to compensate for any inequalities that are undeserved, such as those of natural endowment. Scheffler, "What Is Egalitarianism?".

21. See Daniels and Rawls, *Collected Papers*, 371.

22. Scheffler, "What Is Egalitarianism?" 31.

23. For approaches of this type, see Carl Knight, *Luck Egalitarianism: Equality, Responsibility, and Justice* (Edinburgh: Edinburgh University Press, 2009).
24. Kok-Chor Tan, "A Defense of Luck Egalitarianism," *Journal of Philosophy* 105 (11) (2008), 669ff. Tan's distinction between basic needs and justice seems counterintuitive in at least one way. How society treats its most disadvantaged is often thought of as a test of whether that society is just. E.g., the coverage and effectiveness of a society's health system, which typically includes those suffering from bad option luck, is a good indicator of whether a society is a just one. Why should we think that the well-being of those who are suffering greatly should not be a concern of justice? See also Tan, *Justice, Luck and Institutions* (Oxford: Oxford University Press, 2012).
25. See Arneson, "Luck Egalitarianism and Prioritarianism."
26. Dworkin, *Sovereign Virtue.*
27. Arneson, "Luck Egalitarianism and Prioritarianism," 344.
28. Scheffler, "What Is Egalitarianism?" 22.
29. E.g., see Anderson, "What Is the Point of Equality?" 321–322.
30. Scheffler, "What Is Egalitarianism?" 22.
31. On this point, see Fleurbaey, "Egalitarian Opportunities," 527; Scheffler, "What Is Egalitarianism," 22ff.
32. See Tan, "A Defense of Luck Egalitarianism."
33. See J. Moss, "Against Fairness," *Journal of Value Inquiry* 41 (2007).
34. Anderson, "What Is the Point of Equality?" 318.
35. Ibid., 327–328; Scheffler, "What Is Egalitarianism?" 22.
36. Tan, "A Defense of Luck Egalitarianism," 690.
37. Note too that democratic egalitarianism does not have to depend on an idea of reciprocity. Recall that Tan argued that luck egalitarianism was superior to democratic egalitarianism partly because it could more readily support a theory of global equality. Yet there are other versions of democratic egalitarianism that do not rely on a principle of reciprocity. One could have an "associational" conception of obligation, where duties were generated via being part of the right kind of association (this idea is explored in Chapter 4). Sanyal, e.g., defends a version of "political equality" that seeks to base egalitarianism on the removal of certain sorts of inequalities – namely, subjection and domination. Political egalitarianism requires not simply reciprocity but that we not be unequal in terms of autonomy and nondomination. S. Sanyal, "A Defense of Democratic Egalitarianism," *Journal of Philosophy* (2012), 22ff.
38. Fleurbaey, "Egalitarian Opportunities," 527.

4 Global Egalitarianism

1. Thomas Pogge, "Cosmopolitanism and Sovereignty," *Ethics* 103 (1992), 89.
2. I. Ortiz and M. Cummins, "Global Inequality: Beyond the Bottom Billion – A Rapid Review of Income Distribution in 141 Countries," United Nations Children's Fund (UNICEF) (New York, April 2011, http://www.unicef.org/socialpolicy/index_58230.html.
3. Oxfam, *Rigged Rules and Double Standards* (2002), www.maketradefair.com.
4. B. Milanovic, "Global Income Inequality," *Poverty in Focus* (June 2007), International Poverty Centre, 6.

5. Kok Chor Tan, *Justice without Borders: Cosmopolitanism, Nationalism and Patriotism* (Cambridge: Cambridge University Press, 2004), 21; emphasis in original.
6. See, e.g., Thomas Pogge, *World Poverty and Human Rights*, 2nd ed. (Cambridge: Polity Press, 2008).
7. David Miller, *National Responsibility and Global Justice* (Oxford: Oxford University Press, 2007), 248ff.
8. For a fuller discussion of the differences between these concepts, see Allan Buchanan, "Justice and Charity," *Ethics* 97 (1987); Philippe Van Parijs, "International Distributive Justice," in R. Goodin, P. Pettit, and T. Pogge (eds), *A Companion to Contemporary Political Philosophy*, 2nd ed. (Oxford: Blackwell, 2007); Pablo Gilabert, *From Global Poverty to Global Equality* (Oxford: Oxford University Press, 2012), "Introduction."
9. Andrea Sangiovanni, "Global Justice, Reciprocity and the State," *Philosophy and Public Affairs* 35/1, 2007.
10. Simon Caney, *Justice beyond Borders: A Global Political Theory* (Oxford: Oxford University Press, 2005), 265.
11. John Rawls, *Justice as Fairness* (Cambridge: MA: Harvard University Press, 2001), 10.
12. John Rawls, *Political Liberalism* (New York: Columbia University Press, 1996), 258.
13. Rawls, *Justice as Fairness*, 6.
14. John Rawls, *A Theory of Justice* (Oxford: Oxford University Press, 1971), 457, 7–8.
15. Brian Barry, "Humanity and Justice," in *Democracy, Power and Justice: Essays in Political Theory* (Oxford: Oxford University Press, 1989), 446.
16. For other recent statements, see Andrea Sangiovanni, "Global Justice, Reciprocity and the State"; Brian Barry, "Humanity and Justice"; Samuel Freeman, "Distributive Justice and *The Law of Peoples*," in Rex Martin and David A Reidy (eds), *Rawls's Law of Peoples: A Realistic Utopia?* (Oxford: Blackwell, 2006). For those who support cooperation but think that there is a global form of cooperation, see Darryl Moellendorf, *Cosmopolitan Justice* (Boulder, CO: Westview Press, 2002), and *Global Inequality Matters* (Basingstoke: Palgrave Macmillan, 2009); Charles Beitz, *Political Theory and International Relations*, 2nd ed. (Princeton, NJ: Princeton University Press, 1999).
17. E.g., see Elizabeth Anderson, "What Is the Point of Equality?", *Ethics* 109 (1999), 287–337, 321–322. See also Sangiovanni, "Global Justice, Reciprocity and the State."
18. For views of this sort, see Rawls, *A Theory of Justice*; Freeman, "Distributive Justice and *The Law of Peoples*"; Barry, "Humanity and Justice"; Sangiovanni, "Global Justice, Reciprocity and the State"; Michael Walzer, *Spheres of Justice* (New York: Basic Books, 1983).
19. See, here, Moellendorf, *Cosmopolitan Justice*, and *Global Inequality Matters*; Beitz, *Political Theory and International Relations*.
20. Beitz, *Political Theory and International Relations*, 131.
21. Ibid., 149.
22. Moellendorf, *Global Inequality Matters*, 37.
23. Tan, *Justice without Borders*, 33.

24. Charles Beitz, "Cosmopolitan Ideals and National Sentiment," *Journal of Philosophy* 80 (10) (1983); Arash Abizadeh, "Cooperation, Pervasive Impact and Coercion: On the Scope (Not Site) of Distributive Justice," *Philosophy and Public Affairs* 35 (4), 2007; Tan, *Justice without Borders*, 33.
25. Abizadeh, "Cooperation, Pervasive Impact and Coercion," 324.
26. See Beitz, "Cosmopolitan Ideals and National Sentiment," 595.
27. Tan, *Justice without Borders*, 27–33; Moellendorf, *Global Inequality Matters*. The pervasive impact interpretation might also serve to expand Rawls's focus on institutions as the site of justice. For this, see Cohen and responses by Murphy and Pogge.
28. Michael Blake, "Distributive Justice, State Coercion and Autonomy," *Philosophy and Public Affairs* 30 (2001), 271.
29. Thomas Nagel, "The Problem of Global Justice," *Philosophy and Public Affairs* 33 (2005), 140.
30. Ibid., 130.
31. Tan points out that Nagel acknowledges that there are some duties that we owe to others irrespective of associations, duties such as freedom of speech and movement. Tan, "The Boundary of Justice and the Justice of Boundaries: Defending Global Egalitarianism," *Canadian Journal of Legal and Jurisprudence* 19 (2) (2006), 327.
32. See also Moellendorf, *Global Inequality Matters*, ch. 2.
33. Beitz, "Cosmopolitan Ideals and National Sentiment," 595.
34. For a relational version of the arbitrariness argument, see Sangiovanni, "Global Justice, Reciprocity and the State."
35. See also Gilabert, *From Global Poverty to Global Equality*, ch. 6.
36. Hillel Steiner, "Left Libertarianism and the Ownership of Natural Resources," *Public Reason* 1 (1), 2009.
37. Caney, *Justice beyond Borders*, 107. See also Gilabert, *From Global Poverty to Global Equality*, for a statement of the moral personality argument.
38. P. Singer, *One World* (Melbourne: Text Publishing, 2002). See Gilabert, *From Global Poverty to Global Equality*, for a more recent defense of the moral personality argument.
39. Moellendorf, *Cosmopolitan Justice*, 31.
40. Simon Caney, "Cosmopolitanism and Justice," in T. Christiano and J. Christman (eds.), *Contemporary Debates in Political Philosophy* (Oxford: Blackwell, 2009).
41. See, e.g., Miller, *National Responsibility and Global Justice*; Barry, "Humanity and Justice."
42. Tan, *Justice without Borders*, ch. 2.
43. P. Casal, "Progressive Environmental Taxation: A Defence," *Political Studies*, Jan. 2012.
44. Beitz, *Political Theory and International Relations*, 139; Barry, "Humanity and Justice," 198.
45. Hillel Steiner, "Just Taxation and International Redistribution", in I. Shapiro and L. Brilmayer (eds), *Global Justice*, NOMOS XLI (New York: NYU Press, 1999), 171–191.
46. Barry, "Humanity and Justice," 199.
47. On this point, see Caney. Other rights theorists include Pogge, *World Poverty and Human Rights*; Henry Shue, *Basic Rights. Subsistence, Affluence and U.S. Foreign Policy*, 2nd ed. (Princeton, NJ: Princeton University Press, 1996).

48. Caney, *Justice beyond Borders*, 143; Shue, *Basic Rights. Subsistence, Affluence and U.S. Foreign Policy.*
49. Beitz, *Political Theory and International Relations*, 141.
50. Steiner, "Just Taxation and International Redistribution," 175.
51. The sense of ownership is common rather than joint. Joint ownership implies that people must have a say over a distribution for it to be just, whereas common ownership does not rely on this kind of consent.
52. Ibid., 176; H. Steiner, *An Essay on Rights* (Oxford: Blackwell, 1994), ch. 8.
53. Steiner, "Just Taxation and International Redistribution", 175.
54. Beitz, *Political Theory and International Relations*, 141.
55. Simon Caney, "Justice and the Distribution of Greenhouse Gas Emissions," *Journal of Global Ethics* 5 (2) (2009), 130. See also M. Blake and M. Risse, "Immigration and Original Ownership of the Earth," *Notre Dame Journal of Law Ethics and Public Policy* 133 (2009), 141.
56. Miller, *National Responsibility and Global Justice*, 56ff.
57. Rawls, *The Law of Peoples* (Cambridge, MA: Harvard University Press, 1999), 117.
58. Leif Wenar, "Property Rights and the Resource Curse," *Philosophy and Public Affairs* 36 (1) (2008).
59. Pogge, *World Poverty and Human Rights*, 203.
60. "Nations (or persons) may appropriate and use resources, but humankind at large still retains a kind of minority stake, which, somewhat like preferred stock, confers no control, but a share of the material benefits.... One may use unlimited amounts, but one must share some of the economic benefit." Pogge, "An Egalitarian Law of Peoples," *Philosophy and Public Affairs* 23 (1994), 200–201.
61. N. Stern, *A Blueprint for a Safer Planet* (London: Bodley Head, 2009), 54.
62. Moreover, when the anticipated investments in current and future nonrenewable energy generation capacity are factored in, the amount looks smaller still. See M. Wright et al., *Zero Carbon Australia Stationary Energy Plan*, http://beyondzeroemissions.org/.
63. Intergovernmental Panel on Climate Change (IPCC), *Climate Change 2007: The Physical Science Basis. Contribution of Working Group I to the Fourth Assessment Report of the Intergovernmental Panel on Climate Change*, ed. S. Solomon, D. Qin, M. Manning, Z. Chen, M. Marquis, K. Averyt, M. M. B. Tignor, H. L. Miller Jr., and Z. Chen (New York: Cambridge University Press, 2007).
64. IPCC, *Climate Change 2007*; German Advisory Council on Global Change (WBGU), *Solving the Climate Dilemma: The Budget Approach*, Berlin, 2009, http://www.wbgu.de/en/publications/special-reports/special-report-2009/.
65. WBGU 28. This figure excludes emissions from land use.
66. Ibid., 16.
67. For the latest summary of climate change science, see IPCC, "Climate Change 2013: The Physical Science Basis," http://www.ipcc.ch/report/ar5/wg1/#.Ulor8SQ6dCg.
68. Ibid., 28.
69. K. A. Baumert, T. Herzog, and J. Pershing, "Navigating the Numbers: Greenhouse Gas Data and International Climate Policy" (Gallan: *World Resources Institute*, 2005), 22.

70. P. Baer, "Equity, Greenhouse, Gas Emissions, and Global Common Resources" 401. See also T. Athanasiou and P. Baer, *Dead Heat: Global Justice and Global Warming* (New York: Seven Stories Press, 2002), 28.

71. Beitz *Political Theory and International Relations*, 141.

72. P. Singer, *One World* (Melbourne: Text Publishing, 2002), 39.

73. P. Casal, "Progressive Environmental Taxation: A Defence," *Political Studies*, Jan. 2012, early view: http://onlinelibrary.wiley.com/journal/10.1111/%28ISSN%2 91467–9248/earlyview.

74. Inheritors of the Lockean tradition also give a role to equality. Locke famously argued that original ownership of the natural world rests with humanity, and one can only appropriate it under certain conditions or provisos (John Locke, *Two Treatises of Government*, bk. 2, ch 5). Left libertarians such as Otsuka and Steiner marry self-ownership with an egalitarian proviso. For Steiner equality is an intrinsic feature of justice and extends to us having equal rights over our bodies and to the world's natural resources. Any acquisitions over and above an equal share generate claims on the part of the dispossessed to restitution (H. Steiner, "Just Taxation and International Redistribution," in *Global Justice*, I. Shapiro and L. Brilmayer (eds.), *Global Justice*, NOMOS XLI (New York: NYU Press, 1999), 171–191, esp. 174–175.). Or as Otsuka argues, appropriation of unowned resources can only occur so long as everyone else can equally acquire a share that is as advantageous as yours (M. Otsuka, *Libertarianism without Inequality* [Oxford: Oxford University Press, 2003], ch. 1).

75. A. Meyer, *Contraction and Convergence: The Global Solution to Climate Change* (Dartington, UK: Green Books, 2000), 20; Baer, "Equity, Greenhouse, Gas Emissions, and Global Common Resources."

76. See Meyer, *Contraction and Convergence*; M. Hillman and T. Fawcett, *How We Can Save the Planet* (London: Penguin, 2004), ch. 7.

77. Baer, "Equity, Greenhouse, Gas Emissions, and Global Common Resources," 401. See also Athanasiou and Baer, *Dead Heat*; A. Gosseries, "Cosmopolitan Luck Egalitarianism and the Greenhouse Effect," *Canadian Journal of Philosophy*, 31 (2005).

78. D. Jamieson, "Adaption, Mitigation and Justice," *Perspectives on Climate Change: Science, Economics, Politics, Ethics: Advances in the Economics of Environmental Resources* 5 (2005), 231. See also Singer, *One World*; Brian Barry, *Why Social Justice Matters* (Cambridge: Polity, 2005), 266ff.

79. S. Vanderheiden, *Atmospheric Justice: A Political Theory of Climate Change* (Oxford: Oxford University Press, 2008), ch. 7; H. Shue, "Subsistence Emissions and Luxury Emissions," *Law and Policy* 15 (1) (1993).

80. Ibid.

81. Ibid., 130.

82. Ibid., 131. See also S. Caney, "Just Emissions," *Philosophy and Public Affairs*, 40/4, 2012.

83. Derek Bell, "Carbon Justice? The Case against a Universal Right to Equal Carbon Emissions," in Sarah Wilks (ed.), *Seeking Environmental Justice* (Amsterdam: Rodolphi, 2008), 248; E. Page, "Intergenerational Justice of What: Welfare, Resources or Capabilities?," 2008, 2ff.

84. R. M. Dworkin, *Sovereign Virtue: The Theory and Practice of Equality* (Cambridge, MA: Harvard University Press, 2000).

85. David Miller (2008), "Global Justice and Climate Change: How Should Responsibilities Be Distributed?," *Tanner Lectures on Human Values*, http://tannerlectures.utah.edu/lectures/documents/Miller_08.pdf.

86. Miller's claim that there are only shallow pragmatic reasons for equality is also not borne out by his other claims. He argues that two deep reasons for valuing something equally occur when it is disrespectful to allow an inequality and when a resource is scarce and there are reasons of fairness not to permit inequalities. Either of these reasons could plausibly apply in the emissions case. Countries might, think they and their citizens are being disrespected by an unequal division. Emissions are also arguably precisely the type of scarce resource that needs an equal division. Miller's solution is also compatible with potentially very large inequalities of emissions generation within societies as he opts to leave the internal distribution of emissions to the country in question. So, in principle, a country could decide to allocate all its emissions to its royal family or a whimsical nation-building program. Miller (2008), "Global Justice and Climate Change: How Should Responsibilities be Distributed?"

87. Caney, "Justice and the Distribution of Greenhouse Gas Emissions," 130.

Bibliography

Abizadeh, Arash. "Cooperation, Pervasive Impact and Coercion: On the Scope (Not Site) of Distributive Justice." *Philosophy and Public Affairs* 35 (4) (2007): 318–358.

Ackerman, Bruce, and Alstott, Anne. *The Stakeholder Society*. New Haven, CT: Yale University Press, 1999.

Ackrill, John L. "Aristotle on Eudaimonia." In *Essays on Plato and Aristotle*. Oxford: Clarendon Press, 1997.

Anand, Sudhir, Peter, Fabienne, and Sen, Amartya (eds). *Public Health, Ethics, and Equity* Oxford: Oxford University Press, 2004.

Anderson, Elizabeth. "Justifying the Capabilities Approach to Justice." In *Measuring Justice: Primary Goods and Capabilities*, edited by Harry Brighouse and Ingrid Robeyns. Cambridge: Cambridge University Press, 2010.

Anderson, Elizabeth. "What Is the Point of Equality?." *Ethics* 109 (2) (1999): 287–337.

Arneson, Richard. "The Cracked Foundations of Liberal Equality." In *Ronald Dworkin and His Critics*, edited by Justine Burley. Oxford: Basil Blackwell, 2005, 79–98.

Arneson, Richard. "Distributive Justice and Basic Capability Equality: 'Good Enough' Is Not Good Enough." In *Capabilities Equality: Basic Issues and Problems*, edited by Alex Kaufman. London: Routledge, 2005.

Arneson, Richard. "Egalitarianism and Responsibility." *Journal of Ethics* 3 (3) (1999): 225–247.

Arneson, Richard. "Equality and Equal Opportunity for Welfare." *Philosophical Studies* 56 (1989): 77–93.

Arneson, Richard. "Equal Opportunity for Welfare Defended and Recanted." *Journal of Political Philosophy* 7 (4) (1999): 488–497.

Arneson, Richard. "Human Flourishing versus Desire Satisfaction." *Social Philosophy and Policy* 16 (1) (1999): 113–142.

Arneson, Richard. "Luck Egalitarianism: A Primer." In *Responsibility and Distributive Justice*, edited by Carl Knight and Zofia Stemplowska. Oxford: Oxford University Press, 2010.

Arneson, Richard. "Luck Egalitarianism and Prioritarianism." *Ethics* 110 (2) (2000): 339–349.

Arneson, Richard. "Welfare Should Be the Currency of Justice." *Canadian Journal of Philosophy* 30 (4) (2000): 497–524.

Athanasiou, Tom, and Baer, Paul. *Dead Heat: Global Justice and Global Warming*. New York: Seven Stories Press, 2002.

Barry, Brian. "Humanity and Justice." In *Democracy, Power and Justice: Essays in Political Theory*. Oxford: Oxford University Press, 1989.

Baumert, K. A., Herzog, T., and Pershing, J. "Navigating the Numbers: Greenhouse Gas Data and International Climate Policy." Gallan: *World Resources Institute*, 2005. Available at http://www.wri.org/publication/navigating-numbers

Beitz, Charles. "Amartya Sen's Resources, Values and Development." *Economics and Philosophy* 2 (1986): 282–291.

Beitz, Charles. "Cosmopolitan Ideals and National Sentiment." *Journal of Philosophy* 80 (10) (1983): 515–529.

Beitz, Charles. *Political Theory and International Relations*, 2nd ed. Princeton, NJ: Princeton University Press, 1999.

Bell, Derek. "Carbon Justice? The Case against a Universal Right to Equal Carbon Emissions." In *Seeking Environmental Justice*, edited by Sarah Wilks. Amsterdam: Rodolphi, 2008.

Benbaji, Yitzhak. "Sufficiency or Priority." *European Journal of Philosophy* 14 (3) (2006): 327–348.

Blake, Michael. "Distributive Justice, State Coercion and Autonomy." *Philosophy and Public Affairs* 30 (2001): 257–296.

Blake, Michael, and Risse, Mathius. "Immigration and Original Ownership of the Earth." *Notre Dame Journal of Law Ethics and Public Policy* 133 (2009): 133–165.

Bognar, Greg. "Can the Maximin Principle Serve as a Basis for Climate Change Policy?." *Monist* 94 (3) (2011): 329–348.

Boleyn-Fitzgerald, Patrick. "Misfortune, Welfare Reform, and Right-Wing Egalitarianism." *Critical Review* 13 (1999): 141–163.

Bovens, Luc. "A Lockean Defense of Grandfathering Emission Rights." In *The Ethics of Global Climate Change*, edited by Denis Arnold. Cambridge: Cambridge University Press, 2011, 124–144.

Brighouse, Harry, and Swift, Adam. "Equality, Priority, and Positional Goods." *Ethics* 116 (3) (2006): 471–497.

Broome, John. *Weighing Goods*. Oxford: Basil Blackwell, 1995.

Brown, Campbell. "Priority, Sufficiency...or Both?." *Economics and Philosophy* 21 (2) (2005): 199–220.

Buchanan, Allan. "Justice and Charity." *Ethics* 97 (1987): 558–575.

Caney, Simon. "Cosmopolitanism and Justice." In *Contemporary Debates in Political Philosophy*, edited by Tom Christiano and John Christman. Oxford: Blackwell, 2009.

Caney, Simon. "Cosmopolitan Justice and Equal Opportunities." *Metaphilosophy* 32 (1) (2001): 113–134.

Caney, Simon. "Just Emissions." *Philosophy and Public Affairs* 40 (4) (2012): 256–300.

Caney, Simon. "Justice and the Distribution of Greenhouse Gas Emissions." *Journal of Global Ethics* 5 (2) (2009): 125–146.

Caney, Simon. *Justice beyond Borders: A Global Political Theory*. Oxford: Oxford University Press, 2005.

Casal, Paula. "Progressive Environmental Taxation: A Defence." *Political Studies*, (January 2012): 419–433.

Casal, Paula. "Why Sufficiency Is Not Enough." *Ethics* 117 (2007): 296–326.

Cavanagh, Matt. *Against Equality of Opportunity*. Oxford: Clarendon Press, 2002.

Christiano, Thomas. *The Constitution of Equality: Democratic Authority and Its Limits*. New York: Oxford University Press, 2008.

Clayton, Matthew, and Williams, Andrew (eds). *The Ideal of Equality*. London: Palgrave Macmillan, 2002.

Cohen, Gerald. *If You're an Egalitarian, How Come You're So Rich?*. Cambridge, MA: Harvard University Press, 2000.

Cohen, Gerald. "On the Currency of Egalitarian Justice." *Ethics* 99 (4) (1989): 906–944.

Crisp, Roger. "Egalitarianism and Compassion." *Ethics* 114 (2003): 119–126.

Crisp, Roger. "Equality, Priority and Compassion." *Ethics* 13 (2003): 745–763.
Crocker, David. "Functioning and Capability: the Foundations of Sen's and Nussbaum's Development Ethic." In *Women Culture and Development*, edited by Martha Nussbaum and Jonathan Glover. Oxford: Clarendon Press, 1995.
Daniels, Norman. "On Liberty and Equality in Rawls." *Social Theory and Practice* 3 (2) (1974): 149–159.
Darwall, Stephen. "Two Kinds of Respect." *Ethics* 88 (1997): 36–49.
Dworkin, Ronald. *Sovereign Virtue: The Theory and Practice of Equality*. Cambridge, MA: Harvard University Press, 2000.
Dworkin, Ronald. "Sovereign Virtue Revisited." *Ethics* 113 (2002): 106–143.
Elster, John. "Sour Grapes – Utilitarianism and the Genesis of Wants." In *Utilitarianism and Beyond*, edited by Amartya Sen and Bernard Williams. Cambridge: Cambridge University Press, 1982, 219–238.
Finnis, John. *Natural Law and Natural Rights*. Clarendon Law series. Oxford: Clarendon Press, 1980.
Fleurbaey, Marc. "Egalitarian Opportunities." *Law and Philosophy* 20 (5) (2001): 499–530.
Fleurbaey, Marc. "Equal Opportunity or Equal Social Outcome?." *Economics and Philosophy* 11 (1995): 22–55.
Frankfurt, Harry. "Equality and Respect." *Social Research* 64 (1997): 3–15.
Frankfurt, Harry. "Equality as a Moral Ideal." *Ethics* 98 (1987): 21–42.
Frankfurt, Harry. "The Moral Irrelevance of Equality." *Public Affairs Quarterly* 14 (2000): 87–103.
Freeman, Samuel. "Distributive Justice and *The Law of Peoples*." In *Rawls's Law of Peoples: A Realistic Utopia?*, edited by Martin Rex and David A. Reidy. Oxford: Blackwell, 2006.
Gardiner, Stephen. "Is Arming the Future with Geoengineering Really the Lesser Evil? Some Doubts about the Ethics of Intentionally Manipulating the Climate System." In *Climate Ethics: Essential Readings*, edited by Stephen Gardiner, Simon Caney, Dale Jamieson, and Henry Shue. New York: Oxford University Press, 2010, 284–312.
Gardiner, Stephen. *A Perfect Moral Storm: The Ethical Tragedy of Climate Change*. New York: Oxford University Press, 2010.
Gardiner, Stephen. "Saved by Disaster? Abrupt Climate Change, Political Inertia, and the Possibility of an Intergenerational Arms Race." *Journal of Social Philosophy* 40 (2) (2009): 140–162.
German Advisory Council on Global Change (WBGU). *Solving the Climate Dilemma: The Budget Approach*, Berlin, 2009, www.wbgu.de/en/publications/special-reports/special-report-2009/.
Gilabert, Pablo. *From Global Poverty to Global Equality*. Oxford: Oxford University Press, 2012.
Goodin, Robert E. "Egalitarianism, Fetishistic and Otherwise." *Ethics* 98 (1987): 44–49.
Goodin, Robert E., and Scmidzt, David. *Social Welfare and Individual Responsibility*. Cambridge: Cambridge University Press, 1998.
Gosepath, Stefan. "Equality." *The Stanford Encyclopedia of Philosophy*, http://plato.stanford.edu/.
Gosseries, Axel. "Cosmopolitan Luck Egalitarianism and the Greenhouse Effect." *Canadian Journal of Philosophy* 31 (2005): 279–309.

Gosseries, Axel. "Historical Emissions and Free-Riding." *Ethical Perspectives* 11 (1) (2004): 36–60.

Griffin, James. *Well-Being: Its Meaning, Measurement and Importance*. Oxford: Clarendon Press, 1986.

Harsanyi, John. "Morality and the Theory of Rational Behaviour." In *Utilitarianism and Beyond*, edited by Amartya Sen and Bernard Williams. Cambridge: Cambridge University Press, 1982, 39–62.

Hart, H. L. A. "Postscript: Responsibility and Retribution." in Hart (ed.), *Punishment and Responsibility*. Oxford: Oxford University Press, 1968.

Hillman, M., and Fawcett, T. *How We Can Save the Planet*. London: Penguin, 2004.

Hinton, Timothy. "Must Egalitarians Choose between Fairness and Respect?." *Philosophy and Public Affairs* 30 (2001): 72–87.

Hiskes, Richard P. *The Human Right to a Green Future: Environmental Rights and Intergenerational Justice*. Cambridge: Cambridge University Press, 2008.

Hurley, Susan. *Justice, Luck and Knowledge*. Cambridge, MA: Harvard University Press, 2003.

Hurley, Susan. "The 'What' and the 'How' of Distributive Justice and Health." In *Egalitarianism: New Essays on the Nature and Value of Equality*, edited by Nils Holtung and Kasper Lippert-Rasmussen. New York: Oxford University Press, 2007.

Hyams, Keith. "A Just Response to Climate Change: Personal Carbon Allowances and the Normal-Functioning Approach." *Journal of Social Philosophy* 40 (2) (2009): 237–256.

Intergovernmental Panel on Climate Change (IPCC). *Climate Change 2007: The Physical Science Basis. Contribution of Working Group I to the Fourth Assessment Report of the Intergovernmental Panel on Climate Change*, edited by S. Solomon, D. Qin, M. Manning, Z. Chen, M. Marquis, K. Averyt, M. M. B. Tignor, H. L. Miller Jr., and Z. Chen. New York: Cambridge University Press, 2007.

Jamieson, Dale. "Adaption, Mitigation and Justice." *Perspectives on Climate Change: Science, Economics, Politics, Ethics: Advances in the Economics of Environmental Resources* 5 (2005): 217–248.

Jamieson, Dale. "Climate Change and Global Environmental Justice." In *Changing the Atmosphere: Expert Knowledge and Global Environmental Governance*, edited by P. Edwards and C. Miller. Cambridge, MA: MIT Press, 2001, 287–307.

Julius, A. J. "Basic Structure and the Value of Equality." *Philosophy and Public Affairs* 31 (2003): 321–355.

Kawachi, Ichiro, and Kennedy, Bruce P. "The Relationship of Income Inequality to Mortality: Does the Choice of Indicator Matter?." *Social Science and Medicine* 45 (1997): 1121–1127.

Keller, Simon. "Welfare as Success." *Nous* 43 (4) (2009): 656–683.

Knight, Carl. *Luck Egalitarianism: Equality, Responsibility, and Justice*. Edinburgh: Edinburgh University Press, 2009.

Korsgaard, Christine. "Two Distinctions in Goodness." *Philosophical Review* 92 (1983): 169–195.

Kymlicka, Will. *Contemporary Political Philosophy: An Introduction*. Oxford: Oxford University Press, 2002.

Lang, Gerald. "Luck Egalitarianism, Permissible Inequalities and Moral Hazard." *Journal of Moral Philosophy* 6 (2009): 317–338.

Lippert-Rasmussen, Kasper. "The Insignificance of the Distinction between Telic and Deontic Egalitarianism." In *Egalitarianism: New Essays on the Nature and*

Value of Equality, edited by Nils Holtung and Kasper Lippert-Rasmussen. New York: Oxford University Press, 2007.

Macleod, Colin. *Liberalism, Justice and Markets*. Oxford: Oxford University Press, 1998.

Marmot, Michael. "Social Causes of Social Inequalities in Health." In *Public Health, Ethics, and Equality*, edited by Sudhir Anand, Fabienne Peter, and Amartya Sen. Oxford: Oxford University Press, 2004.

Mason, Andrew. "Egalitarianism and the Levelling Down Objection." *Analysis* 61 (2001): 246–254.

Matravers, Matt. *Responsibility and Justice*. Malden, MA: Polity Press, 2007.

Matravers, Matt. "Responsibility, Luck and the 'Equality of What Debate?.'" *Political Studies* 50 (3) (2002): 558–572.

McKerlie, Dennis. "Equality." *Ethics* 106 (1996): 274–296.

Meyer, Aubrey. *Contraction and Convergence: The Global Solution to Climate Change*. Dartington, UK: Green Books, 2000.

Meyer, Lukas H. "Compensating Wrongless Historical Emissions of Greenhouse Gases." *Ethical Perspectives* 11 (1) (2004): 20–35.

Meyer, Lukas H., and Roser, Dominic. "Distributive Justice and Climate Change: The Allocation of Emission Rights." *Analyse & Kritik* 28 (2) (2006): 223–249.

Milanovic, B. "Global Income Inequality." *Poverty in Focus* (June 2007), International Poverty Centre.

Miller, David. "Global Justice and Climate Change: How Should Responsibilities Be Distributed?." *Tanner Lectures on Human Values*, 2008, http://tannerlectures.utah.edu/lectures/documents/Miller_08.pdf.

Miller, David. "Justice and Global Inequality." In *Inequality, Globalization, and World Politics*, edited by Andrew Hurrell and Ngaire Woods. Oxford: Oxford University Press, 1999, 187–201.

Miller, David. *National Responsibility and Global Justice*. Oxford: Oxford University Press, 2007.

Miller, David. "National Responsibility and International Justice." In *The Ethics of Assistance: Morality and the Distant Needy*, edited by Deen Chatterjee. Cambridge: Cambridge University Press, 2004, 123–147.

Moellendorf, Darryl. *Cosmopolitan Justice*. Boulder, CO: Westview Press, 2002.

Moellendorf, Darryl. *Global Inequality Matters*. Basingstoke: Palgrave Macmillan, 2009.

Moss, Jeremy. "Egalitarianism and the Value of Equality." *Journal of Ethics and Social Philosophy* 2 (2009): 1–6.

Moss, Jeremy. "The Ethics and Politics of Mutual Obligation." *Australian Journal of Social Issues* (2001): 1–14.

Moss, Jeremy. "Justice and Capabilities: Does Personal Responsibility for Capabilities Matter?." *Ethics and Economics* 2 (2) (2005): 1–18.

Nagel, Thomas. *Equality and Partiality*. New York: Oxford University Press, 1991.

Nagel, Thomas. *Mortal Questions*. Cambridge: Cambridge University Press, 1979.

Nagel, Thomas. "The Problem of Global Justice." *Philosophy and Public Affairs* 33 (2005): 113–147.

Nozick, Robert. *Anarchy, State, and Utopia*. Oxford: Blackwell, 1975.

Nussbaum, Martha. "Aristotle, Politics, and Human Capabilities: A Response to Antony, Arneson, Charlesworth, and Mulgan." *Ethics* 111 (1) (2000): 102–140.

Nussbaum, Martha. "Capabilities as Fundamental Entitlements: Sen and Social Justice." In *Capabilities Equality: Basic Issues and Problems,* edited by Alexander Kaufman. New York: Routledge, 2006.

Nussbaum, Martha. *Creating Capabilities: The Human Development Approach.* Cambridge MA: Harvard University Press, 2011.

Nussbaum, Martha. *Frontiers of Justice: Disability, Nationality, Species Membership.* Cambridge MA: Harvard University Press, 2006.

Nussbaum, Martha. *Women and Human Development.* Cambridge: Cambridge University Press, 2000.

Olsaretti, Serena (ed.). *Desert and Justice.* Oxford: Clarendon Press, 2003.

O'Neill, Martin. "What Should Egalitarians Believe?." *Philosophy and Public Affairs* 36 (2008): 119–156.

Otsuka, Michael. *Libertarianism without Inequality.* Oxford: Oxford University Press, 2003.

Otsuka, Michael, and Voorhoeve, Alex. "Why It Matters That Some Are Worse Off Than Others: An Argument against the Priority View." *Philosophy and Public Affairs* 37 (2) (2009): 171–199.

Oxfam. *Rigged Rules and Double Standards,* 2002, www.maketradefair.com.

Page, Edward. "Intergenerational Justice of What: Welfare, Resources or Capabilities?." 2008.

Parfit, Derek. "Equality or Priority." *Ratio* 10 (3) (1997): 202–222.

Parfit, Derek. *Reasons and Persons.* Oxford: Oxford University Press, 1984.

Persson, Ingmar. "Why Levelling Down Could Be Worse for Prioritarianism Than for Egalitarianism." *Ethical Theory and Moral Practice* 11 (2008): 295–303.

Pogge, Thomas. "Can the Capability Approach be Justified?." *Philosophical Topics* 30 (2) (2002): 167–228.

Pogge, Thomas. "Cosmopolitanism and Sovereignty." *Ethics* 103 (1992): 48–75.

Pogge, Thomas. "A Critique of the Capability Approach." In *Measuring Justice: Primary Goods and Capabilities,* edited by Harry Brighouse and Ingrid Robeyns. Cambridge: Cambridge University Press, 2010, 17–60.

Pogge, Thomas. "An Egalitarian Law of Peoples." *Philosophy and Public Affairs* 23 (1994): 195–224.

Pogge, Thomas. *World Poverty and Human Rights,* 2nd ed. Malden, MA: Polity Press, 2008.

Posner, Eric A., and Sunstein, Cass R. "Climate Change Justice." *Georgetown Law Journal* 96 (5) (2008): 1565–1612.

Putnam, Robert D. *Bowling Alone: The Collapse and Revival of American Community.* New York: Simon and Schuster, 2000.

Rawls, John. *Justice as Fairness: A Restatement.* Cambridge, MA: Harvard University Press, 2001.

Rawls, John. *The Law of Peoples.* Cambridge, MA: Harvard University Press, 1999.

Rawls, John. *Political Liberalism.* New York: Columbia University Press, 1996.

Rawls, John. "Social Unity and Primary Goods." In *Collected Papers.* Cambridge, MA: Harvard University Press, 1999, 159–185.

Rawls, John. *A Theory of Justice.* Oxford: Oxford University Press, 1971.

Raz, Joseph. *The Morality of Freedom.* Oxford: Oxford University Press, 1986.

Roemer, John. "A Pragmatic Theory of Responsibility for the Egalitarian Planner." *Philosophy and Public Affairs* 22 (1993): 146–66.

Roemer, John. *Egalitarian Perspectives: Essays in Philosophical Economics*. New York: Cambridge University Press, 1994.

Rousseau, Jean-Jacques. "The Social Contract." In *The Social Contract and Discourses*, trans. G. D. H. Cole. London: Dent, 1983.

Sangiovanni, Andrea. "Global Justice, Reciprocity and the State." *Philosophy and Public Affairs* 35 (1) (2007): 3–39.

Sanyal, Sagar. "A Defense of Democratic Egalitarianism." *Journal of Philosophy* 109 (7) (2012): 413–434.

Satz, Debra. "International Economic Justice." In *Oxford Handbook of Practical Ethics*, edited by Hugh LaFollete. Oxford: Oxford University Press, 2002, 620–642.

Scanlon, Tim. "The Diversity of Objections to Inequality." In *The Ideal of Equality*, edited by Matthew Clayton and Andrew Williams. London: Palgrave Macmillan, 2002.

Scanlon, Tim. "Preference and Urgency." *Journal of Philosophy* 72 (19) (1975): 655–669.

Scanlon, Tim. *What We Owe to Each Other*. Cambridge, MA: Harvard University Press, 1998.

Scheffler, Samuel. "Choice, Circumstance, and the Value of Equality." *Philosophy, Politics, and Economics* 4 (2005): 5–28.

Scheffler, Samuel. "What Is Egalitarianism?." *Philosophy and Public Affairs* 31 (1) (2003): 5–39.

Sen, Amartya. "Capabilities, Lists, and Public Reason: Continuing the Conversation." *Feminist Economics* 10 (3) (2004): 77–80.

Sen, Amartya. "Capability and Well-Being." In *The Quality of Life*, edited by Martha Nussbaum and Amartya Sen. Oxford: Clarendon Press, 1993.

Sen, Amartya. *Development as Freedom*. Oxford: Oxford University Press, 1999.

Sen, Amartya. "Equality of What?." In *The Tanner Lectures on Human Values*, edited by I. S. M. McMurrin. Cambridge: Cambridge University Press, 1979.

Sen, Amartya. *The Idea of Justice*. London: Penguin, 2009.

Sen, Amartya. *Inequality Reexamined*. Cambridge, MA: Harvard University Press, 1995.

Sen, Amartya. "The Place of Capability in a Theory of Justice." In *Measuring Justice: Primary Goods and Capabilities*, edited by Harry Brighouse and Ingrid Robeyns. Cambridge: Cambridge University Press, 2010.

Sen, Amartya. "Rational Fools: A Critique of the Behavioral Foundations of Economic Theory." *Philosophy and Public Affairs* 6 (4) (1977): 317–344.

Sen, Amartya. "Well-Being, Agency and Freedom." *Journal of Philosophy* 82 (4) (1985): 169–221.

Shiffrin, Seana Valentine. "Egalitarianism, Choice-Sensitivity, and Accommodation." In *Reason and Value: Themes from the Moral Philosophy of Joseph Raz*, edited by R. J. Wallace, P. Pettit, S. Scheffler, and M. Smith. Oxford: Oxford University Press, 2004.

Shiffrin, Seana Valentine. "Paternalism, Unconscionability Doctrine, and Accommodation." *Philosophy and Public Affairs* 29 (2000): 205–250.

Shue, Henry. *Basic Rights. Subsistence, Affluence and U.S. Foreign Policy*, 2nd ed. Princeton, NJ: Princeton University Press, 1996.

Shue, Henry. "Subsistence Emissions and Luxury Emissions." *Law and Policy* 15 (1) (1993): 39–60.

Simmons, A. John. "Justification and Legitimacy." *Ethics* 109 (4) (July 1999): 739–771.

Singer, Peter. *One World*. Melbourne: Text Publishing, 2002.

Steiner, Hillel. *An Essay on Rights*. Oxford: Blackwell, 1994.

Steiner, Hillel. "How Equality Matters." *Social Philosophy & Policy* 19 (2002): 342–356.

Steiner, Hillel. "Just Taxation and International Redistribution", in I. Shapiro and L. Brilmayer (eds), *Global Justice*, NOMOS XLI. New York: NYU Press, 1999, 171–191.

Steiner, Hillel. "Left Libertarianism and the Ownership of Natural Resources." *Public Reason* 1 (1) (2009): 1–8.

Stern, Nicholas. *A Blueprint for a Safer Planet*. London: Bodley Head, 2009.

Stieglitz, Joseph. *Inequality*. New York: Norton, 2012.

Sumner, Larry W. *Welfare, Happiness and Ethics*. Oxford: Clarendon Press, 1996.

Sunstein, Cass. *Free Markets and Social Justice*. New York: Oxford University Press, 1997.

Tan, Kok Chor. "The Boundary of Justice and the Justice of Boundaries: Defending Global Egalitarianism." *Canadian Journal of Legal and Jurisprudence* 19 (2) (2006): 319–344.

Tan, Kok Chor. "A Defense of Luck Egalitarianism." *Journal of Philosophy* 105 (11) (2008): 665–690.

Tan, Kok Chor. *Justice, Luck and Institutions*. Oxford: Oxford University Press, 2012.

Tan, Kok Chor. *Justice without Borders: Cosmopolitanism, Nationalism and Patriotism*. Cambridge: Cambridge University Press, 2004.

Temkin, Larry S. "Egalitarianism Defended." *Ethics* 113 (2003): 764–782.

Temkin, Larry S. "Equality, Priority and the Levelling Down Objection." In *The Ideal of Equality*, edited by Matthew Clayton and Andrew Williams. Basingstoke: Palgrave Macmillan, 2002.

Temkin, Larry S. *Inequality*. New York: Oxford University Press, 1993.

UN Development Program, "Human Development Reports." Oxford: Oxford University Press, 1990–2007.

Vallentyne, Peter. "Equality, Efficiency and the Priority of the Worst Off." *Economics and Philosophy* 16 (2000): 1–19.

Vanderheiden, Steve. *Atmospheric Justice: A Political Theory of Climate Change*. Oxford: Oxford University Press, 2008.

Van Parijs, Philippe. "Equality of Resources versus Undominated Diversity." In *Dworkin and His Critics with a Reply by Dworkin*, edited by Justine Burley. Oxford: Blackwell, 2006.

Van Parijs, Philippe. "International Distributive Justice." In *A Companion to Contemporary Political Philosophy*, 2nd ed., edited by Robert Goodin, Philip Pettit, and Thomas Pogge. Oxford: Blackwell, 2007.

Van Parijs, Philippe. *Real Freedom for All*. Oxford: Oxford University Press, 1995.

Van Parijs, Philippe. "Why Surfers Should Be Fed." *Philosophy and Public Affairs* 20 (2) (1991): 101–31.

Van Parijs, Philippe. (ed.). *Arguing for Basic Income*. London: Verso, 1992.

Walzer, Michael. *Spheres of Justice*. New York: Basic Books, 1983.

Wenar, Leif. "Property Rights and the Resource Curse." *Philosophy and Public Affairs* 36 (1) (2008): 2–32.

Wiggins, David. "Claims of Need." In *Needs, Values, Truth*. Oxford: Blackwell, 1991, 1–58.

Wilkinson, Richard. *The Impact of Inequality*. New York: New Press, 2005.

Wilkinson, Richard, and Pickett, Kate. *The Spirit Level: Why More Equal Societies Almost Always Do Better*. London: Penguin Books, 2009.

Williams, Andrew. "Dworkin on Capability." *Ethics* 113 (2002): 23–39.

Wolff, Jonathan. "Fairness, Respect, and the Egalitarian Ethos." *Philosophy and Public Affairs* 27 (1998): 97–122.

Wolff, Jonathan, and de-Shalit, Avner. *Dealing with Disadvantage*. Oxford: Oxford University Press, 2007.

Young, Iris. "Five Faces of Oppression." In *Readings for Diversity and Social Justice*, edited by M. Adams. New York: Routledge, 2000, 35–49.

Index

Made in the USA
Columbia, SC
09 January 2020